THE PIG & I

Kristoffer Hatteland Endresen

TRANSLATED BY
LUCY MOFFATT

The Tale
of Our
Relationship
With a Beast
We Eat

THE
PIG & I

GREYSTONE BOOKS
Vancouver/Berkeley/London

First published in English by Greystone Books in 2023
Originally published in Norwegian as *Litt som oss: En fortelling om grisen*,
copyright © Kristoffer Hatteland Endresen, 2020, by Spartacus.
Published in agreement with Northern Stories and their
sub-agent 2 Seas Literary Agency Inc. (All rights reserved.)
English translation copyright © 2023 by Lucy Moffatt

23 24 25 26 27   5 4 3 2 1

Greystone Books Ltd.
greystonebooks.com

Cataloguing data available from Library and Archives Canada
ISBN 978-1-77164-990-2 (cloth)
ISBN 978-1-77164-991-9 (epub)

Editing for English edition by Paula Ayer
Proofreading by Alison Strobel
Indexing by Cameron Duder
Jacket and text design by Jessica Sullivan
Jacket photo by Kevin Horan

Printed and bound in Canada on FSC® certified paper at Friesens. The FSC® label
means that materials used for the product have been responsibly sourced.

Greystone Books thanks the Canada Council for the Arts, the British Columbia Arts
Council, the Province of British Columbia through the Book Publishing Tax Credit,
and the Government of Canada for supporting our publishing activities.

This translation has been published with the financial support of NORLA.

Canada

Greystone Books gratefully acknowledges the xʷməθkʷəy̓əm (Musqueam),
Sḵwx̱wú7mesh (Squamish), and səlilwətaɬ (Tsleil-Waututh) peoples on
whose land our Vancouver head office is located.

Contents

Prologue

IN 1386, a remarkable event took place in Falaise, northern France.

When the bells began to toll in the town square, the blacksmiths laid their hammers on their anvils, the seamstresses folded up their fabrics, and the old people rolled out of their daybeds. From nearby alleys, people poured across the open square, craning their necks to peer at the scaffold. The raised platform where local criminals were executed was empty, but the rope dangling from the gallows indicated that an arrival was imminent. The day's event must have aroused particular excitement because the condemned party was guilty of the most heinous of all crimes: child murder. The victim—a little boy—had been horribly mutilated and abandoned on the street; the culprit's identity was never in any doubt.

In premodern Europe, there were two ways of hanging people: the conventional method, where the rope was drawn tight around the neck of the condemned person; and a rarer and more humiliating method—the one that would soon play out before this crowd of onlookers—where the noose was fastened around the criminal's feet, suspending them upside down. In the Middle Ages, when the pall of anti-Semitism lay heavy over Europe, this punishment was often reserved for Jews. But it was no Jew who was led to the gallows that day. Nor was it a Christian—or a heathen for that matter. The criminal was not even a human: it was a pig.

What's more, the sow that staggered up onto the scaffold and had a noose placed around her hind legs was clad in human clothing, in a jacket and breeches, with white gloves on her forefeet. And that wasn't all: fastened to her snout was a mask portraying a human face.[1]

Prior to the execution, a trial had taken place at the tribunal in Falaise, where the sow was found guilty of the crime, according to laws and moral principles created in a human universe utterly beyond the scope of her comprehension. When the noose was tightened around her hind legs and the sow was hoisted up, wriggling and squealing in desperation, the spectacle had a dual meaning for the onlookers. On the one hand, it was an insult to all Jews, who risked the same punishment as the animal with which they had such a strained relationship. On the other, this absurd humanization of the pig was part of a long tradition of mirroring the pig in humans—and the human in pigs.

All kinds of animals were tried in the Middle Ages and the Renaissance; even birds and insects might appear in court. But no animal found itself more frequently in the dock than the pig, and in few cases did the outcome involve such a dramatic degree of human projection as in the trial of the Normandy sow.

An Impossible Meeting

IT SEEMS HUMANITY HAS ALWAYS recognized something in the pig.

Forty-five thousand years ago, a human being stands in a cave in what is now Indonesia, scratching at the rock face with a piece of red sandstone. There is undoubtedly an intention behind her sketch, but once she has finished and steps back to consider the result, both she and her clan are surprised by her achievement. For the first time in history, the lines have converged to form a recognizable object and everyone can see what it is: humanity's first known figurative drawing is a sketch of a pig.[1]

The oldest artistic expressions of the Paleolithic Age are symbols that are assumed to have been of spiritual significance. The drawing of the pig in Indonesia could therefore be considered the first example of the human race's capacity to think in such abstractions. Or to put it another way: if, as many claim, abstract thought is what distinguishes humans from animals, then a drawing of a pig is the first known expression of what it means *to be human.*

Perhaps Winston Churchill saw something of this in the pig when, many millennia later, he remarked: "Dogs look up to you, cats look down on you. Give me a pig. He just looks you in the eye and treats you as an equal."[2] But whatever the connection between us, it has been of little benefit to the pig. Because the story of the relationship between pigs and humans is largely a tale of contempt.

The pig was already an outcast in the Middle East long before the ancient sacred texts prohibited Jews and Muslims from eating pork. Jesus had no time for swine, either. He who elevated the lamb to the symbol of innocence simultaneously tarred the pig as the devil's beast. Perhaps it is this ancient animosity that still taints our everyday speech when we use the pig as a living metaphor for all that is vulgar, tasteless, shameful, and sinful.

You know you've done something terribly wrong if somebody shouts "swine!" at you on the street. "Pig" isn't quite so bad: a quick hygiene fix will sort that out. "Dirty old pig," on the other hand, is impossible to shake off, reflecting, as it generally does, the accumulated sins of a lifetime. We could continue in this vein for quite some time, every instance an example of our millennia-long tradition of demonizing *Sus scrofa domesticus*, the domestic pig.

ROUGHLY TWO THOUSAND YEARS would pass between the time Jesus forced a herd of swine to hurl themselves off a cliff in an act of collective suicide and the moment when someone dropped an apparently trivial news item into my Facebook feed. This was a few years back, and the story was simple enough to be encapsulated entirely in its headline: "More Pigs Than People in Rogaland."[3] The porcine and human populations of this Western Norwegian county were both close to half a million.

At this point, I was living in Oslo and had little contact with the landscape back home in Jæren,* a district of Rogaland, yet I felt at once that something was amiss. Why had I never seen a single pig? I'm no farmer's son, it's true—I come from the urban belt of North Jæren—but I've spent my life wandering and driving across the plain that forms the heartland of industrial agriculture in Norway. In my mind's eye, I saw the many animals that populated the landscape, but one thing was for sure—the pig was not among them. Admittedly, I'd seen a specimen or two at hobby farms and petting zoos, but I'd never seen a *proper* pig, the kind that finds its way into the industrial meat production statistics.

This realization came at a time when I had the freedom to spend endless hours at the kitchen counter with the passionate intensity typical of those in their twenties, convinced that I had just as much to offer as the great food writers I followed with such devotion. No one could capture the experience of sinking your teeth into crispy pork crackling better than Anthony Bourdain (may he rest in peace). And he was probably also the writer who first taught me that there was more to pork than dry-fried chops and soggy sausages. When it came to meat, pork became my undisputed favorite, and the pig was the animal I ate most of by a long stretch. And, of course, Bourdain and I were not alone in this preference.

Long before our own era, Pliny the Elder noticed that "all the other [animals] have their own peculiar flavor, but the flesh of the hog has nearly fifty different flavors."⁴ It is, quite simply, "a wonderful, magical animal!" as Homer Simpson declares when his daughter Lisa points out how much of the food he eats comes from the pig.⁵ For many, bacon is the delicacy that secures the pig its culinary standing: the very "spice of life," as

*Jæren is pronounced "YA-ren," with a rolled "r."

Denmark's Price brothers put it in their food show, *Spise med Price* (Dine with Price). And let's not forget the caramelized aromas that waft from cuts of neck and rib after they've been roasted and glazed in an oven for hours on end, then shredded with a pair of forks and left to soak in their own juices. To this day, I recall the very first time I loaded a brioche bun with juicy pork neck and topped it off with an equally generous dollop of coleslaw as one of my landmark culinary moments.

Those days are gone and Bourdain is dead. As for me, I've abandoned all attempts to salt my own bacon and only rarely seek out cuts of meat that require hours of preparation. Caught up in new commitments, I now live in the age of the sausage, with its recurring questions about how many halal sausages you'll need for your kid's birthday barbecue. Now that I'm the provider for a crowded household, pork consumption has become almost exclusively a question of finances and logistics. Throughout the week, our fridge is kept stocked with pig in abstract form: cooked ham, sausages, salami, liver pâté, and bacon. The pig has become the nutritional glue that holds our week together.

IT HASN'T ALWAYS BEEN THIS WAY. Since the 1950s, the Western diet has undergone a meat revolution. In Norway, where per capita meat consumption rose from 73 pounds in 1959 to almost 148 pounds in 2017, the trend is less evident than in other countries. While the average for European Union countries is at the same level as in Norway, Canada devoured 180 pounds of meat per capita in 2017, and the average American managed to wolf down an astonishing 274 pounds of pure meat per year.[6] That's almost twice as much as the average European. But whereas U.S. pork consumption has always ranked second or third behind the favorites, beef and chicken, pigs are the leading meat animals in Norway and several other European countries. Based on current levels of meat consumption, the average European will have devoured more than thirty whole pigs by the time they die. A slaughter pig weighs more than 200 pounds before having its throat cut and its belly sliced open. If left to grow to its full potential, it would weigh over 700 pounds. In 2016, the peak year, more than 1.5 billion pigs were sent to slaughter globally.[7] Over the past half century, no animal has been more widely eaten in the world than the pig.[8]

How can an industry on such a massive scale and based on living animals of such enormous size be utterly invisible to us? What has this done to us—and what has it done to them?

BACK IN 1977, the British author and critic John Berger wrote about the loss of daily eye contact with domestic animals. In an essay entitled "Why Look at Animals?" he speaks of how this has left us in a confusing and unresolved situation where we are no longer certain how to relate to animals as food.[9] In the olden days, when most of us were small-scale farmers, our relationship with domestic animals was clearly defined through our continual contact with them. We recognized something of ourselves in their gaze while simultaneously perceiving an unbridgeable abyss. This existential dualism—between *like* and *unlike*—made the relationship between us complex but at the same time secure, he writes. We both worshipped *and* sacrificed animals. But with the decline in the peasant class and the emergence of industrial society, the bonds between us were severed. People moved to the city, while the animals remained in the rural communities in ever fewer and larger herds. As a result, the eye contact vanished too, along with our ability to keep those two ideas of worship and sacrifice in our heads at the same time.

In 2002, the American food writer Michael Pollan wrote that animals and our attitudes toward them had been marginalized and polarized into "either/or" by idealistic vegans on the one hand and ignorant meat eaters on the other: neither camp appeared to grasp the complexity of the original relationship between humans and domestic animals.[10]

I identify neither as an idealist nor an ignoramus, although my dietary habits clearly reveal where I belong. A lot has happened since Berger and Pollan wrote their essays: the free-range or organic alternatives that have become a fixture over recent decades and set high standards of animal welfare appear to be an attempt to regain something of that old principle of worship and sacrifice. The question is how far it succeeds, and whether the consumers of these alternatives are actually any less indifferent to the animals they eat than consumers of regular commercial pork. The products in the supermarket refrigerators are often just as vacuum-packed, processed, and abstract as any other prefabricated industrial product. And even if you do buy meat from animals you believe have lived a good life, thereby displaying a form of remote empathy, you have not formed a relationship with the animal itself, looked it in the eyes, and valued the individual in the way Berger describes. Nor can we ignore the wider context when it comes to meat consumption. Organic meat is still a marginal niche, and the majority of consumers who take up the offer tend to be inconsistent. Of all the pork consumed in Norway in 2019, the organic share amounted to just 0.4 percent. Things don't look much better elsewhere. Whereas U.S. sales of organic chicken and beef have rocketed, the opposite is true of pork.[11] The trend is the same throughout the West. We all belong to nations of industrial meatheads.

The question is whether it's even possible to find our way back to that ancient relationship with our domestic animals given the environment pigs now live in. If I want to find the answer to that question, I must at the very least look some of them in the eye.

THE SKIES ARE HIGH over Jæren, people say. That's certainly true right now, given the system of high pressure over Norway's southwestern coast. It's early May and I'm driving along the Nordsjøveien coastal road, sea and shoreline to the west and a rolling patchwork of fields to the east. The openness of this landscape gives many people the impression of having an over-view, of clear-sightedness. But that's just an illusion, of course, because Jæren conceals so much.

The cattle lie sprawled in the grass, sleepy eyed. It isn't so long since they were let out of the cattle sheds again after six months indoors. There's always a melancholy beauty to the sight of these great, ungainly beasts emerging into the fresh spring air and picking up speed as they head down into the fields. Many people from the more urban districts turn up spe-cially to witness the event, the cows' springtime release—and this is clearly how we like to see our animals: brimming with vital energy and well-being. There are horses here and there too. Heads lowered, glossy-flanked in their white enclosures, they call to mind a tycoon's fleet of highly polished cars. The conditions in which these spirited, stately creatures are main-tained still bear witness to their social status in days gone by. But horses are only a marginal part of the bigger picture; as always, the animals that truly dominate the landscape here are sheep. These woolly white wisps dotted across field and heath-land have become almost ubiquitous in Norway. And yet none of these domestic quadrupeds in Jæren come anywhere close in number to the pigs. If all the pigs in Rogaland County were to reach slaughter age simultaneously, the combined weight of their meat would add up to 150 million meals.[12] That's enough to treat the combined populations of Germany and the United Kingdom to one vast dinner party.

I TURN OFF the main highway and onto a potholed gravel road that will supposedly take me to a production facility—or a farm, as they're still popularly known. But it isn't clear what I'll get out of my visit since I haven't spoken to anyone in advance. I found this place through an internet search. The producer is apparently among Norway's largest pig breeders, yet beyond an address provided in a list of board members and shareholders, the business offers absolutely no information to the outside world. I looked up the chairman of the board and the company director in the telephone directory; they proved to be the same person. But when I called the listed landline, I heard that familiar female voice: "The number you have reached is not in service." So I contacted the Norwegian Farmers Union instead. I asked for an overview of local producers whom it might be worth my while to visit. But that proved to be out of the question: the union does not provide information about individual companies, the communications department informed me.

"No information?"

"No, we've stopped providing it, I'm afraid."

"Why?"

"It's a privacy issue."

IF WE ARE TO BELIEVE the animal welfare organizations, human and corporate privacy is better protected than animal welfare. Over the past decade, it has become increasingly clear that pigs are at the bottom of the agricultural pile. The problem is global. In country after country, animal welfare activists have infiltrated piggeries, filming and exposing the shocking, heartrending conditions there. You'd have to have been living under a rock to have missed the images. In 2019, it was Norway's turn—the country that markets itself as offering "world-leading animal welfare." The video footage aired by national broadcaster NRK revealed an inferno of violence and suffering. But once the nausea had subsided and the tears had dried, most people returned to their sausages and ham, voracious appetite unabated. The statistics couldn't be clearer: pork sales suffered no impact whatsoever.[13] And yet it's not inconceivable that all these images and reports have left ever more of us in a state of cognitive dissonance about our dietary habits; the bitter ethical aftertaste of this meat is increasingly coming to the fore. Personally, I have had moral qualms about eating industrial pork for more than a decade without this ever spurring me to any action worth speaking of. The truth is that I—like most other people—don't actually *want* to stop eating cheap pork. But how can we industrial meat eaters hope to regain our dignity in a world where our ethics are increasingly measured by what we put in our mouths?

GOOGLE MAPS TELLS ME I've arrived, but I still can't see what this place has to do with pigs. The car rolls down toward a lone white wooden house with a somewhat ramshackle air. The property is surrounded by a protective wreath of unkempt shrubbery. As I step out of the car, I catch a faint whiff of ammonia in the air.

I walk down to the house and knock on the door. Once, then a second time. The place gives the impression of being uninhabited or let on a short-term lease. Through a window, I catch a glimpse of the fixtures: spartan furnishings, a mattress leaning up against one of the walls. Still, the lawn has been mowed, so the place can't be totally dead.

Down in a hollow in the terrain, I spy what I take to be the roof of the industrial premises. That's consistent with the map, at any rate—and with the smell that increases in intensity as I approach. At the far end of the property, I come up against a wall, and beyond it a steep slope that I don't feel inclined to tackle. I follow the wall until I reach a stone fence at the northern end. I climb over that and push my way through birch and hazel scrub until I emerge on a tractor trail on the other side. It leads down to the building.

As I round the bend, I come to an abrupt halt: there it is. In broad daylight, in all its naked, pink glory, a pig lies sprawled on a cement slab—clearly dead. A swarm of flies swirls up as I bend down to take a look. Its tongue lolls from its mouth and its eyes are squeezed tight shut. The sight is unappetizing and rather sad. In another place, under other circumstances, I might have jammed an apple between its jaws, speared its body with a skewer, and brushed it with marinade. I might have drunk a beer and experienced a kind of therapeutic satisfaction.

Appetite and aversion: both are fragile concepts.

AROUND ME THE FIELDS stretch out in all directions, interrupted only by stands of planted spruce that provide shelter against storms and gales in this otherwise exposed, windswept landscape. As I sit by the dead animal, I feel an oppressive silence hanging over the area and have a sudden sense of being unwelcome, of having seen something I am not meant to see, of being in a place where I should not be. I advance farther along the windowless rectangular building. If it weren't for the small ventilation hatches just below the ridge of the roof, the entire system would be hermetically sealed. But there is life inside the building, no doubt about it. The acoustics must be tremendous because every time a pig grunts, the air ducts emit a rumble.

A car is parked midway along the building. It must have arrived by a different route than the one I took. It appears to belong to some kind of cleaning firm. So at least there's a hope I'll get to speak to someone. But at the same time, there's no misinterpreting the sign outside the front door: "No entry!" Still, there's nothing to stop me looking in through the window in the door. I cup my hands around my eyes and lean against the glass. I see a narrow passageway with walls of yellowed pine paneling. The passage leads toward yet another door, with a notice that reads: "PPE must be worn when entering the shed." I open the outer door a crack and stick my head in.

"Hello? Is anyone there?"

My voice doesn't carry; there's no sign anyone has heard me.

From the doorway, I can see into an office. It contains a writing desk, shelves, and racks, but there's little to indicate that it has ever been in use. The whole place is filled with a clutter of bags and plastic paraphernalia.

I respect the signs and walk to the other end of the building, which turns out to be just as empty and desolate as the rest of the place.

A CHILL BLAST OF WIND from the west rustles the leaves on a cluster of birch trees. I turn around and walk back to the entrance. I sit down on the porch there and wait for someone to turn up.

The curlews fly low over the fields, rending the silence with their piping cries. Perhaps they're warning of the cold front that has built up out to sea. High pressure is always a short-lived, transient phenomenon in this corner of Norway. But for all I know, they may well be cries for help. These wading birds with their stalklike legs and drinking-straw beaks are becoming ever rarer in Jæren. No one knows for certain what is causing their decline, but there is much to suggest that agriculture is to blame.[14] A hundred and fifty years ago, the whole of the Jæren plain was almost uninterrupted wetland, full of bogs, deep pools, and marshes—an El Dorado for curlews, sandpipers, woodcocks, and snipes. But as the boggy areas were drained to make way for grass production and vegetable crops, the wading birds' natural habitats vanished. In a few years, there will probably be none of them left here in Jæren.

I check the time. It's been nearly half an hour and still no one has turned up. I'm getting sick of this, so I open the door again. I shout and listen.

Answer comes there none.

HOW DID WE END UP HERE—me on the outside and the pig on the inside, like an impossible face-to-snout encounter? If we trace the lines of history from a pig farm in Jæren, they branch out across the fields and into the forests; some shoot across the sea, connecting landmasses and continents. What they all tell us is that the pig's fate was shaped by humanity's powers of creativity and judgment. We were the ones who bred them and we were the ones who ultimately shut them away. The story of the pig is therefore just as much a story about ourselves.

Eating
Like a Pig

SO, LET'S START WITH OURSELVES.

By the time Charles Darwin published *The Descent of Man* in 1871, scientists were already unearthing proof of the theory of evolution he had proposed in *On the Origin of Species* in 1859. The new element in the 1871 book was that Darwin didn't just apply his theory to the animal kingdom; his model now incorporated humans, who had evolved from the apes through "sexual selection." What came as a shock and an insult to many met with ecstatic enthusiasm from others. And at the same time, it sparked a burning ambition in many a scientist: to become first to find *the missing link* between apes and humans.

Darwin was firmly convinced that humans had originated in Africa. But when the Dutch natural scientist Eugène Dubois left Europe in 1886, he had Asia in his sights—Indonesia, to be precise. After several years of excavations on the islands of Sumatra and Java, parts of a skull and a tooth were unearthed in this first attempt to prove Darwin right. The find, dubbed "Java man," is now known as *Homo erectus*. While deeply controversial, even in scientific circles, it nonetheless attracted a great deal of attention, and Java man convinced many people that science was really onto something.

The excavations continued, and in 1907 a lower jaw containing teeth was found in Heidelberg, Germany. This turned out to belong to an even closer relative of us humans than Java man. *Homo heidelbergensis* was duly placed on the timeline of human evolution. Later, in 1912, bone fragments of a prehistoric human primate, dubbed "Piltdown man," were found in Sussex, England. Forty years later, the find was unmasked as a hoax, but at the time, it was grist to the mill of the evolutionists. Finally, during a dig near Beijing in 1921 led by Swedish archaeologist Johan Gunnar Andersson, traces of what would later be known as "Peking man" appeared. It seemed proof of human evolution could be found anywhere those days.

Against this backdrop, it's easy to imagine the elation of the celebrated director of the American Museum of Natural History, Henry Fairfield Osborn, when, one day in March 1922, he slit open an envelope in his office and an apparently human tooth fell into his palm. The tooth—a molar—had been found during an excavation in the state of Nebraska and had been sent to Osborn personally, since few people had greater expertise and authority in the field than him (among other feats, Osborn had famously described and named the iconic dinosaur *Tyrannosaurus rex*).[1]

It must have struck Osborn at once: a molar, not unlike his own, shaped to chew a variety of food. Could it really be true? A prehistoric human species in North America? For Osborn, it wasn't just a matter of seeing his own name inscribed even more decisively in the annals of science. The molar had been found on a continent so lacking in traces of humanity's purported origins that this might prove to be one of the most staggering paleontological finds ever made. And the timing couldn't have been better. Osborn was in the midst of an intense debate

with the creationist William Jennings Bryan about the theory of evolution and whether it deserved a place in America's school curriculum.[2] What if this was the coup de grâce for
Bryan? Or better yet—marked the ultimate triumph of science
over literalist biblical doctrine?

Osborn wasted no time. Within a month, he had announced
the discovery, and his findings were published in *Nature* that
summer. *Hesperopithecus haroldcookii*, North America's first
anthropoid ape, was a reality.[3] "Nebraska man" instantly became
a global sensation, and the *New York Times* was quick to claim
that Osborn's tooth showed "Mr. Bryan is wrong and Darwin
was right."[4]

Osborn didn't just enjoy the resulting personal fame; the
polemical power of the sensational discovery left him puffed up
with bravado, and in a fit of hubris, he took a swing at Bryan. To
make the humiliation complete, he told Bryan to take out the
Bible he interpreted so literally and consult a certain passage
in the book of Job: "Speak to the earth and it shall teach thee."[5]

But as always—pride came before a fall.

In his euphoria and haste, Osborn had made a fateful mis-
judgment that would not just tarnish his name forever. He also
ended up handing the enemy enough ammunition to sustain
its opposition to the theory of evolution all the way up until
the present day. On closer inspection, an article in the journal
Science revealed, the tooth turned out not to belong to a human
ape. It didn't even belong to a lower primate. It belonged—
yes, you've guessed it—to a pig.[6] It was an irreparable blunder.
"Nebraska man" was swiftly renamed "Pig man," and to this day
creationists rarely pass up a chance to use Osborn's error of
judgment in their mockery of science. "I believe this is a case
in which a scientist made a man out of a pig and the pig made a
monkey out of the scientist," Duane Gish gleefully declared to
the Institute for Creation Research half a century later.[7]

The improbability of Osborn mistaking a pig for a human has led many to assume that the research was intentionally faked in the service of the theory of evolution. But there is little to suggest that this is true. Yet how could a scientist as eminent as Osborn get it so emphatically wrong? His blunder revealed an important truth: pigs and humans are often astonishingly alike.

The tooth from which Osborn drew his over-hasty conclusions belonged to a foremother of the American peccary. Osborn's problem was that the tooth was pretty worn after spending several million years in the sandy Nebraska soil. And once the enamel on a pig's tooth is gone, there is, practically speaking, nothing to distinguish it from that of a human.[8]

PERHAPS TEETH ARE a natural starting point in a tale of pigs and humans. Like humans, pigs have a dental system adapted to the task of tearing meat from bones, as well as chewing and grinding plants, nuts, roots, and tissue. The pig is, in other words, omnivorous—just like us. This is what we might call a primitive trait, because omnivores are descended from a prehistoric creature whose mold was cast in the era before mammals' food intake and digestive systems specialized into narrow niches. Cows and sheep chew grass and plants, while cats and dogs prefer to wolf down animal protein. The primitive mammal developed a taste for *everything*. So, if we really want to understand the expression "eating like a pig," we need to take a trip back in time. A long way back: 65 million years—to the threshold of the Paleocene epoch.

We all remember the story from science class: a meteor struck our planet with the force of millions of nuclear bombs. Ash, dust, and smoke swirled up into the atmosphere and spread a dark blanket across the globe. The layer of dust blocked out the sunlight, halting photosynthesis. When the plants withered, the herbivores starved and so, ultimately, did the carnivores. The giant lizards' 150-million-year dominion of the earth may have ended in one short year.

When the dinosaurs kicked the bucket, the stage was set for a group that had previously been mere bit players in the earth's great symbiosis to take on a starring role: mammals. The most numerous mammals weren't much bigger than rats when the dinosaurs died out. For millions of years, their evolution had been kept in check by a competitor they could never hope to challenge in the battle for food. Instead, these little creatures had found their niche high up in the trees, in burrows, or on the forest floor, where they lived off a varied diet of insects, plants, and other organic material overlooked by the dinosaurs.

There are two reasons mammals escaped extinction: hidden away in their burrows, they were protected from the extreme temperatures that scorched the face of the earth when the meteor struck. Then afterward, when they peered out across the postapocalyptic landscape, what they saw was food. Blissfully ignorant of what had happened or how blessed they were by fate, they scurried across the dusty steppes and found that they could eat much of what they stumbled across.

These primitive mammals fell into three main species groups: those that laid eggs, of which just five obscure species remain today, all native to Oceania; marsupials, which have evolved into kangaroos, koalas, and a few others; and animals with uteruses, the forebears of most modern-day mammals, including the pig and us humans. The idea that everything from mice and whales to pigs and humans descended from these rat-like little creatures may appear so abstract that one almost sympathizes with the creationists' claim that the whole business is "too stupid to be true." But only almost.

Unlike Osborn and his peers, though, we have no difficulty finding proof that Darwin was right: there's a wealth of evidence, which gives a spectacularly clear picture of what happened. In the first (millions of) years after the meteor strike, mammals underwent an evolutionary explosion, competing ruthlessly with one another for dominance and rank on the food chain. By the beginning of the Miocene epoch, 23 million years ago, all the main groups of mammals living today were in place. Over a (relatively) short period, some of them had grown into mighty mastodons while others remained small, insignificant creatures. Some had specialized in eating plants and herbs and evolved into ruminants, while others had become carnivores. In addition, a few species retained the original tradition of eating *everything*.

Pigs eat everything—and humans eat everything too. This is the primitive tradition we still share with the pig and take with us to our dinner table every single day. Next time you sink your teeth into a double-decker burger and relish the way bread, vegetables, and meat blend into a nutritionally complex mush, consider the fact that the same meal would be equally appealing to a pig, and that our common ratlike foremothers' indispensable capacity to digest such varied combinations of food is the very reason we mammals survived into the twenty-first century.

WHAT WE EAT changes rapidly by evolutionary standards, so both of us may well have shifted in and out of our omnivorous existence several times before reaching the point where we are today. Still, one thing's for sure: we have both eaten far more plants than meat—as we can confirm by taking a look at our closest relatives. Humans are primates, which are largely herbivorous. And cloven-hoofed animals, of which the pig is one, are definitely plant eaters. It isn't clear exactly when we started to supplement our diet with meat and other animal products. In the case of humans, it probably happened while we still went by the name of *Homo habilis*—some 2.5 million years ago. Pigs probably started even earlier. But regardless of when we first tasted blood, there is little doubt that meat-eating has been a beneficial strategy for both species. From an evolutionary point of view, it has made us into some of the most successful mammals in existence.

Like that primitive mammal whose flexible and adaptable approach to food enabled it to scrabble together an existence and escape extinction, its omnivorous descendants—including pigs and humans—have been major beneficiaries of the same trait. And it isn't just that we've come a long way: we've both become so dominant that some claim we deserve to be defined as *invasive species*—species that take over habitats where they don't belong, crowding out the original native species.[9] That would place us in the excellent company of other notorious omnivores such as the rat and the Spanish slug.

JUST AS HUMANITY had the world at its feet, the pig had the world at its hooves. But whereas humanity came out of Africa, the pig originated in Asia. Since the emergence of the *Sus* genus, the pig has evolved into a number of different subspecies, which, in turn, fall into four main groups, the most dominant of which is the Eurasian wild boar—*Sus scrofa*. It's also the most important, being the rightful ancestor of the modern domestic pig.

The pig spread across Asia, Europe, and Africa unaided but failed to make it to Oceania and America under its own steam: it arrived there only when the Europeans took it along on their voyages of conquest as a source of protein. So, what about that multimillion-year-old pig molar in Nebraska that Osborn mistook for the tooth of an archaic human? In strictly taxonomic terms, the peccary is not a proper pig; despite sharing many of the true pig's traits, it's more like a cousin in evolutionary terms. To some extent, their relationship is comparable to that of humans and Neanderthals: two species from different branches of the same evolutionary family tree. And just as the

Neanderthals perished after being outcompeted by a more adaptable relative (us), the Eurasian peccary became extinct when its cocksure cousin came on the scene. Since the pig failed to cross the Atlantic or the Pacific, the peccary initially held its own in America, but it's difficult to say how much longer it will be able to cling on. When Christopher Columbus came to the Caribbean for the second time, in 1493, he released the domestic pigs he had brought with him. Hernando de Soto did the same thing in Florida in 1539. And this process has been repeated countless times over the intervening centuries. It's hard to gauge the thinking behind this, since the pigs fled the second their trotters touched dry land. There is no accurate record of how many wild boars or "feral hogs" there are in the United States today, although the estimates run to many millions. In the worst-hit state, Texas, the annual cost of the havoc they wreak on crops and infrastructure runs to around US$400 million. Nationwide, the damages are estimated at around US$1.5 billion.[10] These hogs have become the most destructive invasive species in the United States.

The moral of this story? The less picky we are in our eating habits, the greater our resilience to new climates and new surroundings. And no species are more vulnerable than those with a restricted diet. Polar bears, which eat meat—primarily seal—have specialized in catching their food from drifting ice floes. But this hitherto efficient and successful strategy has the drawback of leaving the polar bear severely exposed to ecological change. When the ice vanishes, the opportunities to hunt seal go with it. And once seal-hunting opportunities are gone, it won't be long before polar bears follow. The future looks even bleaker for the koala, which managed to specialize in eating the leaves of a very particular eucalyptus tree—a species found only in limited areas of Australia. This is one of the reasons the forest fires there are particularly heartbreaking: the koalas

have no place to go other than the few areas where these euca-
lyptuses grow. Of course, efforts can be made to protect them
through relocation, but this seems unlikely to help: they are too
set in their dietary ways.

History seems to be repeating itself. The question is whether
flexible, adaptable omnivores will once again emerge victorious
from the ongoing mass extinction. And even if they do, it's quite
another matter whether our shared destiny will do anything to
ease the strained relations between pigs and humans.

"TELL ME WHAT YOU EAT and I'll tell you who you are," wrote
the French gastronomist Jean Anthelme Brillat-Savarin in *The
Physiology of Taste* (1825). He meant that food is often a marker
of identity and cultural belonging for us humans. But the quo-
tation has far broader implications than Brillat-Savarin had in
mind or could even conceive of.

First of all, what we eat shapes the construction of our digestive system. The cow's enormous stomach system with its four
compartments is the evolutionary outcome of its specialization
in plants—particularly fiber-rich, hard-to-digest grass. The carnivore, on the other hand, has a small stomach and a short gut
without the enzymes needed to break down a fiber-heavy plant
diet, while the stomachs of pigs and humans reflect their evolutionary history as omnivores. At the same time, the construction of our stomachs may also have helped shape the way our
heads work.

Evolutionary theorists have long been interested in how
and why animals evolved different-sized brains. While no one
has yet found the definitive answer, some have come close.
In the early 1990s, scientists Leslie Aiello and Peter Wheeler
unearthed a hitherto unknown connection that would provide
the foundation for some of the most significant work ever done
on brain evolution. Like the rest of us, Aiello and Wheeler were

mostly interested in themselves. For evolutionary scientists, that means focusing on primates in general and Homo sapiens in particular. But to understand the significance of their finding and its relevance to pigs and humans, we need to establish a few anatomical premises.

A large, fully functioning brain is something of a mixed blessing for the body it inhabits, because brains are extremely energy intensive. At rest, the human brain accounts for 20 to 25 percent of our total energy use. Its main energy source is glucose, and this mysterious, intricate clump of fat and soft tissue devours a massive 60 percent of the glucose stores in our body. But unlike our other organs, the brain cannot produce or store its own nutrients, so it leeches off our other organs. And this is where Aiello and Wheeler's line of reasoning comes in.

If we are to maintain a brain of a certain size without our resting metabolism going haywire and starving us to death, there is a limit to how much energy the other tissues in our body can use. According to the "expensive-tissue hypothesis" the two scientists proposed in 1995, we humans have been able to evolve a big brain because, as omnivores, we have consumed a varied and easily digestible diet; this, in turn, has given us a small digestive system that doesn't hog too much energy, leaving our body with a large energy surplus that can be used to maintain our substantial brain mass. In short: a big brain indicates a varied diet and a small stomach.[11]

And that takes us smartly back to our primitive appetites and the legacy of our ratlike Paleocene foremothers. But before getting too excited about the fact that we can apply the same explanatory model to the brains and intelligence of pigs and humans, or citing the cow's enormous stomach as proof of its uncommon stupidity, we need to take a look at that party pooper of the science world, the follow-up study.

Although Aiello and Wheeler's hypothesis is valid when studying primates, other scientists disagree about how applicable it is as a general rule for the animal kingdom. When a young scientist called Ana Navarrete embarked on a doctoral thesis at the University of Zurich, she decided to study a question to which the answer had perhaps been taken for granted: Is the hypothesis applicable to mammals in general? After several years of painstaking dissection, measuring, and weighing of bodies and organs, Navarrete's results were published in *Nature* in 2011.[12] They utterly disproved the general applicability of the hypothesis. However, her findings were far from uncontroversial and her paper sparked a debate that rumbles on to this day.

IF TEETH AND GUT can tell us about *how* certain species have acquired larger brains than others, they tell us little about *why* a species would bother to be bright in the first place. What caused humanity to become superior in this respect? Once again, it looks suspiciously as if it might have a lot to do with pigs.

Lions eat meat and gazelles eat grass. They are what evolutionary psychologist Paul Rozin calls "the specialists."[13] They live simple lives, preprogrammed by nature, and neither needs to waste any brainpower deciding what to eat for dinner. Life is even simpler for the hyperspecialized koala. Often enough, it doesn't even have to think about drinking because that need is also covered by its eucalyptus diet. At the other end of the scale are what Rozin calls "the generalists"—like us omnivores. These are species whose nutrient intake includes a wide range of food sources depending on what is on offer in a given environment and a given season. And the generalist doesn't just need to use its brainpower to decide what to eat; it must also actively weigh up what *not* to eat. Fungi, berries, nuts, and roots—some are vital and some are lethal. The generalist's task is to work out which is which, and that makes curiosity a biological imperative for the omnivore. Without its penchant for the unknown and potentially dangerous, the omnivore would soon miss out on essential nutrients. As a result, pigs and humans are always caught between the two contradictory traits of "neophilia" and "neophobia." The first is an exaggerated taste for the new, while the second is an exaggerated aversion to it. Among us humans, the dinner table is the perfect place to identify which camp people fall into. And it's easy to work out which of your dinner guests would have ensured the clan's survival in the state of nature by seeking out new potential food sources and which would have made no contribution whatsoever.

That said, curiosity alone is not enough: an omnivore must also have well-developed taste buds, so no mammals have more taste receptors on their tongues than omnivores, and no omnivore has more than the pig. Whereas we humans have around six thousand receptors on our tongues, pigs have three or four times as many.[14] But curiosity and good taste buds are not sufficient to ensure the omnivore's success either. It will also need an excellent memory. And we're not just talking from one day to the next; ideally, it should be capable of retaining memories from year to year. In natural surroundings, the omnivore will always eat according to season. At the end of a year, an individual's ability to recall the location of different food sources in any given season may be the key to getting enough food to build a strong, dominant position in a social hierarchy.

In addition to all this, the omnivore must be a quick learner. As long as its food intake is not preprogrammed by nature, the quest for food will involve a great deal of trial and error. And failure to learn from one's errors can easily prove fatal. This is reflected in the hunt for meat—an efficient foodstuff that provides a wide range of vitamins and minerals that are essential to us. But it is not risk-free. The omnivore rarely kills its own prey: pigs never do, and nor did humans initially.[15] Instead, both of us have a long tradition of scavenging the carrion left by predators that have eaten their fill. The challenge for the omnivore is to weigh up how much food it is willing to forgo before exposing itself to the risk of falling prey to a lion or tiger that may still be lurking in the vicinity.

This eternal need to identify the most suitable food source at any given time is what Rozin has called "the omnivore's dilemma."[16] It's a dilemma that has cost innumerable calories in brainpower and has helped shape the brains of humans and pigs over millions of years. So it should come as no surprise to hear that the pig's brain comes equipped with numerous features that we also find in the human brain and therefore associate with high intelligence.[17]

In case the connection between a varied diet and intelligence in pigs and humans still doesn't seem sufficiently compelling, let's take another look at the koala. Once upon a time, it was also an omnivore. The million-dollar question is what happened the day it clambered up into a eucalyptus and began to specialize in eating leaves. The most likely answer is that it fell asleep. Up in the trees, the koala evolved into an idler that needed twenty-two hours of sleep a day. But if we study the skull of the koala's ancestor we can also see this: its brain has shrunk to the size of a walnut.[18]

GIVEN ALL THE SIMILARITIES between pigs and humans, you'd almost think that the porcine race—rather than primates—might just as easily have achieved global hegemony, with dominance over all the other species. Just why it was *us* and not *them* is, of course, a highly complex question, and scientists may never agree on the answer. But if we're to believe primatologist Richard Wrangham of Harvard University, part of the answer may lie in the fact that humans began to cook their food, while pigs did not.[19]

Between the point 2.5 million years ago when humans first began to eat meat and the moment we lit our first campfire some 1.7 million years later, we ate our food the same way as the other animals did: raw. And, like the pig, we sourced our meat from carcasses. Nowadays, the idea of going out into the forest in search of carrion and devouring it on the spot without any kind of preparation would certainly arouse aversion in most people. With good reason, you might say, because over time, we've evolved away from the traits that would enable us to eat rotten meat without becoming sick. And yet the fact is that some 13 percent of us are probably still capable of doing that.

The scavengers among us are those who still carry the same gene that, hundreds of thousands of years ago, enabled us to live the way wild boars do. It's called Apolipoprotein E or APOE and occurs in three different variants: E2, E3, and E4. Strictly speaking, all humans have this gene, but we carry different variants. When *Homo habilis* began to eat meat, everyone had the E4 variant, but in the intervening time, the gene has mutated to either E2 or E3 in most of us. In other words, those of us who still carry the E4 variant have remained unchanged in this respect since the days of the earliest archaic humans. It's pretty cool, of course, but it does have a darker side. If you are one of these people, there's a high chance that you'll also have chronically high cholesterol and be at risk of early death from cardiovascular disease or Alzheimer's.[20] As a carrier of the E4 allele, you are simply not adapted for life in today's affluent society, with its limitless access to meat and dairy products. Biologically speaking, you would do better to live in step with the existence we had before we learned to make fire. In other words, eating animal fat only once in a while. A bit like the pig.

Those of us who have mutated to E2 or E3 aren't entirely safe either. We might have a diminished immune response and become more prone to food poisoning than those with E4. That said, we do have one benefit that comes in handy in an affluent society: we have a high tolerance for animal fat. The big question is why that constitutes an evolutionary advantage.

Wouldn't it be better to live more like the wild boars—eating our meat raw and getting most of our food from plants?

Well, that may have been a good life, but it didn't make us especially bright, according to Wrangham. Cooked food was easier to digest. That caused our stomachs to shrink even further, and the surplus energy could be transferred to our brains. That additional brain volume enabled us to develop tools and weapons, to learn hunting techniques and bag big game by ourselves—which, in turn, gave us access to even more meat. Unlike modern industrial meat, the meat we find in nature is packed with nutrients. All it took to complete our diet was a spot of honey and a few sugary roots to provide us with carbohydrates.

If we are to believe Wrangham, fire is what sent us racing past the pig and the rest of the animal kingdom. Or as he puts it: "Cooking made us human."[21]

There's something to think about next time you listen to the pork crackling sizzle in the oven: the pig ended up in there, I ended up out here.

Quarantine

"SO, YOU'RE STARTING WORK as a pig farmer?"

As she asks the question, my doctor holds up a long, thin metal stick with a cotton swab on the end.

"Yeah, maybe," I blurt out.

"Can you just tip your head back a bit?"

She places a hand on my forehead and directs the instrument toward my nostrils.

"Say 'stop' if it hurts," she says.

Her point becomes clear at once. The swab isn't just going inside, it seems: it's going in, up, farther still, *behind*. It feels like it's touching my brain. Tears spring to my eyes.

Visiting a piggery turns out to be more stressful than I'd imagined.

IT ALL STARTED WITH a telephone call to a pig farmer a few days earlier. He sounded so steady and down-to-earth that I was at a loss to understand how I'd made such a mystery of this essential, self-sacrificing profession.

"Just drop by," he said, calm and unassuming. I was ready to head down there the very next day, but a few hours later, he called me again.

"By the way, have you had a MRSA test lately?"

"MRSA? Lately? No—should I have?"

"Well, we'd rather not have to cull our entire herd after you've stopped by, so yes."

It turns out there's a lot at stake. The Norwegian pork industry is currently battling against what the United Nations has described as one of the greatest threats to human health of our age: multiresistant bacteria.

"In the old days, I'd take a sow and a couple of piglets to the town square on Farmers' Day to show them off to people. But times have changed. If my pigs got infected, it could spell financial ruin. It's not a risk I want to take," the farmer said over the phone.

MRSAS—methicillin-resistant *Staphylococcus aureus*—are strains of staphylococcal bacteria that have developed immunity to methicillin- and penicillin-based antibiotics. They pose the greatest threat to people with weakened immune systems, but that doesn't make MRSA harmless to the healthy either. If you have the misfortune to suffer blood poisoning caused by these bacteria, you face imminent danger of death. Luckily, it doesn't happen all that often. Today, around 2 percent of the world's population carry MRSA on their skin or in their mucous membranes without even realizing it.

But what does MRSA have to do with pigs? And why is the farmer so worried that I might infect his pigs and not the other way around? It's a bit of a paradox, it turns out, since MRSA is totally harmless for pigs.

Prior to the 1960s, what we now know as MRSA was a perfectly ordinary *Staphylococcus aureus* bacterium. From the microorganism's perspective, of course, it wasn't totally ordinary. *Staphylococcus aureus* is one of the most successful pathogens in existence, unrivaled in its ability to spread and cause multiple infections in humans. One of the reasons for this is its special structure, which allows it to attach itself to pretty much anything it comes into contact with. It's particularly good at sticking to smooth surfaces, such as walls, doorknobs, medical equipment, skin, and mucous membranes—all the places we'd much rather *not* have bacteria.

Given that the oldest *Staphylococcus aureus* ever found (admittedly in fossilized form) is over a billion years old, perhaps it isn't so surprising that it has evolved this tremendous capacity to spread and adapt.[1] Yet regardless of how flexible *Staphylococcus aureus* is, there's one type of environment where it flourishes better than anywhere else: in places that are warm, dry, and dusty. In piggeries, in other words. As a result, pig farms risk becoming reservoirs for bacteria that can pose an enormous danger if they find their way into hospitals.

BEFORE ALEXANDER FLEMING discovered penicillin in 1928, infections caused by *Staphylococcus* and other bacteria often had dramatic consequences for people who got them under their skin. But with the advent of penicillin and then other antibiotics, infections that were once deadly or severely disabling suddenly became trivial. It was a medical miracle beyond compare.

And yet, when Fleming received the Nobel Prize in Physiology or Medicine in 1945, he warned the world that antibiotics were a mixed blessing. If they were not used carefully, there was a risk that bacteria would develop immunity or resistance.[2] Fleming had observed how liberally the U.S. and British armies had handed out antibiotics to their soldiers toward the end of the Second World War. Unfortunately for Fleming (and the rest of us), no one listened. During the Vietnam War, soldiers took penicillin with them to brothels and gave it to the women—a kind of preventive measure to eliminate any gonorrhea bacteria on their genitals.[3] Unfortunately, the soldiers didn't know a great deal about microbiology.

What happened in the brothels of Southeast Asia has clear parallels with what has happened in agriculture, especially in the pork industry. When the penicillin wiped out all the gonorrhea bacteria that were susceptible to it, the women were left with a few gonorrhea cells that happened to be immune to the medication. Under original, natural conditions, these cells would have accounted for barely a thousandth of the total gonorrhea flora. And their chances of spreading would have been slim, since the mutation they had undergone rarely enjoyed any evolutionary advantages in the microbial world. But all that changed when the women's systems were flooded with antibiotics. The soldiers' treatment provided the conditions these resistant cells needed to thrive by creating an empty landscape in the women's genitals—and leaving the resistant cells free to spread unhindered. In optimal conditions, a single-cell microorganism takes just twelve hours to reproduce from one cell to seventy billion. The soldiers had created a bacterial bomb.

And this is why overuse of antibiotics poses a danger to society: eliminating the sensitive bacteria cells that can be wiped out by the antibiotics actually worsens the situation by leaving the field clear for the resistant cells. Or to put it in evolutionary biology terms: unrestricted use of antibiotics is equivalent to actively selecting bacteria that may claim millions of human lives every single year over the long term. And this is the UN's prediction for 2050—unless drastic action is taken in the interim.[4] We will find ourselves back in the pre-antibiotic age, with health conditions reminiscent of those in the nineteenth century. In other words, it's no small matter that pigs and other domestic animals have been wolfing down feed laced with antibiotics ever since the 1950s. In some countries, as much as 90 percent of all antibiotics are channeled into agriculture. The truly tragic thing about all this is that most of the medicine hasn't even been used to cure animal disease but—hold on to your hat—to make the livestock *grow faster*.

"How are you holding up?" That's my doctor again.

I squint down at the instrument.

"Is there much farther to go?"

"A little bit more," she says, a trace of pity in her eyes.

"Go ahead." I shut my eyes and clutch the seat of the chair.

Last stage: "Ouch!"

It's out; my body collapses. But it seems we're not done.

"I'm going to need you to pull down your pants and lie on the examination table," she says. "Lie with your face to the wall and bend your knees up as far as they'll go."

I look at the brown protective paper spread over the table. Perhaps she thinks I'm having second thoughts.

"It's okay—there's nothing going in," she says in a detached tone.

While I do as I'm told and crawl up onto the table, she adds: "I'm just going to take a swab of your perineum." At which point I discover what a *perineum* is. Couldn't she just have said "taint"?

When my pants are back on, she runs a cotton swab around the inside of my mouth, and that's the end of the MRSA test.

"You'll get your results in the mail in two weeks," she says before I leave.

And with that, I'm sentenced to an agricultural *quarantine*— all this just to get a peek at a pig. How did we end up this way?

IT WAS IN 1950 that researchers in New York discovered the growth-enhancing effect of antibiotics on pigs. And Norway also played an unexpected role in the complex series of events that led up to this finding.

As the American historian Maureen Ogle has shown in her book *In Meat We Trust*, the backdrop to the discovery was a major meat crisis that struck the United States during the First World War. Consumers ran amok, smashing up butchers' shops in protest against low meat availability and exorbitant prices. Desperate to ease the discontent, the agricultural industry feverishly searched for solutions in animal feed: What was the optimal food that would make the animals grow quickly and put on the maximum possible weight?

Without quite understanding the mechanisms behind it, they rapidly discovered that animals like pigs and chickens, which have only one stomach (unlike ruminants, which have several), enjoyed better health and higher growth rates if their feed included animal fats and protein. The only problem was that feeding animals with animals was expensive. The solution the United States came up with was to import cheap fish meal from Japan and cod-liver oil from Norway. The animals grew more quickly, meat production increased, and consumers could put bacon and chops on their dinner table without risking financial ruin. Everyone was happy. Until a new world war broke out.

Suddenly, Japan was the United States' archenemy and Norway was occupied by German Nazis. As a result, deliveries to the American agricultural sector ground to a halt. In the absence of any immediate alternative pig feed additives, and with the meat protests of the First World War still fresh in its memory, the U.S. agricultural industry entered a phase of experimentation, driven by the White House and the Pentagon. There was no end to what they stuffed the pigs with: soybeans, sweet potatoes, and amino acids mixed with various vitamins. But no matter what they tried, nothing could match the impact of Norwegian cod-liver oil and Japanese fish meal.

Then, in 1948, came the breakthrough: the pharmaceuticals company Merck discovered a hitherto unknown vitamin, B_{12}.

But this vitamin couldn't be found just anywhere—it was isolated in animals' livers. This posed two key questions for the agricultural sector. Was B_{12} responsible for the impact animal and vegetable protein had on the growth of pigs and chickens? And if so, was it possible to produce B_{12} artificially? Merck was also asking itself the latter question—although not for agricultural purposes: it was mulling the possibility that B_{12} could be the key to curing the wave of anemic deficiency diseases that had spread after the war. The challenge for Merck was that the enormous amounts of liver needed to extract the vitamin made the product commercially unviable. A ton of animal livers yielded a meager twenty milligrams. The solution was to produce B_{12} synthetically, and this is where the miracle medicine, antibiotics, came into the picture.

Antibiotics were produced in huge vats of fermented microbes. The process produced vast amounts of waste, which was steeped in antibacterial microorganisms. This residue, among other components, was used in the artificial manufacture of B_{12}. When researchers at an American conglomerate, American Cyanamid, tested the effect of the B_{12} vitamin on chickens in 1950—primarily to investigate its impact on the animals' health and survival rates—they were in for a surprise. By chance, the chickens had received B_{12} produced using two different types of pharmaceutical industry waste. One came from the manufacture of the antibiotic Aureomycin, while the other did not contain antibacterial agents. The chickens that were fed B_{12} containing Aureomycin were not only healthier than the others but also grew 50 percent faster. At first, the scientists thought they had stumbled upon yet another unknown vitamin. But on closer inspection, they discovered the secret: antibiotics stimulated growth.[5] They turned out to have the same effect on pigs, and worked just as well on sheep and cattle.

Just why antibiotics have this impact remains something of a mystery, although we may have a partial explanation: human and animal guts are packed with bacteria that aid digestion. Of course, there is a cost. The reason bacteria flourish in the gut is that they get plenty of nutrients from the food we eat. In other words, gut bacteria are freeloaders. In the case of pigs, the bacteria snaffle roughly 6 percent of all food that reaches the gut. So, what happens if antibiotics kill the gut bacteria? That's right: the pig may suffer a bout of constipation, but—and this is much more significant for agriculture—those freeloaders are no longer siphoning off 6 percent of the nutrients, which go straight into the pig's body instead.[6] The pigs pile on the pounds, their slaughter weight increases, and customers get cheaper meat.

The expensive animal protein the Americans had so feverishly sought to replace had become inefficient and irrelevant overnight. In the early postwar years of intensive agriculture, antibiotics rapidly became a standard component of all animal feed. Alexander Fleming and other scientists could warn about antibiotic resistance until they were blue in the face: the people wanted meat—cheap meat.

IN THE MEANTIME, antibiotics were gaining a foothold in hospitals and doctors' offices. But in 1960—just a decade after they found their way into piggeries—the British microbiologist Patricia Jevons discovered that several cultures of *Staphylococcus aureus* bacteria had developed a new enzyme. The problem was that the new enzyme bonded to any penicillin that came into contact with the bacteria, preventing the antibiotic from destroying it. *Staphylococcus aureus* had become penicillin resistant.

By then, the pharmaceutical industry had thrown its full weight behind the antibiotic boom, developing numerous alternative medications. As a result, the hullabaloo over this resistance was short lived. Penicillin was switched out with methicillin, which had a slightly different effect. But almost at once, new *Staphylococcus aureus* cultures were discovered that were resistant not only to penicillin but to methicillin too. And thus the multiresistant bacteria MRSA was born.

But even methicillin resistance wasn't enough to make the agricultural authorities heed Fleming's warning—despite the fact that *Staphylococcus aureus* was far from alone in gaining immunity. By the 1960s, more than 90 percent of all pathogenic bacteria strains in the world had developed cultures that were resistant to penicillin. But the pharmaceutical industry was riding a wave of new discoveries, and there were still plenty of other good medications to choose from. Even so, the battle against the bacteria was increasingly starting to look like an arms race, with medical science always one step behind the mutations. Today, MRSA has become resistant to first-generation tetracycline and streptomycin antibiotics, as well as to all types of amoxicillin and oxacillin, and the medicine drawer is starting to look empty. MRSA is in the process of becoming unstoppable.

More than half a century would pass between the point when the Americans discovered the growth-stimulating effects of antibiotics on livestock and 2006, when the European Union decided to prohibit all nonmedical use of antibiotics in agriculture. The question was how far its member countries were prepared to toe the line: in 2016, around three hundred milligrams of antibiotics went into every kilogram (2.2 pounds) of pork produced in the highest-usage EU countries, including Spain and Italy, and not a single restriction had yet been introduced in the meat-loving United States.[7] But by 2017, antibiotic usage had stopped there too. The same year the American ban came into force, almost twenty thousand Americans died of infections caused by resistant bacteria.[8]

Despite these measures, there is barely a country in the world where MRSA has not thoroughly infiltrated the pork industry. A 2016 study in Denmark showed MRSA to be present in 88 percent of herds—even though nonmedical use of antibiotics was phased out in the Danish pork industry as early as the 1990s.[9]

Of all the pork-producing countries, there is just one that stands out from the rest: Norway is the outpost that has managed to keep both piggeries and hospitals free of MRSA, all thanks to the fact that we—again the only country to do so— have pursued an active strategy of keeping the resistant bacteria at a safe distance from our piggeries. And this is the system I've become caught up in at a doctor's office in Stavanger.

Given the measures adopted by the global pork industry and the agricultural sector to date, you might think we were at least heading in the right direction. But that doesn't seem to be the case. Between 2000 and 2018, total antibiotic resistance in agriculture more than tripled. And even though the European Union and the United States have halted their nonmedical use, 73 percent of the world's antibiotics are still used on pigs, chickens, and other livestock. It's the same old story: whenever multilateral global cooperation is needed to solve an international crisis, there's always someone prepared to throw a wrench in the works. On this occasion it's the pork-loving republic of China. Until recently home to roughly half of all the world's pigs, China is now an epicenter of antibiotic resistance. But it's not alone. Chicken production in India, Pakistan, and Turkey also plays a central role. And countries including Brazil and Kenya are rapidly becoming new hot spots.[10]

The nineteenth century is right around the corner.

THREE WEEKS HAVE PASSED since my visit to the doctor's office. I've finally received the letter from Stavanger University Hospital that contains the results I need if I'm ever to get anywhere near a real industrial pig. I take a knife out of the kitchen drawer, slit open the envelope, and pull out the letter. My eyes run across it: the answer is… negative—which, as we all know, is the most accurate terminology doctors and micro-biologists have at their disposal when they wish to convey the message that a test result is unequivocally positive.

I step into my boots, get in my car, and drive back across the Jæren plains.

The First
Encounter

THE ROAD WINDS ALONG the foot of the hills that rise to the
east. Up here is where most of the pigs live. Whereas the low-
land plain is dominated by vegetable production, the highland
is the domain of livestock. Rugland Farm lies at the top of a
ridge with a view of the sharply defined coastline that borders the ocean to the west. That's the origin of Jæren's name. It
comes from the Old Norse word *jaðarr*, meaning "edge" or "rim."

The gravel crunches beneath my tires as I drive into the
farmyard, in among the three, four, five, six, seven buildings
(*eight* counting a garage). In front of the barn is a boulder with
a black-lettered inscription: "Rugland." On top of it is a gilded
bronze pig—as if to remove any lingering doubt about what is
concealed here. Outside one of the buildings stands a solitary
figure. Tall, with a good-natured air, he is dressed roughly the
way you'd imagine, in overalls and rubber boots. This must be
Eirik Rugland. He can't be far off my own age, probably in his
mid-thirties. But although he is officially the farmer here at
Rugland, I'm actually here to meet someone else.

Just as I'm greeting Eirik, a door opens in the building behind him. The man who emerges is older and shorter. This must be his father, Leiv. I get the impression that he is scowling at me from behind his son's back. The sun-bronzed face beneath a head of silver-gray hair lends a sharp clarity to his sky-blue eyes. He comes around and holds out a rough hand.

"Leiv Rugland," he says, from deep in his chest, as he shakes my hand. He reminds me of an old athlete whose body still retains a residue of his former strength. He's actually retired but still has energy enough to tend the pigs on the farm.

I QUICKLY GET a feeling that all is not well. Eirik and Leiv exchange brief glances as if communicating a thought they are both privy to. The farmers here are famed for their taciturn disposition, but this is something else. Something is bothering them. On the telephone, everything seemed so straightforward, but something has changed. Leiv sees no reason to leave anything unsaid.

"We're skeptical about this."

I hasten to fish out the sheet of paper with the result of my MRSA test.

"I expect you want to see my test result," I say, holding it out to them.

Leiv barely glances at the certificate. "Oh, yes—that. I'm sure it's fine," he says, waving it aside. They've taken their own precautions anyway. Eirik hands me a face mask, plastic gloves, and an anti-contamination suit wrapped in plastic.

"You can just leave your boots in the car. We'll give you some special footwear," Leiv says.

For an instant I'd been afraid they were going to turn me away, so it's initially a relief to be given the gear they want me to dress up in. But an edge of doubt soon creeps in. Protective gear? What was the point of making me take the test? Why are they walking around in ordinary clothing themselves? Is all this a subtle display of power directed at a person they don't really trust? It's all a bit much. First there was the Farmers Union being unable to give out information about pig breeders because of "data protection." Then there was my own fumbling and failed attempt to visit a pig farm. Next came the painful MRSA test, followed by three weeks' quarantine from farms before the result arrived—and now anti-contamination gear. All this just so that I, a simple carnivore, can catch a glimpse of the animal I love to eat.

"Is this really necessary?" I ask as I unwrap the suit and stick my foot into the first pant leg.

"That's just the way it is. It's all about contagion," Leiv says.

This is no time to quibble. I pull up the zipper, coax the plastic gloves over my fingers, place the mask in front of my mouth, and draw the hood over my head. I see my reflection in the car window: I look like a health worker about to enter an Ebola zone. Or maybe more like a crime scene investigator, since they clearly suspect there's something I want to look into, something I want to expose. Leiv stops on the threshold.

"We don't know what kind of a guy you are," he says.

"We talked about this on the phone, though," I say, words muffled by the face mask.

"Well, yes. But it isn't so easy to tell who you're dealing with nowadays."

I'm genuinely starting to become uncertain myself. All I wanted to do was meet a pig. How difficult can it be?

IT ISN'T HARD TO SEE THINGS from Leiv's point of view. He and Eirik are embroiled in what they perceive as an escalating cultural conflict. It's actually the age-old story of the tension between town and country, center and periphery. But in the past decade, the pivot of this conflict has increasingly shifted from people to animals—and in few areas is it more heated than in pig farming. According to Leiv and Eirik, the profession is under attack, and they believe their opponents are playing dirty.

"So you're wondering if I have a hidden agenda?" I ask.

Leiv ponders this for a while. "Well, it is a bit suspicious—you turning up here saying you want to meet the pigs. It isn't what you'd call an ordinary request. But you said you were open, that you'd listen to both sides, so I'll just have to take your word for it."

Leiv seems to have guessed my intentions. Although I wolf down industrial pork in one form or another pretty much every day, my worldview has long been shaped by forces that work *against* this way of life. For years I have met the arguments of the animal welfare movement with an assenting nod. From the standpoint of moral philosophy, they strike me as pretty unassailable—given my position as a person remote from any form of animal husbandry. After all, why should we eat food from animals we doubt have lived good lives when we can simply stop doing so? It just isn't good enough to resort to "tradition" or "because it suits us." That's too reminiscent of the sort of self-justification that robbed women and vulnerable ethnic groups of their fundamental human rights in times gone by. Nor is the fact that we are carnivores by nature a good enough argument to justify the neglectful treatment of animals: it fails to take into account the fact that humans are an omnivorous species with a capacity for critical reflection. The problem is that I have an essential flaw, which I would say is just as profoundly human: I am lazy and struggle to practice what I preach. In order to avoid living my life as a hypocrite, I wish—among other things—to get some help from the person who knows the industrial pig best. But now I sense some unease.

"The animal welfare movement has a stranglehold on the media these days. They don't seem to think we should be here at all."

What is this—the swan song of the Norwegian pig farmer? An elegy to industrial livestock? One last grunt from the farmyard before it all crumbles to dust?

According to the U.K. newspaper the *Guardian*, 2018 was the year that vegetarianism and veganism became mainstream in the West.[1] In bookstores, vegetarian and vegan recipe books now account for a significant share of the cooking section, and all self-respecting restaurants now offer vegetarian dishes that are as imaginatively prepared and appetizing as any meat-based meal. Even McDonald's offers vegan burgers these days. But who is actually eating all this?

"It's odd the way there's been so much talk about this," Leiv says. "After all, what do most people eat?" Of course he wants me to yell "industrial meat!" And why shouldn't I indulge him? Even though membership numbers in environmental and animal welfare organizations have rocketed in the past couple of years, there are still no reliable statistics for how many people have cut out meat entirely. Based on how many pigs have been slaughtered in the past few years, it wouldn't seem to have been all that many: after adjusting for the decline caused by the 2019 African swine fever outbreak, consumption of industrial pork has remained more or less stable over the whole of the past decade.[2]

If animal welfare were as important as it often appears to be in the media, we might reasonably assume that organic farming of happy free-range pigs is the future. But there is little to suggest that this is true: in recent years, the organic share of the meat market has fallen in real terms in many countries. And even where there *has* been growth, there is still no country where organic pork has a share of more than 5 percent of the pork market. In other words, the trend in many countries appears to be that ethically aware consumers leapfrog over organic animal husbandry entirely and head straight for the vegetables.[3] It's become a matter of either/or: eat or don't eat, kill or don't kill. So Leiv has a point when he says:

"What's the alternative for Eirik, now that he's taken over the farm? There's a limit to how many organic farmers can make a living in this country."

He falls silent for a moment. We stand there, taking in the panoramic view across the sea. The light falls in columns through the perforated cloud cover like organ pipes—as if the awesome gray-blue canvas of sky and sea could blast out a crescendo any second.

Then he adds:

"I honestly don't know how you'd farm organically. I'm not remotely interested, and given how mucky pigs get and how they root around in the soil, I don't think it looks especially appetizing either."

It's ironic that Leiv should choose to make this particular comment right before we go in—because the second we step over the threshold of his piggery, I feel like throwing up.

FORTUNATELY, IT ISN'T the sight that sets off my retching reflex; we're still only standing in the entranceway. It's the smell. The intense, penetrating stench of ammonia and acetone, which scorches my mucous membranes and is worse than almost anything I've ever experienced. I must have said something because Leiv's face is a picture of bewilderment.

"Do you think it smells?" His question turns out to be absolutely genuine.

"Can't *you* smell it?"

"Not enough to think about it, anyway."

Leiv has spent almost every day of his sixty-six-year life in the piggery. It must have done something to his receptors, I think. At the same time, I have a feeling he thinks the opposite: "Here's a sensitive city nose that's come to the countryside and finally found out what smell is."

Once the olfactory shock has died down, I can at last take in what I came for. Because here they are—sows, in this case. We're standing in a large room with four enormous pigpens, each containing roughly ten fully grown sows. The naked mounds of flesh lie together in great clusters, partly on top of one another—not unlike a colony of walruses. The association is further underscored whenever any of these long-bodied, short-legged, 650-pound biological paradoxes of a beast heave themselves up onto their cloven hooves. It's a helpless struggle against the laws of nature—some of them barely manage to stand up. It's hard to grasp that once, far back in prehistoric times, these animals would have been neat, spritely wild boars.

I reach over the edge of the pigpen and scratch one of them behind the ear. She seems to like it; when I withdraw my hand, she oinks and tosses her head as if asking for more.

The piggery is divided into four sections: one for breeding sows, one for young sows waiting to reach sexual maturity, and two for slaughter pigs. In addition, there's a separate slaughter pig section in the neighboring building. In all, fifty-two sows produce more than a thousand slaughter pigs per year. That is a significant-sized business by Norwegian standards, although it would barely rank as a hobby farm compared with businesses in other countries. In China, the largest complexes are several stories high and can house up to thirty thousand sows, which produce around 850,000 slaughter pigs per year.[4]

"You've timed it nicely," Leiv says once we're inside the next section. He leans into one of the pigpens and pulls the umbilical cord off a naked little newborn who's crawling around in the wood shavings by the sow's backside.

It turns out I've arrived in the middle of farrowing. There are twenty smaller pigpens in this section, each housing a sow that is either farrowing or waiting for things to start moving. We stand there beside pigpen number thirteen, where the sow is midway through this process. She lies on her side, groaning and snorting, as her newborn piglets butt unsteadily against her teats. It isn't easy to spot, but a power struggle is underway among the piglets. They are battling for ownership of the teats, establishing a hierarchy that will last for the whole of their short lives.

As Leiv and Eirik explain the cycle here—insemination, birth, growth, and slaughter—I become aware of a low, muffled whine. Who is squealing? I look around but can't work out where it's coming from. Can it be from a piglet that's on its way out? I look at Leiv and Eirik. They also seem a bit puzzled.

"One of them has probably ended up underneath," Leiv says, going in and slapping the sow on her backside. But she doesn't stir. Another slap, two slaps. She has no intention of moving. The thin wail continues, and now Eirik gives him a hand. They rock the enormous body and eventually manage to winkle out an exhausted little fellow from beneath the mound of flesh. Leiv inspects the tiny creature. Unbelievably, there's no sign of injury. So he slings it nonchalantly over to the rest of its siblings, who are crawling around by the teats.

The fact that sows can crush their young to death is an unfortunate by-product of recent Norwegian animal welfare legislation. Previously sows were kept immobile during birth in a farrowing crate that prevented them from moving to the sides. For days, the sow was deprived of all movement while her young escaped being crushed by their mother. The ban on immobilizing breeding sows has obviously been beneficial for the sows themselves, but has undoubtedly caused painful deaths for some of their young—and greater wastage for farmers.

So far, twelve piglets are out, but there may well be more on the way. Litters of piglets usually number between ten and fifteen, and it's unusual for there to be more than twenty. The larger litters can easily become a problem, because sows normally have only fourteen teats and, since the piglets establish a fixed hierarchy, that generally means some will go short of food. So it's also a fight for survival, and the piglets come into the world equipped with razor-sharp fangs. However, survival of the fittest isn't the only rule that applies here: the pigs are also subject to a first-come-first-served principle. Studies have shown that the last piglets to arrive are twice as likely to die as those that get to the food early. Nonetheless, there is hope for the latecomers: since piglets are hairless, sows don't lick their young. As a result, the bond between mother and offspring is not as strong as in many other animals. That makes it easy to sneak some of the piglets into a different pigpen with better access to teats.

THE TIGHT FACE MASK is cutting into the top of my nose. After adjusting it a few times to relieve the pressure, I end up pulling it down below my chin. At first it feels like a liberation, but I soon find I'm dry-mouthed and my throat starts to prickle. I swallow, clear my throat, and growl. Steam from the urine and feces has mingled with particles of wood shavings, scurf, and mites—and now it's coating my mucous membranes.

Previously, it wasn't unusual for pigs to suffer from this problem too. Many developed chronic respiratory problems as a result of the poor air quality in the piggeries. But following the introduction of new, stricter rules on ventilation in Norway, there are few signs that pigs suffer such problems today. I'm not so lucky. In an effort to achieve some respiratory relief, I breathe in through my nose for the first time. It immediately proves to be just as bad an idea as it was when we came in.

THE AFTERBIRTH OOZES OUT into the wood shavings. After piglet number twelve, the sow in pigpen thirteen is done. The fact that pigs have so many young is a taxonomic aberration.

Animals with cloven hooves rarely give birth to more than two per litter. In this respect, pigs are more like dogs and cats. But unlike the offspring of predators and like most herbivores, piglets are quick to get to their feet. This is a typical trait in prey animals that need to be able to move fast to avoid danger.

Whereas cows and sheep generally need a bit of assistance from the farmer during birth, pigs usually get by on their own. That means Leiv doesn't need to spend the night in the piggery and oversee the process. But one thing is important: he must always inspect the pigpens for afterbirth. Because if the piglets have arrived and there's no afterbirth, there are probably still some piglets left inside the sow. That means he'll have to stick his arm in and pull them out.

Leiv picks up the last arrival and wipes it clean with a handful of straw. Then he sticks his fingers in the piglet's mouth and forces its jaws apart.

"Feel this."

I stick a finger in cautiously. Its canines feel like needles. Leiv pulls out a little gadget that looks like an electric shaver. He pushes the jaw fully open and places the device inside the mouth. It only takes a couple of seconds for the first tooth to be ground down. Leiv tells me the piglets feel no pain and he could have used a nail clipper instead.

"Do you want to hold it?"

I arrange the piglet with its head resting in the crook of my elbow and its belly against my lower arm—roughly the way I might hold a newborn baby. It doesn't make a sound but is clearly frightened. Its body trembles and its heart hammers beneath its ribs. I stroke its back gently and feel the bumps of its vertebrae through its naked skin. Less than a week ago, I was at the hospital taking my own son in my arms. This probably accounts for the nagging sense of concern I suddenly feel for the newborn, humanlike creature. I try to shake it off, try to say to myself "I'm going to eat you," but somehow I can't force the sentence out—not even in my head.

Like Alice in Wonderland, I'm suddenly finding it difficult to see any great difference between a baby and a pig—although admittedly Alice experiences it the opposite way around. During a visit to the Duchess's kitchen, Alice is asked to look after a baby. She picks it up and decides to take it for a little stroll. The minute she gets outside, she hears some small grunts from the child. On inspecting its face, Alice sees to her surprise that it is gradually taking on the features of a pig: "This time there could be *no* mistake about it: it was neither more nor less than a pig, and she felt that it would be quite absurd for her to carry it further. So she set the little creature down, and felt quite relieved to see it trot away quietly into the wood."[5] I'm finding it less easy to let go.

"Looks like you want to take him home with you," Leiv says with a grin. His comment makes me think of something I read about Papua New Guinea. Nowhere else in the world is the pig held in higher esteem. All its offspring must be cared for, including piglets that aren't really strong enough to survive. If there's a lactating woman in the village, the creature will be placed on the woman's breast and raised like a human child.

"My wife's breastfeeding. Maybe it'd be possible?"

We laugh and that tense atmosphere between us is dispelled.

"The question is what you'd do in six months," Leiv answers. And he obviously has a point. At birth, a piglet is just a third of the weight of a human baby. After sixteen weeks, the human child weighs around fifteen pounds. By that time, the pig weighs in at 150 pounds. This growth rate is something Canadian couple Steve Jenkins and Derek Walter experienced close up when they adopted what they thought was a six-month-old—and fully grown—mini pig. That rapidly proved to be a lie. After a year, the sow was well on her way to 600 pounds and had outgrown their small home. But the couple liked their pig, Esther, so much that they didn't want to give her up. Nowadays, they live with a 630-pound sow in the living room at their farm, which doubles as a sanctuary for abused farm animals.[6]

I ask Eirik and Leiv if they've ever thought of taking a piglet into the house with them, just to cuddle and play with it.

"Pigs are industrial animals. They're not for cuddling," is the curt response to my question. Suddenly, the cozy atmosphere has evaporated. *Industrial animal?* What is the distinction between an industrial or production animal and a pet? Of course, it's all just a matter of language and social constructs. But Leiv's comment highlights a key point: how we *use* our animals determines how we *classify* them; and how we *classify* them determines how we *treat* them. A single word allows us to shut pigs away in factorylike units, to stop interacting with them, and, ultimately, to eat them.

As I put the piglet down, I catch sight of one of its siblings. It's trembling helplessly in the corner of the pigsty and is just half the size of the others.

"That one probably won't amount to anything," Leiv says with the faintest trace of empathy in his voice.

It's a long way from Papua New Guinea to Jæren.

IN THE CAR on the way home, I cough and clear my throat as I drive. I feel as if I'm *breathing* pig. I turn into a gas station and buy a bottle of water. When I go to pay, I get the impression the girl behind the counter is shrinking away from me. I really can't blame her, because there's no doubt about it: I stink. I open the bottle on my way out of the sliding doors and chug it down between the gas pumps. It feels better, but I still haven't gotten rid of that tickle in my throat, and the taste of caged pigs persists—a disturbing element at the back of my gullet. I feel the need to be outside, to breathe in the sea breeze and air out my body.

When I left the farm, we agreed that I would spend a lot of time at the piggery in the months ahead, so I could get to know the pigs and learn how to be a pig tender. I use the breathing space to travel back to a time when pigs and humans both lived beneath the open skies. Because if there has ever been a trace of equality between us, it was then. It's only a short drive north across the plain.

The Animal
That Domesticated
Itself

OAK TREES BEND their crooked branches over a rocky outcrop, framing a deep hollow in the rock face. The cave isn't large—just ten feet high, sixteen feet wide, and thirty feet deep. Nonetheless, Vistehola (the Viste cave) in North Jæren is the place that comes closest to giving us an idea of how cave dwellers lived in Norway. The cavern is so rounded, so elegant, its location facing the shore to the south so perfect, that the place has an almost artificial air. The enormous outcrop that provides the opening with a protective overhang does little to dispel the impression that the place is a planned construction. But the only non-natural elements here are the neatly clipped lawn outside and the information board down the road. For hundreds of millennia the sea surged in here, scouring the rock face with sand and sediment until the ocean retreated and people arrived.

It would take a surprisingly long time, roughly three thousand years, for the first settlers in Rennesøy—a mere half-hour car trip north of here—to find their way to Vistehola, some eight thousand years ago. But once they did arrive, they came to stay. For more than six thousand years, they remained within these walls.[1] They hunted and fished, slept and reproduced, and did so in a climate and amid a fauna very different from those we see today.

A SOLITARY GULL glides above the oak trees on a thermal. The others flurry over something in a field off in the distance. These scavengers of the sea are more or less the only wild species to be found here nowadays. But when archaeologists first examined the cave in the early twentieth century, they uncovered an entirely different biodiversity: the people of Viste left the remains of more than fifty different animal and fish species behind them. They had a casual approach to waste disposal, simply throwing the animal bones, fish spines, and shells onto the floor of the space where they lived and slept. As a result, the cave was one vast mound of prehistoric food waste when the archaeologists set to work. The "cultural layer" was more than five feet high—and would have been even higher if a local farmer in the early twentieth century hadn't shoveled out a massive amount of these precious vestiges of history and spread them over his fields to fertilize his crops. Even so, the finds offer a unique insight into the eating habits of humans over thousands of years.

From the sea, they ate mussels, fish, and seals, and from the land, they ate everything from elk and venison to bear, fox, and lynx. But there was one animal the people of Viste ate more often than any other: the pig. Pork accounted for such a large share of their diet that we could accurately describe the inhabitants of Vistehola as specialized wild boar hunters. And this same dietary trend is evident in Stone Age locations over large swaths of ice-free Eurasia. Everyone ate pork. In massive quantities.

TAKING IT IN THE CONTEXT of human evolution, one might almost make the claim that wild boar hunting marked the birth of the thinking human. Although some sparse proof suggests that archaic humans would occasionally bag a wild boar or two, they generally did not. The Neanderthals didn't hunt boars either—they weren't bright enough—and the same applies to other early hominids.[2] There's a reason for this: wild boar hunting involves numerous risks that can only be tackled with a great deal of thought. A wild boar at top speed can run at over thirty miles an hour—far faster than most dog breeds. What's more, these animals are notoriously aggressive when they sense a threat. And the wild boar's tendency to go for the groin when it attacks does little to reduce the perils of the hunt. Over the millennia, many a family line has been cut short and even more hunters have limped home empty-handed with mutilated shins and thighs.

As a result, the wild boar was left in peace for most of the history of humanity, along with various other animals that were too dangerous to hunt in earlier times—lions, mammoths, and rhinoceroses. But then, apparently overnight, something changed. Suddenly we became capable of sophisticated planning and were able to make weapons and tools that were far more precise than before. This cognitive leap changed everything. The hunt was on.

Before long, humans had wiped out most of the Eurasian megafauna—cave bears, mammoths, rhinoceroses, and lions. By about seventeen thousand years ago, these same animals had disappeared from the American continent too. Over time, the Eurasian aurochs (precursors of the cow) and most wild horses became extinct. But humans were never an existential threat to the wild boar. Adaptable and hyper-reproductive, they have almost always been numerous wherever they have lived. However, robust populations are not necessarily the sole reason that wild boar bones are so commonly found at Stone Age sites like Vistehola. A further explanation may be that, once we'd cracked the code, the method we used to hunt them proved extremely efficient. Hunting prey like elk, deer, or bears was time-consuming and exhausting. The prey had to be found and tracked over vast areas, then transported home over long distances. Not so the wild boar. Its indiscriminate eating habits made it easy to trap by laying out carrion and other waste: it's quite possible that much of the hunting may have taken place right outside the mouth of the cave.

The boar's meat and offal had to be eaten at once, because the art of food preservation had not yet been discovered. Then our forebears stretched out the hides with straps and cleaned them with flint scrapers. After that, they sewed clothes, foot-wear, pouches, and bags using needles carved from the bones. Bones also became fishhooks and arrows, which could be used to hunt new prey, and thus the circle was closed.

I STEP INSIDE, onto the muddy floor of the cave. It's damp and chilly, and I have to step over large puddles to avoid getting my feet wet. A layer of algae coats the walls and forms a dark crescent beneath my nails when I run my fingers over the rock. The place is apparently not as cozy as it first seemed. Then again, perhaps a twenty-first-century Norwegian is not ideally placed to judge what constituted comfort for a Stone Age human.

The archaeologists also found a person here, a fourteen-year-old boy. He was one of the pioneers who arrived here around eight thousand years ago. They found him buried deep inside the cave, at the point where the wall curves down to meet the ground. His is the oldest complete human skeleton ever to be found in Norway. It isn't difficult to conjure up scenes from his life, but when we do, it's a bit like observing an animal—all behavior and silent movement, the sound permanently switched to mute. Although there are no traces of language or thought here, it's still possible to catch a glimpse of his worldview. But to do so, we'll need to look at Stone Age finds from other places.

THE MOST EXTENSIVE SPECIMENS of older Stone Age art were found in the Chauvet and Lascaux caves in France, and the Cave of Altamira in Spain. Other than a few handprints, they exclusively depict animals. Nothing but animals. This is the common denominator of all artistic expression from that time, regardless of its geographic location. Existence revolved around humanity's relationship to animals. Humans may have been predators who hunted in flocks, but we were just as often prey to other species. This symbiosis engendered respect, humility, and awe for the other beings on the plains and in the forests. Animals were both life and death. Animals became spirits and they became gods. Some became inferior to us, others superior. This life and this position—in the midst of the animal kingdom—was our original state.

Dating Stone Age illustrations is a hopelessly difficult task. As a result, the oldest cave drawings were long thought to be the illustrations in France and Spain, which dated back roughly 30,000 years. But when a group of archaeologists carried out new pigment tests on samples from a cave wall on the Indonesian island of Sulawesi in 2012, the migration map of thinking humans had to be redrawn. The sketch of a pig, until then estimated to be around 17,000 years old, turned out, on closer inspection, to have been produced 43,900 years ago.[3] In 2017, an even older pig painting was discovered in another cave on Sulawesi, dating to at least 45,500 years ago.[4]

There is little doubt that people elsewhere in the world also had boars on their mind. That much is evidenced by the food waste. Yet there is something unique about the animal depicted in Indonesia. Because if there is one typical feature of early Stone Age art, it's that people did *not* draw pigs.

Of all the animals we hunted and fled, some occupied our thoughts more than others. And these were the ones we drew in our caves. Consequently, there is rarely any connection between the food we ate and the animals on the walls. The ones we most admired, the ones to which we assigned the greatest spiritual value, were the big predators. This is clear from the cave paintings, from the strategically placed skeletons and animal skulls, and from the jewelry and carved figures. But when many of the iconic megafauna became first rare and then extinct, we transferred our admiration to the large herbivores. The way horses and deer are depicted on the cave walls leaves little doubt about the fact that we must have seen something graceful and spiritual in them.

It's hard to say why pigs didn't acquire a higher spiritual ranking in the Stone Age. Could it be that the pig was already denigrated for its unappealing appearance? Or might it be that the wild boar was so easy to catch that it failed to capture the imagination of the Stone Age people? As with so much else in our remote prehistory, we are reduced to questions and speculation. Nonetheless, the general absence of pigs in European Stone Age art *may* have an important implication: even back then pigs were considered to be inferior animals.

But the pig would have its revenge. Along with a handful of other species, it helped wipe out an entire spiritual culture and undermine our relationship with the majestic animals we once revered. For unlike most other species, the pig became domesticated. That would change the world beyond recognition.

QUITE HOW AND WHY it happened is still a mystery, but some eleven thousand years ago, people in the Fertile Crescent (which spans parts of the Middle East) began to cultivate

plants and breed wild animals. With the agricultural revolution, humans transitioned from nature to culture in a process
of change that lasted millennia. It's a process whose significance can hardly be overstated. Agriculture enabled people to
settle: first in small groups, then in clusters of houses and vil-
lages, later in towns and civilizations, and ultimately in states
and empires with all their trappings—written language, power
structures, religious systems, money, industry, and consumption. In macrohistorical analyses, the transition to agriculture
has been identified as the main reason we humans ended up in
the ecological predicament in which we're now trapped. If it's
any consolation, there is little to suggest that it was driven by
concrete intent—and the domestication of the pig is a prime
example of this. Whereas cows, sheep, goats, and horses were all
tamed intentionally, there is little indication that this was the
case with the pig.

The most striking thing about the species we keep as livestock these days is how few of them there are. It's fairly likely
that all the big mammals have been *tamed* over the years. Yet
only a minority have ended up as *domesticated* livestock.

Let's clarify some terminology here. "Taming" is often used
synonymously with "domesticating," but in this context, there's
an essential difference between the two. If you take a young
animal from its mother and bring it up to trust humans, you
have tamed it. However, to be able to define your animal as
domesticated, you'll have to put in a bit more work—at least if
you're going to do it the old-fashioned way. First you'll need to
tame several individuals of both sexes, and you'll need to have
selected them from different flocks to ensure viable offspring.
After that, you'll have to ensure that your animals don't give way
to their instincts and bolt the moment they reach sexual maturity. If you manage to avoid that, you'll have reached the most
critical point—the point where many an attempt has come to a
grinding halt: getting them to mate with each other. Both sexes

must become sexually aroused and must breed freely. If you can get over that particular hump and manage to repeat the process often enough for the animals to start to assume traits that set them apart from their wild forebears, you are more or less home and dry.

Now you may, of course, wonder what in the world to do with this creature. Imagine that the animals in question are giraffes. They may be cool, but do your giraffes fulfill a function or have an economic value that will persuade other people to follow your lead? And will your descendants continue this practice in the generations after your death? Perhaps not. That may go some way toward explaining why there are not more species in our cattle sheds and stables, or sleeping at the foot of our bed. However, it doesn't explain why we domesticated wolves and not bears, aurochs and not deer, Eurasian wild horses and not zebras.

An animal is domesticated when humans have taken full control of its reproductive process, access to food, and habitat. The only predators over which we managed to gain such control in ancient times were dogs and cats. The majority of species we succeeded with are herbivores. Humans have probably attempted to domesticate all of the world's 148 species of large herbivorous land mammals at some time or another. Yet only fourteen of those attempts have been successful. And of these, just five have ended up being global successes: mouflon (sheep), wild goats (goats), aurochs (cows), the wild horses of North Caucasus (horses), and wild boars (pigs). The other nine are dromedaries, camels, llamas, donkeys, reindeer, water buffalo, yaks, bantengs (a type of Southeast Asian cattle), and gaurs (sometimes called "Indian bison").[5] Some may wonder why the Asian elephant is missing from this list. But elephants have never been domesticated. Individual animals are still captured in the wild and raised using the method Hannibal adopted with the African elephants that he took on his legendary crossing of the Alps in 218 BCE. There is much to suggest that it would have been perfectly feasible to domesticate elephants if people had really given it a try. Because elephants share a feature common to all the livestock we have successfully domesticated: they are herd animals, with all that this implies in the way of social traits, such as trust and the capacity for submission. These are probably among the single most important factors that determine how well-suited an animal is to domestication. (That also explains why cats don't make such suitable pets as their numbers might suggest.[6]) Yet nothing ever came of elephant herds. There are several possible explanations for this, but two crucial factors stand out: elephants eat enormous amounts of food and grow at a frustratingly slow pace. It doesn't compute.

It was the father of eugenics, Francis Galton, who identified the six key factors that must be in place for an animal to be considered "domesticable." If the candidates failed on just one of them, they would remain in their wild state forever, according to Galton.[7] In addition to the factors mentioned above, the animals in question must not be overly aggressive—which rules out most predators—or overly given to panic—which rules out most deer.[8] If we go through the animal kingdom applying these factors, we find that the number of domesticable species eventually narrows down to the few that were already domesticated in antiquity.[9]

Since wild boars were domesticated, it's perhaps self-evident that they met all of Galton's criteria. But only just—because pigs lack one essential trait that all other livestock possess: they do not produce a valuable by-product. Whereas other domestic animals give us milk, wool, or eggs, pigs only give us meat. It's paradoxical, really, because pigs, with their fourteen teats, undoubtedly produce milk. And it's rich in nutrients too, roughly like cow's milk, only with higher fat content and a waterier consistency. So why don't we wash our supper down with an ice-cold glass of sow's milk?

Because milking pigs can be dangerous. Sows with suckling young are always on the alert and extremely aggressive to anyone who gets too close. Goats don't like being milked either, but whereas goats can only give you a bruise if they kick you, a pig can kill you. If it rams an exposed area with tusks that haven't been properly filed down, you'll be facing a trip to the emergency room at the very least. This must have been hard-won knowledge in the early phases of domestication. And when, against all the odds, people *did* manage to milk pigs, they must have noticed another negative trait—one, by the way, that they share with us humans: lactation serves as a natural form of contraception. Whereas cows can be impregnated and give birth to new calves while they are being milked, pigs can only do one thing at a time. What's more, it's a complicated job milking fourteen teats, each of which yields only a dribble. In short, when it comes to pig's milk, the outcome doesn't justify the effort. Dutch pig farmer Erik Stegink can confirm this. With much effort and the aid of ten assistants, he eventually managed to squeeze out enough sow's milk to make some cheeses. But the price per pound worked out at more than US$1,000.[10]

It's only fair to ask: why were pigs domesticated in the first place? And how did it turn out to be such a great success? To find out, we'll need to go back to where it all began—to the mountains of Anatolia in Turkey some eleven thousand years ago.

THERE WAS AN UNUSUALLY Indiana Jones–like atmosphere to the dig when American archaeologists set to work on the prehistoric settlement of Hallan Çemi in southeast Turkey in 1991. When news emerged that the Turkish government had embarked on a new dam project in Anatolia, archaeologists were spurred to action. Several rivers were to be diverted from their courses to create a new lake in the valley beside the Taurus Mountains. The entire area would soon be flooded, and some newly discovered but as yet unexcavated prehistoric settlements would vanish forever. It was a race against the clock. The drama was further heightened by constant skirmishes between the Turkish military and Kurdish guerrilla groups that were active in the area. As military vehicles patrolled the roads, the archaeologists dug into the sun-scorched hillsides.[11]

They soon unearthed an unusual complex of round clay houses. The big question was whether Hallan Çemi represented one of the first settled hunter-gatherer societies or was an early example of an agricultural society. It proved to be neither.

There was no doubt that these people were hunter-gatherers, and that pork was an absolutely central part of their diet. When the archaeologists took bone fragments from the animals back to the lab for further inspection, nothing about the bone structure itself indicated that these were the remains of domesticated animals. They bore none of the usual features—shorter snouts, alterations in the molars, or a smaller body size. No, the pigs of Hallan Çemi were undoubtedly wild. Or were they?

Gradually, a mysterious pattern emerged among the pig bones: most of the animals were males. And almost all of them were young animals. This couldn't be accidental. It reflected a tendency that could have been cut and pasted from modern animal husbandry: young males had evidently been picked out for slaughter while females were kept alive for further breeding. It became clear that these people had gained control over a herd of wild boars. In other words, these finds dated back to an early phase of a domestication process that must have concluded before the animals had time to develop traits that set them apart from their wild relatives.[12]

This was a breakthrough in two respects: first, it showed that pigs were domesticated some two thousand years earlier than archaeologists had previously assumed. Second, it overturned all earlier assumptions about how the transition from hunter-gatherer to agricultural societies occurred. The established theory was that plants were domesticated first and animals came later. But at Hallan Çemi, there was nothing to indicate that these people had cultivated anything whatsoever. Instead, the archaeologists found wild plants such as corn, almonds, pulses, and pistachio nuts. Hallan Çemi was a transitional society unlike any other.[13]

IN NORWAY, AND NORTHERN EUROPE for that matter, there is nothing to indicate that animals were ever domesticated. Domestication of an animal like the wild boar required continuous human settlement over a period of centuries, so you might assume that the people of Viste had what it took for the wild boar to be domesticated there too. But while Vistehola and other known Stone Age locations in Norway were in use for more than long enough, each of these places served as just one of several alternative bases for hunting and fishing. The constant movement of the population that used them would have been incompatible with breeding a domestic animal like a pig.

Pigs were simply the last of the big domestic animals to find their way to Norway. The oldest traces of them are found near Ruskeneset, just outside the western coastal town of Bergen, and date back to between 1500 and 1400 BCE. By that time, the country had already had cows, sheep, and goats for more than a thousand years.

Even so, the interaction between humans and pigs that played out at Vistehola may not have been all that different from what happened in the earliest phase of the process at Hallan Çemi. In both places people must have noticed that there was something about the behavior of the wild boars that set them apart from other groups of animals. On the one hand, there were the large predators, which could creep up on humans and tear them to shreds. On the other, there were the herbivores, which never displayed any interest in humans, for

good or for bad. The wild boars were different. Like the predators, they might seek out humans, but they were never a specific
threat. Only when they were scared or being hunted could they
pose a direct risk to people. The wild boar's purpose in seeking
out humans was scavenging. The individuals with little intrin-
sic fear of people would come increasingly closer, while the
shier animals would stay away, and the most aggressive ones
would be killed in self-defense. The result was a natural selection of individuals whose temperament was compatible with
proximity to people. This behavior may have led to a unique
coexistence between the wild boars and the people of Vistehola: the wild boars helped themselves to simple meals from
the humans' waste, and from time to time the people would kill
one of them with a spear. It's uncertain how long that kind of
interaction persisted in Hallan Çemi before people took on a
more active role. But by around eleven thousand years ago, the
relationship between people and wild boars must have evolved
into one so close that the inhabitants of Hallan Çemi—without
any clear intention—had begun to monitor the movements
and reproduction of the pigs ever more closely. The herds they
tended and fed probably consisted of sows and piglets, with the
wild and more unruly males sneaking in among them whenever they were in heat.

The process seems to have been so symbiotic and haphazard
that one could justifiably claim that the pigs effectively domesticated themselves.[14] This also helps explain why pigs have been
domesticated many more times than other animals. In the case
of cows, it probably happened twice: once in the Fertile Crescent, and then a second time in India. Sheep, goats, and horses,
meanwhile, were probably only domesticated once and then
spread around to the rest of the globe as tame animals. The pig,
however, is known to have been domesticated in Turkey, Southern Europe, India, Southeast Asia, and twice in China.[15] The list
may well be even longer.

IT'S OBVIOUS THAT a great deal has happened between the time we hunted pigs as wild animals in the forest and the point we've reached now, where we primarily encounter pigs in the form of a processed product in our supermarkets, in the refrigerated section, or among the canned goods. And this development has had consequences, not only for our access to meat. Just as we've transformed our livestock from wild creatures to almost unrecognizable production animals, our livestock has also changed us.

Life in hunter-gatherer societies was relatively peaceful and egalitarian. Groups of people lived spread out over large areas, with little contact between each other. The closest relationship these human groups had was to animals. We probably felt an alliance with them. And the animals weren't nobodies: they became the embodiment of the forces of nature over which people lacked control. But the domestication of animals toppled this entire worldview.

By gaining control over animals, humans went from being "just another species" to being "master of them all." This was clearly reflected in our new spiritual notions: first in the mythologies, where humans come to occupy an ever more prominent place, and later in the world religions, with their omnipotent godheads. Nowhere was this new worldview more clearly expressed than in Genesis, when God said: "Let them have dominion over the fish of the sea, and over the fowl of the air, and over the cattle, and over all the earth, and over every creeping thing that creepeth upon the earth."[16]

And we undoubtedly took Him at his word.

Not on the Same Wavelength

THINGS HAVEN'T GONE quite to plan in Jæren this past week. It's been really hot—well over ninety degrees Fahrenheit. The wind turbines have been at a standstill and the sea beyond the shoreline has been green with algae and full of jellyfish. Perhaps the dog days are simply unusually intense this year, but it's hard to avoid thinking that there's something else behind all this— something more threatening and foreboding.

You'd think the population of Jæren would be better positioned to deal with climate change than other Norwegians. Not because the farmers here are any more stoic than those elsewhere, but because Jæren has always had the kind of climate many people in other parts of the country fear they will see in the years ahead: mild winters and rainy summers. The absence of clearly defined seasons has been one of the main reasons Jæren is such good agricultural country. The soil can be plowed early in the spring, and the growing season lasts until late into the autumn. But in the past couple of years, the farmers seem to have been taken by surprise, and one of the places you can really feel it is in the piggery. Lately, it's felt almost like a sauna, and right now Leiv stands there peering up at the air vent in the ceiling as he scratches his scalp with the peak of his cap.

"No matter how well we air it out, it won't get any cooler in here than it is outside," he says. Hardly ideal conditions for an animal that's incapable of sweating. And the situation isn't helped by the fact that the animals have no water holes or mud to cool down in. They're at risk of heatstroke. And if things get really bad, the stress on the pigs' cardiac and respiratory systems could be enough to kill them.

"It was even worse last year. If this is the new normal, I'm going to have to see if something needs to be done about it."

Leiv is thinking of installing a sprinkler system in the ceiling to shower the pigs with water when the heat gets too intense. But for now, they'll have to content themselves with a good airing and peaceful pigpens.

"As long as the animals keep calm and don't stress, it'll be fine," he says.

"It's all very well for *them!*" I catch myself thinking. "But what about us?"

I'M TROUBLED. I've just heard the UN Intergovernmental Panel on Climate Change present its latest report. It's backed by scientists from fifty-two countries, is based on seven thousand scientific studies, and its message couldn't be more queasily clear: eat less meat. Otherwise, we're not going to make it.[1] Our livestock account for 14.5 percent of all the climate-warming emissions caused by us humans. That's equivalent to the combined emissions of the global transport sector—the impact of every single car, boat, bus, truck, and plane in the world.[2]

It's one thing to worry about being kind to animals. But it's only reasonable to admit that if the food we eat is destroying our children's future, that's a problem in a totally different league. Has my question—can I eat these animals with a clear conscience?—already been answered?

There are so many pitfalls and points of view to take into account in the debate about meat consumption and its climate impact that it's enough to leave most of us thoroughly drained of motivation. It doesn't help matters that the warring fronts in the debate about domestic animals and climate appear to be as rigidly immovable as in the debate about animal welfare—what's more, conflicts of interests seem to be profoundly embedded in the research.

It's common knowledge that the real hornet's nest in the debate about meat and climate involves the cow. One minute it's presented as the worst culprit of all our domestic animals, the next it's held up as the answer to all our problems. The reason for the unexpected reversal that has transformed the cow from climate sinner to climate saint is this: certain studies have shown that *grazing* animals—unlike animals that eat concentrate feed, corn, hay, and silage (fermented grass from bales or siloes)—can increase the amount of carbon sequestered in the soil. This is because ruminants that graze outside stimulate the grass to grow deeper roots, enabling it to absorb far more carbon dioxide (CO_2) than grass that is trimmed mechanically for later use as hay and silage.

However, there are plenty of solid objections to this. First of all, only a tiny minority of the world's ruminants currently live in this state. Even in Norway, where cows and sheep spend a fair amount of time grazing in the open air, the bulk of their diet is still concentrate feed and silage. Second, ruminants that eat a lot of grass produce much more of the potent climate gas methane, which they then burp out into the atmosphere. This increased methane production may erase the benefits yielded by grazing. Third, there are only a few countries where grazing ruminants can become a reliable means of sequestering CO_2. This is because prolonged drought can make grass roots wither, creating a CO_2 bomb. A similar bomb would be created if someone decided to convert grazing land to other use—for example, vegetable production or construction. This type of livestock farming would therefore require countries to adopt a much stricter management of agricultural land use than most apply today.[3]

Norway is often praised as a country where conditions are especially good for grazing ruminants. Little of our land lends itself to vegetable farming, and our wet climate ensures that grass grows readily without imminent risk of withering. But the mere fact that Norway is among the *best suited* countries does not mean that ruminants will necessarily have a positive climate impact there, either. Or at least not as long as the alternative is to grow forests. The fact is that if Norwegian grazing land were converted to forest, the area converted would sequester 1.03 tons more carbon per hectare per year.[4] In short, there's still little to suggest that cows are anything other than a highly destructive force in a climate context.

Luckily, the pig is less complicated in this respect. Since pigs aren't ruminants, they don't eat grass or burp out methane. They do, however, eat concentrate feed—exclusively. Of course, this is problematic in its way: imported soybeans account for a large share of concentrate feed, and most of them are grown in the precious ancient rainforest regions of Brazil. Admittedly, much of the soy imported to Europe and the United States is a so-called sustainability certified product, meaning that it's produced in areas that haven't been deforested since 2004. But if food production in a marginal country like Norway consumes the output of roughly 495,000 acres of Brazilian land—almost ten thousand Brazilian small farms—we can assume that the countries with the highest meat production are placing an enormous pressure on the Brazilian countryside, leading to increased destruction of the rainforest. It's obvious that global pork production is among the worst culprits, as becomes clear when we look at China, which has long been home to almost half of all the pigs in the world. In 2017, some 60 percent of total global soybean production was exported to China, with the vast majority going to animal feed.[5]

To calculate which domestic animals are most sustainable, we have to compare the greenhouse gases emitted by meat production with those produced by beans and tofu—the two most widely consumed vegetable-based protein sources. For every 50 grams of protein produced, they cause emissions of 0.4 and 1 kilogram of carbon dioxide equivalent, respectively. The biggest villain by this same measure is beef, which emits a whopping 17.7 kg of CO_2 per 50 grams of protein. Next in line is lamb, with emissions of 9.9 kg, followed by cheese, at 5.4. Only now does the pig come into the picture, with emissions of 3.8 kg of CO_2 equivalent. Although it's true that chicken and eggs are much less of a burden on the environment, at 2.9 and 2.1 kg of CO_2, respectively, ham is, as we can see, a more sustainable sandwich filling than any kind of cheese.[6] If we take this to its extreme, we could claim that a pork-based diet is basically better for the planet than a cheese-heavy vegetarian diet.

So does that mean we can breathe a sigh of relief and drop our shoulders? Well, the temperature has fallen sharply, at any rate, and rain is forecast in the foreseeable future. Normal summer conditions have resumed in southwestern Norway.

TODAY, I'M DRESSED in regular green overalls. It feels like a declaration of confidence. No face mask, protective gear, or plastic gloves. At last I'm one of them, an ordinary farmhand; not a threat from the outside who risks sullying their herd with scary microbes, or, perhaps more pertinently, an interloper who has come to show the world how bad things are in the Norwegian pork business. That's pretty rich, considering that if there's one thing everyone has been discussing in Norway this summer, it's how appallingly Norwegian pigs are treated.

The reason for this is a documentary called *The Secret Lives of Pigs*, which was aired by Norway's national broadcaster, NRK, shortly after my previous visit. Norun Haugen adopted a fake identity and spent five years traveling around the country with a hidden camera, pretending to be an aspiring pig farmer keen to gain practical experience in a piggery. Many of the herds she visited were in Jæren. She filmed sick animals, castration without anesthetic, blows, and kicks—an unbroken litany of misery throughout the entire hour of the program.

Ever since the documentary was aired, I've worried that it may have ruined my entire project—my plan to get inside a piggery and get to know the modern industrial pig. What if the negative attention from the film made the pig farmers close ranks? But here I am, and I have the impression that they're more trustful than before. Why hasn't Leiv become even more skeptical about having me here?

"You're allowed in here because you've got a positive attitude to our business and because you want to learn. I mean, you told us you aren't one of them. I'll just have to take your word for it," he says.

Not one of them. Positive attitude. There doesn't seem to be a middle point, room for an open-minded and tentatively neutral position. Even though we've been through this several times before, I feel obliged to explain some more.

"I really want to find out about this for myself, without too much input from either side," I say.

"Of course," he says curtly, before continuing. "What she did in that documentary... I just don't know how to put it. Going in with a hidden camera like that and lying to the farmers' faces..."

It's undoubtedly humiliating to be exposed the way the pig farmers were in the documentary—especially for those who felt the recordings didn't reflect their own working lives. Because the program wasn't trying to catch out individual farmers but rather to illuminate a structural problem that, according to NRK and the film producer, permeates the *entire industry*.

"What do you think about the content?" I ask.

"It wasn't good. Some of it was really awful. There was a sow that should definitely have been put down ages ago, and one pig was castrated in a really cruel way. The animals came in for a lot of really rough handling, too. But after all, she *did* spend five years going around with a hidden camera."

Leiv turns out to share some of my own reservations: Regardless of the awfulness and the public-interest aspect, wasn't there also a certain dishonesty about the footage shown? Is what we saw genuinely the reality, given that the film is a mash-up of all the worst scenes Haugen recorded over *five years*? What if the same method were applied to other professions? Where *wouldn't* you find enough material for an hour of grim images, poor judgment, and moral failures? I ask Leiv if he feels threatened after what came out.

"I wouldn't say that. You can say a lot about the activists, but I think the way the food safety inspectors treat us sometimes can be just as bad. The inspectors who show up often have zero expertise and make decisions that have huge consequences for the farmers—often on totally false grounds. It's very obvious they don't like our business."

Over the past year, the inspectors have started conducting all their inspections at pig farms unannounced. The reason for this is that for several years now, the pork business has been seen as the main culprit when it comes to animal welfare violations. Or, as many farmers have come to think since the government decided to phase out the fur industry: "Pigs are the new mink."[7]

"I'd be the first to say that some farmers should never be allowed anywhere near animals. Like all other professional groups, us farmers are bound by regulations. If you don't give a damn about the rules, you shouldn't be in the business. But it's really hard to run a piggery when we're attacked even though we're following regulations, or when the whole industry is condemned just because a few people can't do their job. What the inspectors and a lot of the other people don't get is that we farmers can't be here in the piggery around the clock. And things can happen at night. A pig's tail can get bitten—and that's a bloody business. When you come into the place in the morning, it isn't a pretty sight. And if you're unlucky enough to have people show up at that exact moment, it can cost you dearly."

Even though Leiv appears resigned and irritated, there's a melancholy undertone to everything he says. Leiv and Eirik are, respectively, the fourth and fifth generation of pig breeders at this farm. It's a profession they were born into. It's the only life they know. So I'm interested to hear how their professional pride is doing these days.

"I can't say I especially care about pride. But I like the idea that I'm producing food for people," Leiv says, picking up a broomstick with a metal blade at one end.

"All right. Time to get started."

Leiv demonstrates something that looks fairly straightforward: scraping the floor clean of excrement, shoving the muck through a grate at the end of the pen, strewing the floor with wood shavings, and then slinging in a bit of hay.

"It isn't all that complicated," he says. "Just remember to move slowly as you do it, and it's best to let the pigs have a little sniff of you before you go in. It doesn't take much to stress them out, especially when there are new people in the piggery."

I do as he says and walk up to pen thirteen, where I witnessed the birth last time I was here. Because of the summer season and a clash between my holiday plans and Leiv's, it's taken a bit longer than expected for me to come back. The piglets are almost five weeks old now, are twice as big, and have already become parentless. Their mother has been sent back to the section for breeding sows, where she's waiting for her next estrus.

The piglets will live out their entire life within these sixty-five square feet. Not that it's such a very long existence: less than six months will pass from the day they were born to the day the slaughter truck comes to fetch them. But short or long, there's little doubt that it's a life devoid of content. There is absolutely nothing for them to do here. They just relax and wait for feeding time to come around again. That's it. Nothing to investigate, nothing to apply their instincts to—other than some wood shavings and hay, which don't seem to interest them very much.

I squat down and hold out a hand. At first they don't want to come to me but huddle in the corner of the pigpen like a panicked shoal of fish, just looking at me. "What the hell does he want?" they seem to be thinking.

It doesn't take long for one of them to venture forward. I have no way of telling whether it's male or female. It hesitates, lowers its head, and tentatively sets one cloven hoof in front of the other as if it wants to see whether the floor will give way.

When it has gotten all the way over to me, it touches the back of my hand with its snout. It's damp but feels surprisingly solid, almost hard. I pat the animal gently on the neck, but it gives a start and bounds away frantically.

That was pretty intense. I thought I'd read that pigs were social animals.

I try to lure it back. A little friendly chat: "Here, piggy, piggy, piggy," "Come on now, piggy." It doesn't work. A bit of whistling? Nope. Whistling plus friendly chat? Absolutely not. In the end, I catch myself making some lip-smacking noises, though I don't quite know where they came from, and now all the pigs are staring at me with what I interpret as a terrified gaze. I feel almost embarrassed. What do they see?

The German zoologist Jakob von Uexküll referred to a species' perception of its environment as the Umwelt. Perhaps the concept is easier to grasp if we replace it with the term "sensory world." Pigs live in one sensory world, while I, a human, live in another. Uexküll developed his concept after studying obscure creatures like ticks, sea urchins, and jellyfish—species so far from us humans in evolutionary terms that one seems bound to ask how far we are even capable of adopting the perspective of such creatures. However, the aim of Uexküll's work was not to achieve absolute empathy; he called his experiments "excursions into unknowable worlds."[8]

Although the pig, as a species, is much closer to us than jellyfish and sea urchins, its world is largely closed to us. Whereas we are an upright, visually oriented species, the pig's worldview is low, and it is largely steered by smell and the tactile sensors in its snout. Despite the thoroughly human appearance of pigs' eyes, sight is a secondary sense for them. Of course, we can never know for sure just how well pigs see. In previous times, people believed that the pig (and all other animals apart from the chimpanzee) saw the world in black and white, but nowadays, the consensus is that most mammals perceive color. Yet we know little about how many shades of color they can distinguish and how clearly they perceive the contours of their surroundings.

Although we humans have much sharper vision than pigs, our eyes aren't anywhere close to registering as much of what goes on around us as those of pigs. Our own visual field is 180 degrees, whereas pigs can see almost all the way around their own axis, with a visual field of 310 degrees. This is a typical trait among prey animals, which must always be on guard to avoid danger. That also explains the placement of pigs' eyes, far out to the side of their heads, similar to those of horses, sheep, and cows. By comparison, humans are more like predators. Our eyes are placed in front, their attention fully fixed on what is going on before us, the place we are heading toward, the prey we intend to trap.

Nor are humans and pigs on quite the same wavelength when it comes to hearing. Admittedly, the ears are secondary sense organs for both of us. The problem is that we're set to slightly different frequencies. You might think that the deep grunts of the pig would make it a species whose ears were focused on the lower end of the sound spectrum, but the opposite is true. Pigs are more like dogs when it comes to hearing, with a range from 45 hertz at the lowest up to 45,000 hertz at the highest. For comparison, we humans can pick up what happens between 20 and 20,000 hertz. That doesn't just tell us that the pig's hearing is on a different frequency from our own; the range of sounds it can pick up also far exceeds those we are capable of perceiving.

And then there's the sense of smell. If a pig had its nostrils blocked, it would scarcely be capable of moving, much less seeking out food, recognizing danger, or interacting with other pigs. Whereas the smell center in humans is a tiny little nub hidden away on the underside of the brain, in the pig it's a prominent bump at the front of the brain. Along with the complex receptors in its nose, this equips the pig to pick up smell molecules whose existence we humans could never register. According to studies, a pig that touches one card in a deck with its snout can pick out the same card from the rest of the deck two days later—even after the cards have been thoroughly washed in the interim. My smell doesn't just tell the pig in front of me that I'm a different person from Leiv; based on the scent signals I secrete, it can probably also pick up the emotions that are affecting me: whether I'm scared or stressed, or whether I'm the way I currently feel myself to be—relaxed, if a little uncertain.

This piggish quality is of course something we humans have exploited. The best-known application of pigs' supersniffer skills is in truffle hunting in the deciduous forests of Southern Europe.

The use of pigs as truffle hunters goes all the way back to the Renaissance, when the Italian gastronomist Bartolomeo Platina noticed how much more efficient the quest to find these tuberous delicacies became when one took a pig along. The challenge, Platina wrote, was to stop the pig gobbling the truffles before he had a chance to pick them himself. More recently, further problems with using pigs for truffle hunting have come to light. When the pigs root around in the soil with their snouts, they destroy the fungal spores, preventing new growth. The upshot is that Italy introduced a formal prohibition on all use of pigs in truffle hunting in 1985. Dogs have now taken over the pig's role. As a small consolation to the pig, we should point out that there are some places where pigs have begun to compete with dogs in sniffing out narcotics for the police. One of the first to have a go was a Vietnamese potbellied pig called Tootsie, who graduated with a diploma from an American canine academy in the 1990s.[9] However, there is no record of how much dope she managed to sniff out during her term of service with the New Orleans narcotics squad.

AS I WORK MY WAY THROUGH, cleaning other pigpens, I try to make contact with different piglets. Some experiments are more successful than others, but none are especially so. While I'm doing this, it strikes me that a pigpen really isn't an ideal place for an encounter between a person and a pig. As I squat here, the best I can do is give them a little pat. But I learn nothing about how they're doing, how they would behave if all opportunities were available to them. So what am I supposed to do? Throw some wood shavings up in the air? Get them to jump over the shaft of my scraper? Besides, the piggery is not a place I want to be for any longer than strictly necessary. By the time I've finished my cleaning duties, I have such a terrible tickle in my throat that the only thing I want to do is get away from it all.

At least this makes a positive contribution to my appetite for pork. Whereas I had difficulty even imagining eating the newborn piglet I held in my arms last time I was here, I am now totally at peace with the idea. I'm even capable of declaring to them, face to snout: "I'm going to eat you up!"

A lot of people in the world could never say this. Not because they are so fond of the animals, but because someone has told them that eating pigs is forbidden.

The
Forbidden
Animal

THE WINE WAS BREATHING on the kitchen counter, a game stew was simmering away on the stovetop, and our guests were on their way through the winter-dark streets of Oslo. The stage was set for a cozy, convivial evening.

Once we were all assembled, I set the steaming cast-iron casserole down on the table with a thump that rattled the tableware.

"Dive in!"

Wine was poured and plates were filled with the hearty game stew. And that's when the question came:

"There isn't any pork in this, is there?"

Our guest showed every sign of discomfort—the apologetic grin, the evasive look. He was asking on behalf of his girlfriend, who was of Somali descent. She sat beside him, staring into her lap in embarrassment.

"Oh, no! It's reindeer stew. Help yourselves!"

As I said this, I felt someone nudge me in the ribs. I turned to find myself looking into my partner's alarmed eyes.

"Didn't you...?"

The penny dropped. Yes, I did.

"Hang on a minute..."

Everyone stopped talking and the heat spread across my face.

"Bacon... there's bacon in the stew."

"Oh dear..." someone said. There were a few nervous titters.

"Oh, it's fine," she said quickly, to get the whole situation over and done with. She didn't want to be a nuisance, of course.

I ran into the kitchen to look for substitutes, pulling open the refrigerator and scouring its contents. It was no good. Mushrooms, reindeer meat, vegetables—the whole lot had ended up in the stew. And now it had been defiled by juices of pork belly.

When I came back into the room, she preempted my excuses.

"Don't worry about a thing. I can just have potatoes."

I looked down at her plate. Her meal looked like the wretched dinner of a picky child: two pallid potatoes and a dollop of lingonberry sauce.

"I have some sour cream in the refrigerator. Would you like some?"

"Yes, please."

THE QUESTION OF WHY some of us abstain from pork for cultural or religious reasons is one of the great mysteries of anthropology, and an issue that increasingly affects us in the West. The most obvious answer is simple enough: the holy books of both Islam and Judaism prohibit the consumption of pork. What is less obvious is the origin of that prohibition.

It's debatable just when the first five books of the Old Testament were written, although they probably already existed by around 500 BCE. At any rate, it's here, in the third book, Leviticus, that it says of the pig: "Their flesh you shall not eat, and their carcasses you shall not touch. They are unclean to you."[1] More than a thousand years later, the prohibition was repeated in the Quran: "He has only forbidden to you dead animals, blood, the flesh of swine ..."[2]

There are many potential explanations for the prohibition, but let's start with the one people cite most often: pork was banned on health grounds. The first person to make this point was the great Jewish thinker Moses Maimonides, who claimed in the twelfth century that pork was "unwholesome" and "injurious" to the human body.[3] Nowadays, we know that his claim is supported by fact: pork can contain *Trichinella spiralis*—a parasite or roundworm that causes an infection called trichinosis in humans if the meat is not roasted or boiled for long enough. This is a simple and rational theory. But if there's one thing most people who have tried to get to the bottom of the mystery agree on, it's that neither T. *spiralis* nor other health-related factors offer a satisfactory explanation. T. *spiralis* wasn't even discovered until 1835, and several more decades would pass before the link between the parasite and disease was uncovered. Of course, one could argue that the people of antiquity may have noticed a link between the consumption of pork and incidence of the disease without having any concrete knowledge of the underlying cause, but that isn't self-evident. The symptoms of trichinosis only appear many days after the meat has been consumed—and if other types of meat have been eaten in the interim, the link is hardly so obvious as it might at first appear. Besides, pigs hardly posed more of a health risk than other livestock in antiquity.[4] Cattle, sheep, and goats are all bearers of a far more dangerous and deadly disease—anthrax—which almost never occurs in pigs. If people back then were truly so afraid that the meat they ate would make them sick, wouldn't it have been natural for them to avoid eating all these species? As we know, that didn't happen. Also, why did this prohibition only apply in the Middle East? If trichinosis were the explanation, why wasn't the pig forbidden in other parts of the world as well?

And here's a thought for anyone still inclined to see trichinosis as the culprit and avoid eating pork as a result: in the United States, trichinosis cases averaged just sixteen per year from 2011 to 2015, and tended to be associated with raw or undercooked wild game, while Canada is "considered free of *Trichinella spiralis* in swine raised for commercial purposes."[5]

Another entirely different explanation for the origin of the prohibition was proposed by the influential social anthropologist Mary Douglas. "Dirt is matter out of place" is one of the central tenets of her 1966 classic *Purity and Danger*.[6] In this book, Douglas investigates how ideas of "the pure" and "the impure" manifest themselves in different cultures. According to Douglas, our view of what is clean or dirty is guided by cultural norms about where different materials belong: feces belong in the toilet, not in the sink; dinner belongs on the plate, not on the tabletop. Today, we would largely associate such rules with hygiene, but in previous eras purity and impurity tended to be associated with order and disorder.

According to Douglas, the pig violates Judaism's way of creating order and systems in nature. She points out that the rules of kosher stipulated in Leviticus involved a strict categorization of nature and the animal kingdom, whose central rule was that terrestrial animals were either predators with paws or ruminants with cloven hooves. As God said to Aaron: "These are the animals which you may eat among all the animals that are on the earth: Among the animals, whatever divides the hoof, having cloven hooves and chewing the cud—that you may eat."[7] While the pig does have cloven hooves, it does not chew the cud. As a result it is prohibited—along with several other land animals. Pigs were "matter out of place" and created chaos in Judaism's rigid taxonomic scheme.

The main problem with Douglas's explanation is that it rapidly becomes a circular argument. Rather than being the reason for the pig's impurity, the entire Judaic system could just as well have been constructed in order to legitimize and rationalize a preexisting aversion. Indeed, later in life Douglas herself acknowledged the shaky foundations of her explanation when her book was republished. "I made mistakes about the Bible for which I have been very sorry ever since."[8]

The discipline that knocked the bottom out of Douglas's theory was archaeology. When data from several decades' worth of archaeological digs in the Middle East were examined, archaeologists discovered a striking pattern. From around 1500 BCE, the bones of pigs started to become increasingly rare, practically vanishing in around 1200 BCE. This finding reveals a key fact: the pig was an outcast long before the religious injunctions of the Bible and the Quran were written down. And the archaeologists found another interesting thing in this same data material. Just as the pig vanishes, another species starts to appear in abundance: the chicken. The concurrence of these events leaves little room for doubt that this was a case of systematic substitution. The crucial question is whether the pig was rejected in favor of chickens, or whether the chickens arrived as a welcome substitute for the already unpopular pig.

Archaeologist Richard W. Redding has argued that the pig was replaced for purely economic reasons.[9] Unlike cattle, sheep, and goats, which produce milk and wool, the pig has no function other than providing meat. That said, the pig is extremely efficient in this respect: whereas cattle and sheep require 43,000 and 51,000 liters of water, respectively, to produce one kilogram of meat, the pig needs just 6,000 liters. This made pig husbandry a rational business—but only until the chicken came on the scene, if we're to believe Redding. Chickens require only 3,500 liters of water to produce the same amount of meat. In addition, the chicken outcompetes the pig in terms of pure protein. Whereas 100 grams of pork yields 13 grams of protein, 100 grams of chicken yields 19 grams. Since, in addition, the chicken lays eggs, it naturally outcompeted the pig. Indeed, the benefits may have been so great that it simply became irrational to continue raising pigs.[10]

Redding undoubtedly argues convincingly for the excellence of the chicken. Yet this hardly offers an explanation for the religious prohibition on pigs. First and foremost, it's far from certain that the pig was so easily outcompeted as a source of nutrition as Redding suggests. Although the chicken yielded more protein, the pig provided more calories through its fat—and here of course we should note that the poor reputation of fat is a phenomenon of our modern affluent society: in previous eras, fat has always played a role of crucial significance in human nutrition. One might also query whether the tiny protein gap between chicken and pig was significant enough to be noticed by the people of antiquity. Nor does Redding's reading sufficiently account for the fact that the chicken was not entirely new to the Middle East when it replaced the pig. Archaeologists have made sporadic finds of chicken bone fragments dating as far back as 3900 BCE. If the chicken really was the superior alternative that Redding claims it to have been, why didn't it replace the pig sooner? Why was this phenomenon entirely isolated to the Middle East? And why did Islam consider it necessary to underscore the prohibition on eating pork in the Quran more than 1,500 years after the pig had, to all intents and purposes, vanished?

Redding shores up his theory by referring to the anthropologist Marvin Harris, who focused on climate and ecological conditions in the region.[11] In ancient times, animal husbandry in the Middle East was largely based on nomads driving herds of cattle, sheep, and goats across the dry and barren areas between the Euphrates, the Tigris, the Nile, and the Jordan. The herders would be ordered to bring their herds into the city centers, where the central authorities would then distribute this food. The porcine physiology is ill-suited to this form of husbandry. First of all, pigs can't be herded over large areas in this way, nor would there have been enough fodder for them to survive on in the region the nomads passed through. Whereas the ruminants—cows, sheep, and goats—could feed on scrub and extended patches of grassland, pigs required higher-calorie, more easily digestible food, like carrion, nuts, roots, and grain. And while climate conditions in the Middle East were somewhat different three or four thousand years ago, the region was, then as now, exposed to a burning sun that left the landscape hot and arid. For pigs, which lack sweat glands and are utterly reliant on shade, water, or mud to keep their body temperature down, such living conditions are almost impossible. And thus, as an immobile wetlands animal, it never became part of the trading economy or the central authorities' food distribution policy.

Food logistics during the construction of the Egyptian pyramids offers an illustrative example. Over many decades, Egyptian rulers had to feed thousands of workers as they carved and stacked blocks of stone to the greater glory of the pharaohs. The whole of the Nile Delta was caught up in this process, and cattle, sheep, and goats were herded to the sites at Giza, where they were slaughtered and eaten straightaway. As a result, access to meat was limited for those not involved in the work. The salvation for people living on the margins of society was to keep pigs.[12] And the same pattern is evident at another power center of the ancient world, in Puzrish-Dagan, outside Nippur in modern-day Iraq. Around four thousand years ago, this place also had a centralized economy and a population reliant upon on food distributed by its rulers. Tens of thousands of animals were requisitioned by the city and slaughtered for the population. These included cattle, sheep, and goats, but the archaeologists find no traces of pigs.[13]

This may indicate that animal husbandry in the first great civilizations was a matter of social class. The nomads who herded cattle and other ruminants belonged to the established trading economy and had close links to the elites. Pigs, on the other hand, were the preserve of an underclass who didn't have a stake in that system. For the rulers, pigs may have represented both poverty and an attempt to break away from the important control function implicit in the food distribution economy. If the Old Testament injunctions reflected a strategic regard for power relationships and political currents, it's not inconceivable that the prohibition on pork was a carefully considered attempt to keep on the right side of the influential rulers. One thing is for sure, at any rate: pork was never the food of elites and city dwellers in either Mesopotamia or Egypt.[14]

FROM 2000 TO 1500 BCE, Palestine experienced population growth and increased urbanization along the Jordan River. The pattern was the same as in all urbanization processes in antiquity: the traditional habitats of pigs came under threat.[15] Trees were felled and swamps were drained to channel scarce water resources toward vegetable crops. Pigs had no choice but to look for new places to live. For many of them, the solution was to invade the city streets, where, along with the dogs, they could live in the shade of the buildings and scavenge off human leavings. In a society without waste-disposal systems or knowledge of sanitation, these offered both species a veritable banquet. Pretty much everything they ate was associated with fundamental human taboos: garbage, excrement, and cadavers of both humans and other animals. It's hardly surprising that this behavior provoked aversion. As it says in a Babylonian text: "The pig is impure" because "it makes the streets stink" and "besmirches the houses."[16] At some point, this aversion became severe enough for the Greek historian Herodotus to report in 425 BCE that anyone in Egypt who had the misfortune to brush his hand against a pig "goes to the river and dips himself therein, garments and all." Herodotus also observed that he was aware of the reason for this disgust, but "it was not suitable to be declared."[17]

The pig did not just provoke repugnance. By rooting around in the soil and helping itself to precious crops intended for human consumption, the pig was also a direct threat to many people's sustenance. In this sense, the prohibition of the pig can be interpreted as simple confirmation of an informal rule that had existed for centuries: very few people wished to have anything to do with pigs, let alone eat them. In the case of both the Old Testament and the Quran, prohibiting the consumption of pork was pushing at an open door. The prohibition on pork may simply have been a strategically adopted rule that people could identify with.

However, such aversion to the pig starts to look less "natural" 2,500 years later. And that's precisely why the pig has become a source of such conflict when people of different cultural or religious convictions come into contact with one another. Nowhere is this conflict more evident than the place where the original prohibition emerged: Israel/Palestine.

IT WAS A PERFECTLY ORDINARY spring day in May 2015. The young American-born cadet who had recently joined the Israel Defense Forces and moved in with his grandparents on a kibbutz in Israel was at last ready to serve his state and people. In the morning before he set off to military camp, his grandmother handed him a packed lunch. Little did he know what this innocent sandwich would cost him. At lunch break, some of his fellow trainees noticed his sandwich filling and reported him to their superiors, who immediately confiscated the American's food and placed him under arrest. He discovered that the punishment for bringing in a homemade ham sandwich was eleven days under lock and key.[18]

The IDF is a strict upholder of kosher rules, and soldiers who fail to observe them while they're in service are in violation of military regulations. The case attracted considerable attention in the press and was seen as a brutal overreaction on the army's part. After several challenging questions from journalists and protests from the family, the leaders at the military base decided to revoke the punishment in recognition of the soldier's short time in service and the likelihood that he was unaware of the regulation. While the outcome was not as dramatic as it first appeared to be, the episode drew global attention to a country where the pig has been the subject of more and greater conflicts than anywhere else in the world.

Of the many internal conflicts in Israel, the battle over the pig is among the least frequently discussed. It may perhaps come as a surprise to some that the pig is a topic at all in a state where Jews and Muslims account for the absolute majority of the population. But right from the time the state of Israel was established in 1948, the pig—or "white meat" as the animal is euphemistically known—has been a thorn in the side of the Israeli authorities.

Nowadays, pigs are slaughtered, processed, and eaten on an industrial scale in Israel, to the delight of some and the horror of others. The people with the greatest appetite for pork are kibbutz-dwelling Jews. Kibbutzim started out as collectivist agricultural communities formed by secular Jews, many of whom were originally from Eastern Europe. Consequently, they have little interest in Orthodox kosher rules or other strict dogma. But for ultra-Orthodox Jews, the practice of pork production is seen as nothing short of a massive anti-Semitic conspiracy aimed at wiping out Judaism by forcing people to eat the forbidden animal.[19] This perception is based on a trauma that extends far back in time. It all started with the Ancient Greeks.

AFTER BEING ABSENT from Palestine for more than 1,500 years, the pig was reintroduced when the region was conquered by the Ancient Greeks in 167 BCE. As recounted in the apocryphal Books of the Maccabees, the Syrian king Antiochus IV Epiphanes wanted to wipe out Jewish culture and replace it with Hellenistic rule based on the Greek pantheon. And his approach was brutal, to put it mildly.

The Greeks forbade all rituals and practices that served as markers of Jewish identity. They set up images of the Greek gods in the Jewish holy places in Jerusalem, and they converted the temple into a pig abattoir. But things became truly macabre when the Greeks required Jews to eat the forbidden animal. The grimmest depiction of this is the tale of a mother and her seven sons who were arrested for refusing to eat pork. In order to underscore the gravity of their offense, the soldiers seized one of the woman's sons, cut out his tongue, chopped off his hands, and scalped him. After that, they threw him in a great cauldron, where he was boiled alive. When the rest of the family still refused to give in, the process was repeated, and thus it continued until only the mother was left. In the end, they showed her no mercy either.[20]

By the time the Greeks arrived, the pig had been absent from Jews' lives for centuries; they barely spared the animal a thought. But with the Greek conquest, the refusal to eat pork quickly became an expression of cultural belonging and patriotic resistance to the occupying forces. The battle against the Greeks and the reconquest of the temple in 142 BCE is commemorated by the Jewish festival of Hanukkah, and the Books of the Maccabees have become a tale of Jewish heroism.

After the Jews reconquered Jerusalem, less than a century would pass before the pig became part of the cityscape in Palestine again—this time following the Roman invasion of Jerusalem in 63 BCE. While there's a lot to be said about the Romans, they were certainly less ruthless than the Greeks. The same cannot be said of European Christians in the Middle Ages and Renaissance.

In the fifteenth century, during the Spanish Inquisition, people were once again compelled to eat pork. And this time, the practice was imposed on Muslims too. Eating pork was among the proofs that people had to present to document that they had abandoned their former faith in favor of Christianity. In certain places during the Middle Ages, Jewish children's lips were smeared with lard to emphasize the same point. And when Jews were executed, the pig played a central role: they would often be led to the gallows riding on a pig, and were frequently forced to stand in a pool of pig's blood as they waited for the noose to tighten around their neck. Humiliating depictions involving pigs were another way of mocking the Jews. One particularly widespread example of this was a form of folk art from the late Middle Ages known as *Judensau* (Jews' sow) that was often found in churches and depicted Jews suckling or eating the excrement of a huge sow.

There were verbal pummelings, too. Grossly anti-Semitic statements about Jews and pigs were preached from pulpits and published in theological tracts across the entire continent. Few could surpass Martin Luther for his blazing anti-Semitism: "You are not worthy of looking at the outside of the Bible, much less of reading it. You should read only the Bible that is found under the sow's tail, and eat and drink the letters that drop from there."[21] The pig also became a common metaphor for anti-Semitism in wider society. And it is not inconceivable that certain of the pig-related metaphors that many of us use to this day are historical remnants of that same ancient anti-Semitism.

WHAT MANY OBSERVANT JEWS have asked in more recent times is how any Jews could possibly choose to eat pork of their own free will after all the pain and suffering visited upon Jews because of the pig. According to Israeli historian Giora

Goodman at Tel Aviv University, the answer is relatively simple: "First, they were hungry. Then, it tasted good. And then, there was money in it."[22]

The years that followed the foundation of Israel in 1948 were a time of scarcity and thriftiness, and meat was thin on the ground. Like the people of antiquity, the Jews in the socialist kibbutzim found that pig breeding could give them an easy and efficient source of protein. To start off with, the meat was intended for individual families, but production gradually increased, several families got together, and eventually the express goal of establishing a special "Zionist" pig breed emerged. These secular Jews were, of course, aware of how controversial this activity was. Consequently, the breeding animals were smuggled into the country under secret code names like "white bear" and "midget sheep," but after a few years, the industry had become so big that it was no longer possible to conceal it.

Naturally, rabbis were disgusted by any pig-related activities and condemned all attempts to breed the forbidden animal in the Holy Land. And in the 1960s, the time came to settle matters once and for all in the Knesset. The prime minister, David Ben-Gurion—who was sympathetic to the kibbutzim—found himself on the losing side. In 1961, under pressure from the Orthodox wing, he had to agree to pass a law that would prove to be one of the most invasive and controversial religious regulations ever issued by the Knesset. The pig would be banished from the state of Israel. All pigs were to be confiscated, slaughtered, and destroyed.

The authorities were swift to implement the measures. The process was quick, and soon 70 percent of herds nationwide had been killed. But then inspectors came to a Christian convent outside Jerusalem, which had a pigsty. It became clear at once that the authorities had come up against a religious institution whose power network the Jewish Orthodox promoters of the policy had failed to fully consider. Despite its dominance in Israel, Judaism couldn't hope to compete with the global reach of Christianity. When the Mother Superior at the convent discovered the purpose of the inspectors' visit, her response couldn't have been clearer: "I will enlist the entire world if the Israeli authorities put their threats into action." The nuns unleashed a diplomatic crisis for Israel. The emergency meeting the government called to deal with the so-called pig crisis resulted in a compromise: in order to prevent such conflicts in the future, pork production would be allowed to continue in areas where Christians accounted for the majority of the population. But once again, the authorities failed to see the full implications of their decision. When the pigs were transported and dumped in "the Christian areas," it rapidly became clear that there were at least as many Muslims living there—with a relationship to the pig that was just as strained as that of observant Jews. Now another faith group had been insulted, creating the need for yet another compromise: pork production could be maintained, but from now on it must take place behind closed doors, out of sight of anyone not involved in the business.

Although the years that followed were calm, pork policy in Israel was far from settled. When the conservative politician Menachem Begin became prime minister in 1977, many assumed that this would usher in a new era. In the kibbutzim, people feared that the days of Zionist pig breeding could once again be numbered. But thanks to the appointment of Ariel Sharon as minister of agriculture, the producers spied a crumb of hope. Sharon had a convenient weakness: he could not resist the taste of the white meat. When Sharon took up his new post, he quickly traveled out to visit the producers and assure them that their business had his full blessing. The sighs of relief echoed around the kibbutzim. But they would prove short-lived.

In the 1980s, Israel experienced considerable growth in religious parties. As a result, the pig once again became the focal point of a battle over Jewish identity between Israel's Orthodox and secular citizens. In the Knesset, the battle against the kibbutzim was led by the Orthodox rabbi Yitzhak Peretz, who hammered home a message that could hardly be interpreted as anything other than a head-on attack on secular Jews: "The pig in Israel is not just repulsive in itself, it is first and foremost—and please note this—a symbol of the obscene, a symbol of obsequiousness, a symbol of hypocrisy, a symbol of lies, a symbol of every negative trait in the human spirit." Little did Peretz know what lay in store.[23]

After the fall of the Soviet Union in 1991, Israel experienced an enormous wave of Jewish immigrants from Russia, who had been thoroughly isolated from Jewish practice by seventy years of secular communist rule. And the Russians brought with them an appetite for pork the likes of which Israel had never seen before. Once again, Orthodox Israelis were forced to fight an intense battle over Jewish identity. Thanks to new constitutional amendments in 1992—which, among other things, assured all citizens freedom to choose their occupation—secular Israelis had gained an effective legal argument to counter any religious attempts to crush the pork trade. At the same time, the legal system had a difficult task: figuring out how to apply the principle of freedom of occupation in a way that allowed for balance between the interests of the pork trade and consideration for the faithful.[24] This conflict of interests has colored Israeli's political and legal system all the way up to the present day. Among ultra-Orthodox Jews, eating pork is still considered a fate worse than death—or as Rabbi Yehuda Meshi-Zahav puts it in the 2016 documentary *Praise the Lard*: "If someone kills you, it takes you out of this world. If someone leads you into sin, you are finished in both this life and the next. That is a thousand times worse."[25] At the same time, the Jewish appetite for pork has reached ever new heights in Israel and the rest of the world.

The question is whether the same is true of Muslims.

"Indeed, Allah Is Forgiving and Merciful"

AUGUST 17, 2017, 5:00 PM: La Rambla, Barcelona's famous pedestrian boulevard, is teeming with life. Suddenly there's a wave of panic. A white van zigzags down the street at top speed, mowing down unsuspecting pedestrians. After continuing for more than five hundred yards, it smashes into a crowd of people by the Miró mosaic, and there it stops. As people rush to help the wounded, the driver sneaks out of the car and escapes on foot. He leaves behind thirteen dead and 130 wounded. Islamist terror has struck again in Spain.

At around eleven o'clock that same evening, police arrest two suspects. After being informed of events on the other side of the Atlantic, U.S. president Donald Trump takes to Twitter with a pointed suggestion for the Spanish authorities: execute the terrorists using bullets dipped in pig's blood.

The thinking behind his proposal was clear to all. The risk of being defiled by the forbidden animal would scare radical Islamists and deter them from carrying out future terror attacks. According to Trump, there was even historical proof that his suggestion was an effective deterrent. "Study what General Pershing of the United States did to terrorists when caught. There was no more Radical Islamic Terror for 35 years!" ran his tweet. The event Trump referred to was a story—long before exposed as apocryphal—about how American soldiers dealt with jihadists during the Moro rebellion in the Philippines in the early twentieth century.[1] And Trump had served up this myth to people once before. During a speech in South Carolina ahead of the American primaries in 2016, he discussed the story in greater detail. According to Trump, General Pershing had captured fifty terrorists, then had his soldiers dip fifty bullets in pig's blood and load their weapons with them. In the end, they shot forty-nine of the prisoners, after which Pershing said to the last prisoner (still according to Trump): "You go back to your people and you tell them what happened."[2]

While these events in the Philippines may be lacking in veracity, there is a related story from the middle of the nineteenth century that is thoroughly documented. However, it's far from certain that it would have had the same rhetorical effect for Trump. The event concerned was the Indian rebellion against the Britons in 1857.

After the East India Company seized a monopoly on trade with India, British influence over the Indian subcontinent underwent constant expansion. Discontent over the Britons' behavior began to grow among the Muslim and Hindu populations. To protect their own trading interests, the Britons recruited tens of thousands of soldiers from the local population and equipped them with British rifles. When the soldiers loaded their weapons, they had to bite open the cartridge to release the gunpowder. At the outset, this was no problem for the Hindu and Muslim soldiers—until rumors started to circulate about the substance used to keep the powder in the cartridges dry: the fat of pigs and cows. And this is what sparked the Indian Rebellion of 1857.

In modern times, Trump is far from the only person to have proposed the pig as a weapon in the war against terror. In 2004, an Israeli bus company was said to be placing bags of lard on board its buses to deter Islamist suicide bombers.[3] In the globalized era, the pig has undoubtedly been weaponized, both politically and culturally.

More recently, the use of pigs in cultural conflicts has formed part of China's system of political control. In this authoritarian regime, where there are half a billion pigs and religion is defined as an evil, life is difficult for observant Muslims. And things have become especially bad in the western province of Xinjiang. Bordering Pakistan, Afghanistan, and a number of other Central Asian countries, Xinjiang has always had a high proportion of Muslims. In recent years, it has emerged that minorities such as the Uyghurs and Kazakhs are being subjected to a brutal and ruthless assimilation process.[4] Millions of Muslims have been imprisoned and placed in what human rights organizations describe as "indoctrination camps" for the "cultural cleansing" of minorities.

Here, Muslims are forced to abandon their traditional culture and religion in favor of the communist state ideology. And the tools are familiar: as well as being forced to swear loyalty to the state, the prisoners are forced to consume alcohol, are deprived of opportunities to pray, and are compelled to eat pork.[5]

While it may never have been official policy, the pig has also been used by Americans. When news came out of the abuses at Abu Ghraib prison during the Iraq War, it emerged that pork played a role in the torture of the prisoners. Under the leadership of Charles Graner and Lynndie England, the American soldiers forced pork down the throats of their victims to humiliate them and attempt to rob them of their faith in a better afterlife.[6]

IN EUROPE, THE PIG has lately been used as an instrument of identity politics in the face of multiculturalism. The most widespread manifestation of this has involved individual far-right activists hanging strips of raw bacon from the door handles of mosques or dumping pigs' heads outside Muslim community centers.[7] But with the rightward shift in European politics of the past few decades, the pig has also increasingly become part of the public political discourse on Muslims' cultural and religious lives.

In one of the most extreme cases, Heinz-Christian Strache of the Austrian Freedom Party published a cartoon of himself eating roast pork in 2012. With its caption, "If you eat pork you can come in," the drawing was a clear attack on immigrants and asylum seekers of both Muslim and Jewish origin.[8] Rasmus Paludan of Denmark is another example. As leader of the far-right party Hard Line, Paludan came close to being elected to parliament in the June 2019 elections. To drum up publicity for his policies during the campaign, he opted—among other things—to burn a copy of the Quran wrapped in bacon and hand out pork sausages to people he assumed were Muslim.[9]

A quite different case made the news in Denmark in 2013, when it became known that kindergartens nationwide were rejecting any meat that contained pork. Indeed, in the town of Ishøj, an absolute ban on serving pork was introduced in public sector institutions, and several switched to serving halal meat. Unsurprisingly, in the land of pork meatballs and red sausages, this caused a commotion. In the ensuing debate, dubbed the "meatball wars," many claimed that Danish children were being robbed of an essential part of Danish culture in the name of tolerance. "In Denmark, we eat roast pork and pork meatballs," commented the prime minister Helle Thorning-Schmidt, while the leader of the right-wing populist Danish People's Party, Kristian Thulesen Dahl, opined that the absence of pork was downright discrimination against Danish children.[10]

WHEN PORK AND RELIGIOUS DIETARY RULES turn up as a political topic in Europe these days, it can often appear that the people making the most noise are the ones who don't think their compatriots are eating *enough* pork—as exemplified by Christian Tybring-Gjedde of Norway's right-wing populist Progress Party. When it was reported that only chicken sausages would be served at parliament's Christmas party, his response was crystal clear: "This is cultural capitulation." And he obviously struck a nerve, for just hours later, the party's organizing committee made a U-turn. Ordinary pork sausages would be served too, which prompted Tybring-Gjedde to declare cheerfully: "This is my first ever breakthrough in Norwegian politics."[11]

When it comes to those who do *not* eat pork, the tendency is for Orthodox Jews to be more vociferous than conservative Muslims. This has been especially evident in debates surrounding the methods of ritual slaughter used to produce halal and kosher meat. In order for an animal to be slaughtered according to halal or kosher principles, it must bleed out while still conscious. In this way, its life ebbs out with the blood. From an animal welfare perspective, it isn't hard to see the problematic side of these methods, since several minutes can pass between the time an animal's throat is cut and the moment it loses consciousness. It's an issue that could have been tailor-made for right-wing populists and nationalist conservatives throughout Europe. When a law prohibiting halal slaughter was pushed through the Danish parliament, the then minister for food, Dan Jørgensen of the center-right Venstre party, said that "animal rights come before religion." Animal liberationists and right-wing populists applauded in unison, while others were angered. The law also provoked reactions beyond the country's borders. "European anti-Semitism is showing its true colors across Europe, and is even intensifying in the government institutions," said the Israeli rabbi and minister Eli Ben-Dahan to an Israeli newspaper.[12] In Norway, halal and kosher slaughter have not been such a dominant topic, since it has been mandatory to anesthetize animals before their throats are cut since back in 1929—and Islamic Council Norway still recognizes this method as halal. The Jewish community is stricter, however, and does not recognize the resulting meat as kosher.

One logical explanation for why Orthodox Jews respond more forcefully than conservative Muslims is the long and tragic history of anti-Semitism in the West. At the same time, it's interesting to note the wording of the dietary laws in the Old Testament and the Quran. Whereas the Old Testament is forthright in its rules, the Quran is milder. After listing the prohibitions on eating pork, dead animals, and animals sacrificed to gods other than Allah, the text makes it clear that Allah is ultimately a fair god: "But whoever is forced [by necessity], neither desiring [it] nor transgressing [its limit], there is no sin upon him. Indeed, Allah is Forgiving and Merciful." In the Bible, on the other hand, the dietary rules end thus, curt and strict: "For I am the Lord... You shall therefore be holy, for I am holy."[13] But the fact that Allah appears more merciful than God on this point does not, of course, mean that Muslims have a more relaxed attitude to eating pork. Whereas, according to one U.S. survey, increasing numbers of Jewish people are eating pork, there is no sign of a similar tendency among Muslims.[14] And whereas Norway's Jewish community does not intervene in its members' dietary habits, the imams in Norwegian mosques make no bones about urging their members to alter their dietary habits if they are found to be living in conflict with the laws of Allah.

MY DINNER-PARTY GUEST who was left with a meal of potatoes and lingonberry sauce while the rest of us ate our reindeer stew with bacon grew up in a home steeped in Somali culture, with Islam as her religion. Though not a practicing Muslim, she is an example of how culture can have just as much of an influence on dietary choices as religion. So deep-seated is her culture, in fact, that her secular Norwegian husband has agreed not to feed pork to their Norwegian-born children either.

For many people, it's undoubtedly difficult—not to say pointless—to start eating things they didn't grow up with. That's why many of us pork eaters struggle to eat snake or dog in other parts of the world. At the same time, though, it can be just as difficult to do the opposite—to cut out a food that has always been part of our diet. This is a dilemma the American hip-hop artist Snoop Dogg experienced when he converted to Rastafarianism in 2012. While his conversion handily legitimized his high marijuana consumption, he had failed to realize that Rastafarianism follows the same Old Testament dietary rules as Judaism. When *Rolling Stone* touched on the topic during an interview that same year, Snoop's reply unwittingly hit the nail on the head: "Me and Porky Pig, we agree with each other. You gotta understand, I was fed this shit from a baby."[15]

WHILE SNOOP DOGG and many others may marvel at the continued need to maintain this religious aversion to the pig, here's an interesting question: Why is there no equivalent prohibition in the New Testament? One thing's for certain: Jesus never ate pork. And not only did he not eat it; he also despised the pig and treated it like the demonic animal he considered it to be. Nowhere is this more clearly expressed than in the tale of the Gadarene swine:

> Then they sailed to the country of the Gadarenes, which is opposite Galilee. And when He stepped out on the land, there met Him a certain man from the city who had demons for a long time... Now a herd of many swine was feeding there on the mountain. So they begged Him that He would

permit them to enter them. And He permitted them. Then the demons went out of the man and entered the swine, and the herd ran violently down the steep place into the lake and drowned.[16]

This scene has been a headache for theologians through the ages. What was the intention behind Jesus's actions, and what meaning are the faithful supposed to draw from them? As the philosopher Bertrand Russell points out in his essay "Why I Am Not a Christian": "It certainly was not very kind to pigs to put the devils into them... He could have made the devils simply go away; but He chose to send them into the pigs."[17] Why did he bear so much ill will toward pigs?

For the Church Father Saint Augustine, such biblical episodes were evidence that humanity owed no moral obligations to animals or plants. This was in stark contrast to the pagan cultures that Christianity was attempting to supplant, in which animals and nature usually had spiritual importance. Saint Augustine said: "Christ himself shows that to refrain from the killing of animals and the destroying of plants is the height of superstition." In his view, Jesus's dealings with the Gadarene swine show that "there are no common rights between us and the beasts and trees."[18]

Saint Augustine's position speaks volumes about Christianity's relationship to nature. As the influential moral philosopher Peter Singer has pointed out: "The Old Testament did at least show flickers of concern for their sufferings. The New Testament is completely lacking in any injunction against cruelty to animals, or any recommendation to consider their interests."[19] However, this does not explain why Jesus was so very harsh in his dealings with the pig.

In the Bible, no animal is more prized than the lamb. In ancient times, the lamb emerged as a symbol of innocence—as the pure, innocent, and flawless sacrifice that paid with its life for humanity's sins on earth. In Moses's day, it was mandatory to sacrifice lambs, and the only families who were rescued from slavery in Egypt were the ones who painted their thresholds with the blood of the sacrificial lamb. If John the Baptist later referred to Jesus as "the Lamb of God," it was precisely because Jesus had been sent to earth to fulfill the same function of sacrificial victim previously performed by the lamb.[20] This intimate link between Jesus and the lamb makes it unthinkable that he could have sent the demons into a flock of sheep. Of course, he could have banished them into horses, cattle, or goats, but it wouldn't have seemed natural for him to put a curse on them in this way either.

Jesus chose the pig because he despised it. As he himself said: "Do not cast your pearls before swine, lest they trample them under their feet, and turn and tear you in pieces."[21] Jesus was born Jewish and lived by the Jewish traditions, and his loathing of the pig stayed with him throughout his life. For him, the pig was not just impure and sinful: for Jesus the Jew, it also represented the Roman occupiers, who would persecute him and nail him to the cross.

If anyone had asked Jesus outright: "Should we eat pigs?" he would undoubtedly have answered "No!" But Jesus never said this—at least not according to the writings that made their way into the Bible. On the one hand, he may have found it unnecessary to repeat rules that had already been hammered home in the Old Testament. On the other, the absence of an express taboo—whether conscious or unconscious—may have been necessary to win over the Romans to the new religion. In fact, as early as the first church assembly at Antioch in the third century, it was recommended that the faithful eat pork.[22] In this way, the pig became a symbol of a new religion, which was not merely bidding farewell to Judaism; the recommendation to eat pork was at the same time a clear signal of Christianity's ambitions to expand into heathen territories farther north. As with the Romans, it would have been difficult to imagine that German, Saxon, Norse, or Celtic tribes could ever be won over to Christianity if that also meant abandoning their love of pork.

Appetite
and
Aversion

MY EARLIEST MEMORY of culinary desire dates back to child-
hood. I had a craving for a food that was always out of reach
because it only existed in a comic strip. To this day, those spit-
roasted wild boars in the Asterix books are a source of impossible yearning. While it's certainly possible to prepare a whole
wild boar in the real world of adulthood, I will never be able to
recreate the version in the comic books: those reddish-brown
boars, glistening with grease, that Obelix wolfs down one after
another, leaving a stack of stripped rib cages on the table in
front of him.

As everyone knows, Asterix, Obelix, and all the other Gauls
live tucked away in a tiny hamlet in northern France that
always, inexplicably, manages to resist the might of the Roman
Empire. But there was one thing that united Romans and Gauls
more than the Asterix books fully acknowledge: their appetite
for boar.

In real life, the Romans envied the Gauls their culinary
prowess with pigs. According to the Roman poet Marcus Ter-
entius Varro, the Gauls made the best bacon to be had in the

whole of the Roman Empire, and Rome imported thousands of cured hams from the northern province every single year.[1] This speaks volumes about the Gauls' culinary skills, because if there was one place where people really knew their pork, it was the seat of imperial power in Rome.

IT WOULDN'T BE UNREASONABLE to claim that the art of cooking pork began with the Roman Empire. While the pig had been a prized protein source for millennia before the empire's foundation, it was the dignitaries at the heart of the imperial power who truly refined the art of preparing—not to mention eating—pork. Refined it so much, indeed, that things quickly went over the top.

Few have devoted more effort to recreating the decadence of Ancient Rome than Federico Fellini. His 1969 film *Satyricon* is based on an incomplete text written in around 50 CE by a Roman official called Gaius Petronius. Set in the era of the Emperor Nero, the film is a dreamlike voyage of decadence, eroticism, and mysticism. In the magnificent banquet scene, the guests recline side by side in their finery, gobbling down meat and wine. Everything comes to a climax when the servants trundle in a whole roast pig. But the diners' ecstasy is short-lived, because the second the host sets his eyes on the animal, all hell breaks loose: he accuses the servants of failing to gut the pig before roasting it over the coals. The servants are banished, and the host orders the cooks to be flogged. But before there is time to carry out any of the punishments, one of the servants brandishes a saber, slices open the belly of the beast, and out tumble the cooked entrails, along with sausages, birds, bones, and chunks of meat. As always, Roman excess was a performance—with the pig at center stage.

The most important source of information about the cuisine of Ancient Rome is a collection of recipes called *De Re Coquinaria* (On the subject of cooking), from around the same era as

Petronius's text.[2] Despite uncertainty surrounding the identity of the author, the text is generally attributed to the wealthy Roman merchant and gourmet Marcus Gavius Apicius. According to his contemporary Pliny the Elder, Apicius was not just an inventive gastronome. He was one of Rome's most extravagant gourmands, and the man who developed an extremely niche taste for flamingo tongues. But his lavish banquets would also be his downfall. His profligate lifestyle eventually bankrupted him, driving him to suicide. Nonetheless, his recipes and methods lived on.[3]

Apicius's greatest culinary feat was the invention of the Roman equivalent of the French foie gras. But rather than using goose livers, Apicius used the liver of the animal he prized most highly: the pig. Apicius's pig's liver was one of the most sought-after delicacies in the Roman Empire. That was unfortunate for the pigs of Rome, since the procedure for producing it was macabre, to put it mildly. Apicius's secret was to starve the pig in the run-up to slaughter, then force-feed it dried figs. After that, the pig was made to drink massive amounts of honeyed wine. Once it hit the pig's stomach, the wine caused the figs to swell until the stomach eventually burst and the pig dropped dead. When the Romans cut open the belly and extracted the liver, it had become hugely expanded as a result of all this physical stress. Most important of all, though, the liver had absorbed the flavor of the sweet mixture that had caused the pig to kick the bucket. It was gruesome, it was extravagant, it was Roman haute cuisine.

Other delicacies almost as exclusive as the liver were the sow's vulva, uterus, and teats. One prerequisite for using these private parts was that the animal must be sterile, although Plutarch claimed the uterus itself could also be eaten in a fertilized state, as long as the sow's offspring were first aborted. This was done by applying brute force to the sow's belly region, which "blended together blood and milk and gore" in the milk-filled teats—creating yet another refined tidbit to tickle the Roman palate.[4]

While the recipes in *De Re Coquinaria* are very approximate, they do offer several methods for preparing the vulva. One suggestion is to simply prepare it with herbs, stock, and vinegar. Another is to pickle and then grill it. As for the sow's teats, the recipe runs roughly as follows: Boil the teats, bake them in the oven, make a sauce from wine and raisins, pour it over, and serve. It's perhaps fitting that the recipes in *De Re Coquinaria* are not written in classical but in vulgar Latin—the language of the common people.

The Roman Empire's culinary love affair with the pig was not just vulgar and macabre, though. A number of the dishes have stood the test of time better than others, although some half-hearted modern carnivores may have difficulty understanding why anyone would eat them in the first place. It is true that the Romans liked to mash brains into a soup with a mortar before cracking a few eggs and beating the mixture together into a kind of omelet. They also struck on the idea of stuffing several pig brains into a pig belly, which was then sewn back up and simmered in a pot of stock. The lungs, meanwhile, might be stuffed with egg and honey before being boiled in milk. But in other respects, the Romans weren't all that different from modern consumers who buy their pork at the supermarket: they too fried their chops, boiled their pig knuckles, and salted their bacon. Above all, they loved sausages.

THE HEDONISTIC LIFESTYLE of those at the pinnacle of Roman society was further underscored by the fact that the pig, in particular, was the object of their affections. The horse provided transport, the ox drew the plow, cows and goats gave milk, and sheep produced wool. The pig's only job was to fatten up and wait to be eaten. In Rome, the pig didn't even fulfill the function of waste disposal worker on the city streets. Given the enormous numbers of pigs in and around the city, this method of pig rearing would have made life impossible for the populace. The traditional alternative was for pigs to roam free in the forests, but this was also a problem for the Romans. There were simply too many pigs. Single herds could number as many as several hundred sows and produce thousands of slaughter pigs every year—far larger than even the biggest herds in Norway today.[5] That may sound excessive for a city that existed more than two thousand years ago, but we are, after all, talking about Rome—a metropolis on a scale Europe would not experience again until the nineteenth century. Indeed, the environmental footprint of the Ancient Romans was so enormous that the pollution they caused can still be detected in the Greenland ice to this day.[6]

The Romans undoubtedly knew how to organize things, but they turned to Ancient Greece for the solution to their pig-mania: they shut their animals up in pigpens. And that was how they avoided the human aversion that often arises when pig rearing gets out of hand, as it had in the Middle East several millennia earlier. But the use of pens brought its own set of challenges, introducing a new aspect of animal husbandry. The animals had to be actively fed. And what are pigs to be fed on when their owners aren't producing enough organic waste? Well, the same things the majority of the population lived off: grains, nuts, beans, and chickpeas. And since some herds around Rome were comparable in size to those in today's intensive production units, that made the pig a clear competitor for food resources. Perhaps it's hardly surprising that as much as three-quarters of Rome's food provisions had to be imported from other regions around the Mediterranean.

It wasn't sustainable.

WITH THE COLLAPSE of the Western Roman Empire at the beginning of the fifth century, population levels nosedived. And so did the number of pigs. The pigpens vanished, and the extravagant concept of feeding animals with grain and other food that could otherwise be eaten by people was shelved right up until the modern era.

In Italy and Northern Europe, pigs ended up living in the vast forests around the towns. There they lived in a semi-savage state, foraging for their own food and mingling with their forebears, the wild boar. In certain parts of Italy at the dawn of the Middle Ages, the number of pigs a forest could sustain determined its land value, rather than the forest's size or its tree species. Admittedly, trees meant a lot to the Anglo-Saxons, who imposed severe penalties on anyone who chopped down or harvested from nut-producing deciduous trees, but these nuts were, after all, the primary food source for forest pigs. In other places again, the compensation payable for stealing a pig was higher than for any other domestic animal. For example, the Salian Franks, who lived in the region that now belongs to the Netherlands and Belgium, introduced more laws to safeguard pig farmers than all the laws for owners of goats, sheep, and cattle put together.[7]

The protection of pigs also reflected who was eating them: whereas the farmers survived on a vegetarian diet or ate the meat of old, worn-out sheep and cattle, the pig remained the meat of the upper classes.

MANY HIGH-RANKING PEOPLE in the Middle Ages shared the Romans' appetite for pork. Sometimes they would even revive the more spectacular culinary hits of the Roman Empire— taking a suckling pig and a capon, say, cutting both in two, and then sewing the front of the capon to the rear of the pig—and vice versa.[8] Or they might equip a chicken with a miniature helmet and spear, then sit it astride a spit-roasted suckling pig.[9] But the court cuisine of the Middle Ages did not merely rely on relics of the Roman Empire. It introduced gastronomic innovation of its own, too, not so much in the preparation of the food as in the seasoning.

Roman cuisine involved fairly simple flavors, seasoning with salt, pepper, herbs, and honey. The finest dishes of the Middle Ages, on the other hand, were complex explosions of flavor that would probably be a bit overwhelming for the modern palate. The development of the Eastern trading routes introduced new and costly ingredients into upper-class cuisine. The stock ingredients of a nobleman's kitchen included spices such as cinnamon, cardamom, nutmeg, cloves, ginger, and saffron. A French pie recipe from the fifteenth century includes the following ingredients: minced pork, eggs, almond milk, figs, and dates, together with vast amounts of cinnamon and saffron.[10]

Perhaps these spices were precisely what it took for the elite to continue eating pork until as late as the early Renaissance. Because by that time, something had happened: the pig's status had plummeted.

IN THE CENTURIES after the fall of Rome, European agriculture evolved, pushing the edge of the forests ever farther away from the cities. This was a result of the dramatic population growth that occurred from the 1000s up until the Black Death. People needed grain, and grain needed space. That rapidly came into conflict with pig keeping. When the forests were felled, the pigs' habitat went with them. The mechanisms were the same as in the Middle East some millennia before: as their natural habitats came under threat, the pigs invaded the cities. Once again, they adopted a diet of waste, excrement, carrion, and—worst of all—human cadavers.

The endless military campaigns that ravaged Europe gave the pigs of the Middle Ages ample access to human corpses.

This supply was supplemented by the medieval practice of punishing executed prisoners or people excommunicated from the church postmortem by leaving their bodies to lie and rot unburied.[11] The pigs' new food source did not go unnoticed, of course. "Swine that taste the flesh or blood of men are always forbidden," declared the Irish legal text the Canon of Adamnan as early as the seventh century. Some, such as the Bishop of Canterbury, took a more practical view: pigs that "tear and eat the corpses of the dead, their flesh may not be eaten until they become feeble and weak and until a year has elapsed."[12] But no matter what stance people took on man-eating pigs, there was no getting away from the fact that the pig had once again become a symbol of impurity.

Although the prohibition on eating pork never became Christian dogma, people did not totally disregard the dietary laws of the Old Testament. One important legacy was God's injunction to Noah after the Great Flood: "Every moving thing that lives shall be food for you... But you shall not eat flesh with its life, that is, its blood."[13] As Deuteronomy later hammers in: "Only be sure that you do not eat the blood, for the blood is the life; you may not eat the life with the meat. You shall not eat it."[14] This had several implications for Christians. First of all, eating blood was perceived as impure, so the animal had to bleed out before it could be butchered. What's more, impurity was seen as contagious in the biblical context.[15] As a result, believers always regarded the consumption of predators and carrion eaters as an impure act, even if the animal was drained of blood before being butchered. We in the West maintain this Old Testament tradition by opting to eat herbivores rather than predators and scavengers.

As the pig took over the streets of the medieval cities, its behavior and dietary habits became a conspicuous reminder of the category to which it belonged: this was an animal that ate blood—even human blood. Aversion grew, so much so in some places that people developed their own particular taboos against eating pigs. This was the case in parts of Scotland, where pork didn't find its way back onto dinner tables until the nineteenth century.[16]

ALTHOUGH THE RELIGIOUS TEXTS had long been in existence when this medieval aversion to the pig arose, this attitude was most evident in the field of law. In 1131, pigs were banned from the streets of Paris. By the fourteenth century, the same thing had happened in many cities in Great Britain. In 1301, a law introduced in York stated that "no one shall keep pigs which go in the street by day or by night, nor shall any prostitute stay in the city."[17] A similar regulation was drawn up in London in 1419, albeit with different targets: "Jews, Lepers, and Swine... are to be removed from the City."[18] This association between pigs and people considered to be at the bottom of the social ladder was also evident in the way pigs were treated.

During the many animal trials conducted in Europe during the Middle Ages and the Renaissance, no other animal was more frequently punished than the pig. And it didn't just end up on trial most often—it was also punished most *harshly*. This wasn't just down to a general disdain for the pig; it also reflected the fact that pigs had an unfortunate tendency to come into contact with small children. Such encounters quickly became fatal, first for the child, then for the pig.

The "eye for an eye, a tooth for a tooth" principle was strictly applied in premodern Europe—as evidenced by the trial of the pig that was condemned to death and hanged by its hind legs in Falaise in 1386. When the sow was led up to the scaffold, she not only faced the same fate as the boy she had killed. She had also been subjected to the same agony she had caused her victim when she chewed his hands and face to bits. The gloves and mask in which the sow was clad concealed her mutilated trotters and mangled snout.[19] But the clothing gave her an extra dimension: she became a reflection of that most despised of peoples—the Jews.

There was no limit to the human qualities people ascribed to pigs in that era. It was not uncommon for the carcasses of executed pigs to be placed on display at central sites both in and outside the towns, as a deterrent and a warning. There is little to suggest that this did anything to curtail porcine criminality. In 1394 a pig was hanged after killing and eating a child "although it was Friday"—as if the pig should have understood that it was a day of fast.[20] Before the hanging, several attempts were also made to extract a confession from the accused, using torture, of course.

Now and then, the accused animal also took accomplices with it to the grave. In 1379, three condemned sows were very nearly accompanied to the gallows by two entire herds of pigs in the French town of Saint-Marcel-le-Jeussey. These three sows had attacked the son of the swineherd in charge of one of the herds. At the culprits' trial, the prosecution pointed out that all of the pigs in both herds had hurried to the scene of the crime, displaying agitated and aggressive behavior. For the court, this was proof enough that all had participated in the crime and therefore deserved the same punishment as the three original culprits. Luckily for them, the accomplices had a skilled defense lawyer, who argued that they were not to blame and must be released out of consideration for the financial position of their owner. The court allowed itself to be persuaded.[21]

Some mercy was also shown in 1457 after a sow with young was caught in the act of killing a child. While the sow was condemned to death, the piglets were released in view of their youth and their mother's adverse influence on them.[22]

AT THE DAWN of the Renaissance, one thing had become clear: of all Satan's creatures on earth, none was worse than the pig. It was even said that the natural number of piglets in a litter was seven—one for each of the seven deadly sins.[23] But among the pigs' countless sinful attributes, one in particular was more prominent than the rest. Gluttony.

The pig has never been famed for its seemly behavior—that simply isn't its nature. Whereas cows and sheep, which only eat grass, are slow eaters who rarely need to look far for fodder, the pig is always on the lookout for small, scattered sources of nourishment. As a result, it is constantly in competition with other species, which is why it comes equipped with tusks and reacts aggressively if anyone gets too close. Once pigs do find food, they need to be on the alert and polish it off quickly. Their rapid, chaotic eating style, so reminiscent of human gluttony, is simply an evolutionary product of being an omnivore. But whereas humans are reined in by cultural norms, pigs are not. So it's hard not to see the irony of gluttony being the sin that truly dragged the pig down into the sociocultural gutter: that was, after all, one of the most striking traits of the empire that had once so prized the pig.

IF THE WORLDLY POWERS of the Middle Ages—royalty and nobles—were inclined to take a nostalgic view of the Roman Empire as a historical civilization, the same was certainly not true of the spiritual powers. For monks, priests, and bishops, the cultures of antiquity represented the pagan, the barbaric. By extension, there was also something barbaric about the pig. But the ancient Greeks and Romans were not solely to blame for this: the pig had also enjoyed high standing among the heathens to the north. For the Celts on the British Isles, the pig was an important symbol of war, representing virility, courage, and strength. Ornaments depicting wild boars adorned weapons, armor, buildings, and vessels—an awe-inspiring sight for the first Christian missionaries who arrived on the islands. In Norse mythology, too, the pig was important. The Viking dream was to earn afterlife in Valhalla, whose rewards included feasting at Odin's table, where the pig Sæhrímnir was served up day after day. Every morning he was slaughtered and every night he returned, alive and kicking once again.

The upper classes in the late Middle Ages didn't reject the pig solely on aesthetic and religious grounds: it was also a matter of status. But although the pig gradually became increasingly despised, it could still be found on the nobles' dinner tables to a certain extent. This was particularly conspicuous after the eleventh century, when the population grew and famines began to ravage the continent. By then, eating pig could be an effective marker of wealth, and this held true all the way up until the Black Death.

When the Plague reached Italy in 1347, it took no more than three years for the deadly parasite to infiltrate the entire continent. Half the population of Europe was wiped out, and the population rapidly plummeted to the same levels seen in the eleventh century. The lucky ones who lived to continue their line faced a new era. Vast tracts of land lay open and freely available, and food was easier to come by. This enabled far more people to resume the human species' long evolutionary tradition of eating animals. Meat was democratized, and the pig once again became food for the wider population. And that rapidly became a problem for the elites.

Given the enduring compulsion of the privileged to mark their distance from the masses, it quickly became urgent for them to seek out a culinary niche that could be their sole preserve. It was simply unacceptable that a meal served at court could be recreated by peasants. They found the solution in the forests. The hunting grounds were, after all, reserved for the church, the monarchy, and other landowning nobles. The peasants wisely kept their distance, because the penalty for poaching game was severe. And so the tables of the privileged heaved beneath the weight of hares, deer, and wild boars—not to mention large birds such as swans and pheasants.

Soon, only peasants and the poor were still eating pig: "Pork is the habitual food of poor people," as a visitor to Paris said in 1557. In Scotland, another source remarked that "pork is generally despised, and left to be consumed by the mean populace."[24] For the elites, sausages in particular came to symbolize the vulgar and loathsome eating habits of the masses. At the same time, there is much to suggest that the pig's decline as a food for the upper classes was ultimately a question of *taste*.

When the pig took to the cities, switching from a diet of acorns and truffles to city fare of garbage, excrement, animal carcasses, and human cadavers, this also had an impact on the meat. Our modern palates can easily detect the difference between pigs raised on concentrate feed and Spanish Ibérico pigs that have fed on acorns. It must have been just as easy for the carnivores of the Middle Ages to taste the difference between forest-raised pigs and city swine. Because, unlike ruminants, with their complex stomachs, the pig has a digestive system and metabolism that make it much easier for it to take on the flavors of what it eats. Whereas ruminants have microorganisms that break down and transform the fatty acids in their stomachs, pigs (and humans) do not. Consequently, the fatty acids that are stored in the body retain the form in which they were consumed. Pigs that eat fish taste of fish, and pigs that eat nuts taste of nuts. What's more uncertain is whether eating human and other carrion gave the flesh of the pigs concerned an unpleasant aftertaste. According to a medical text from the Middle Ages, it is barely possible to distinguish between the flavor of pig and human: "Many have eaten man's flesh instead of pork, and could perceive neither by the savour nor the taste but that it had been pork."[25] But considering how much excrement those pigs wolfed down, it isn't inconceivable that their pork eventually took on a slight flavor of... well, *shit*.

The free-range city pigs would prove to be a resilient species. They wandered freely on the streets of Kristiania—now Oslo—until well into the nineteenth century, and continued to do so in other European cities for another century. At the same time, though, it had become clear that this practice could not persist.

Naked
and
Imprisoned

THIS IS AN EVENTFUL DAY at Rugland Farm: five sows are being let out into the open. More precisely, they will walk across twenty yards of gravel from one building to another. That's not far, readers may object, but for an animal that has spent its entire life to date lying on its side, it's a veritable marathon. Over the past four weeks, these five sows have been living in the old barn from the 1960s, where they have farrowed a new litter and suckled their young; but the time has already come for the mothers to be separated from their piglets. The sows will be returned to the section for breeding animals in the modern industrial building, where they will await estrus and another insemination. Their young will remain in this pigpen for another five months, spending their days in a space of roughly three square feet apiece until the slaughter wagon comes for them. It's a passive and monotonous life, but it almost had to be that way.

WHEN THE EUROPEAN FORESTS vanished in the nineteenth century, pig breeding could only continue on one condition: increasingly, the pigs had to be locked away. Enclosed pigpens rapidly became the new normal for European pigs. In many ways, this was a rational system. The pigpens restored the relationship between humans and pigs that had brought them together ten thousand years before: the people fed the pigs on their waste, and the pigs converted it into pure protein in the form of muscle mass. It was a common-sense business. Adam Smith, the founder of modern economics, even devoted a separate chapter to the economic rationality of pig breeding in *The Wealth of Nations* (1776). "The hog finds its food among ordure, greedily devours many things rejected by every other useful animal… A farm can raise a certain number of such animals at little or no expense."[1]

That economic principle didn't just apply to farms, though. The economic expansion of the seventeenth and eighteenth centuries resulted in the emergence of commercial enterprises. Breweries, distilleries, and dairies all produced massive amounts of organic waste, which had to be disposed of. The solution was obvious: these businesses established their own piggeries and the pigs ate the waste, also providing the early capitalists with an efficient source of supplementary income. Consequently, it was the processing industry rather than farming that was first to breed pigs for commercial purposes.[2] Sailors needed salted meat for their long voyages, as did the military, and most of this meat was bought from the commercial operations near the towns. The same pattern occurred in Norway in the 1900s, when dairies rather than farms had the largest herds.[3] This new type of enterprise would mark the beginning of the end for physically active—not to mention *visible*—pigs.

TO GET TO THE SOWS, Leiv has to push open the broad barn door, tramp across the creaking floorboards, and walk past the huge stacks of hay. Partly hidden behind the hay is a plank door so low that we have to bow our heads to get through it, and there, at last, they are. This place feels so hidden away, so provisional that the image of a creepy kidnapper's basement appears unbidden in my mind's eye. But once I'm inside, there's little in this section to distinguish it from the industrial building on the other side of the yard. The pigpens are separated from one another with the same partitions, the water tap is the same, the floor grate where the pigs defecate is more or less the same, and the stink is almost as intense.

While the piglets huddle terrified in the corners, the sows respond more calmly, barely twitching an ear as they lie there. We divide up the tasks: Leiv will get the animals out of the pigpens, and I will stand by the barn door to meet them. That way, we'll be able to herd them all across the yard in a group. It will be an interesting experience because pigs are apparently harder to herd than sheep and cows. Although they are certainly herd animals, they are also individualistic: they have more of a tendency to break away from the group and are more easily distracted by their surroundings. I barricade the opening by standing legs astride with a rectangular panel held out in front of me.

The first sow comes out at once. She can't have found the separation from her young all that difficult. She waddles along, snout to the planks, snorting and snaffling the hay that has drifted down from the stacks. She's followed by another, who shows no interest in the daylight behind me either. And so it continues until four of the five are out. That's when something happens.

From my vantage point, I can see neither Leiv nor the pigs, but I hear something slamming against the partitions and the squeals that penetrate the barn are so loud it's hard to believe that a single animal could make so much noise. But a pig's squeal can reach up to 130 decibels—more than twice as loud as a chainsaw and not far off the noise levels of a jet plane taking off thirty yards away. Is this the sound of separation anxiety?

Regardless of the cause, the sow emerges defeated from her battle with Leiv. Now she comes charging out through the plank door and heads straight for me at full tilt. I clutch the panel in front of me firmly and walk determinedly toward her. Just as I'm readying myself for the collision, she stops dead, cocks her lowered head slightly, and scowls up at me. I can almost hear her pleading with me: "Please, let me out of here." And there we stand surveying each other, separated by a mental gulf, until Leiv comes out.

"She was a bit stubborn, that last sow," he says.

"Do you think it's because she doesn't want to leave her piglets?"

"Dunno, it's hard to say what she's thinking," he says, giving her backside a shove.

When the pigs finally make it outside, they don't look much like animals turned out into springtime pastures. In fact, they don't look much as if they appreciate the fresh air at all. With a tottering gait, they waddle down the ramp from the barn. Some try to turn around and go back inside. We block their path and force them forward.

It's slow going. The pigs' snouts are sensors, and they stop constantly to investigate everything: a tractor rut, a withered dandelion, a few tufts of grass, a hole in the ground.

Suddenly, one of the sows seems to experience a revelation: she can run. Or more accurately *trot*. It happens just as we reach the door the animals are supposed to go through. She breaks away from the herd and heads purposefully down toward the field. Leiv stays behind, herding the others in through the door while I run after her. As soon as I've set off, I realize there's no need for me to run at all. A light jog is more than enough. Her motor skills are so poor that I foil her attempted jailbreak after little more than fifteen yards. If she'd had the same physique as her forebears, I might never have seen her again. But a lot has happened to the pig's body over the past few centuries.

RIGHT UP UNTIL MODERN TIMES, pigs in Europe so closely resembled wild boars that it would have been pretty much impossible for a modern, untrained eye to distinguish between the two. Traditionally, pigs used to be bristly, fast-moving, rugged beasts, well adapted to an outdoor life dashing around in shady woods or marshland. That's how it was in prehistoric times and antiquity, and that's how it was in the Middle Ages and well into the modern era. When the Spanish conquistadors went to America in the sixteenth century, the pigs they took with them on their ships were these wild-boar-like animals. We know this because a group of them still live in isolation on the island of Ossabaw off the coast of the U.S. state of Georgia. Today, the wild hogs of Ossabaw are the closest we can get to the old domesticated pig of Europe.

The European expansion of the sixteenth century also brought European pigs into contact with their Asian cousins. The Chinese were far ahead of the Europeans in many fields, and pig breeding was one of them. Chinese pigs were fatter and had tastier flesh than European breeds. They also grew faster and reproduced more efficiently. In the years that followed, many Asian pigs were loaded onto trading vessels bound for Europe, where they were such a success that it's barely possible nowadays to find a single domesticated pig in the world whose genetic material can't be traced back to these old Chinese animals.[4] But this cross-breeding with Chinese swine is not what created the modern industrial pigs we find in piggeries today. The pigs from Asia were black. In Europe, on the other hand, they had become brown, russet, and, in some places, pale with pink skin. So why did this last type in particular become so successful that it's now the very model of how a pig is supposed to look? It's mostly down to the Danes.

THE BREEDING PROCESS that led to the modern, naked, pink pig has involved intricate interactions across cultures and national borders, with particular input from China, Denmark, and the United Kingdom. While the Chinese genes made the animals fatter and improved their reproductive potential, the Danes' initial contribution was the color.

With the development of different breeds of domestic animals in the nineteenth century, breeding became both sport and big business for many farmers. Soon there was status to be gained from exhibiting their largest and finest animals. When status and prestige came into the picture, cattle were the livestock farmers initially worked hardest to compete with. Once pigs were also included, the main criterion—unsurprisingly—was how big and fat people could breed them. In this respect, the American boar Big Bill from Tennessee was second to none.

When he was born, there was nothing to indicate that the little Poland China piglet was destined for global fame. Farmer Walter J. Chappell bought him for just over three dollars when he was a few weeks old and started to feed him a blend of cornmeal, sweet potatoes, and sorghum molasses. Chappell quickly noticed that little Bill was a bit hungrier than the other pigs. And he grew quicker too. Much quicker. There seemed to be no end to it. After two years, Bill was the weight of an adult ox. By the time Chappell sent the hog to the Chicago World's Fair in 1933, he weighed in at 2,552 pounds.[5] Sadly, Big Bill never had a chance to wow the crowds in Chicago. The two men hired to transport the hog stopped along the way to settle a bet about how much Big Bill weighed. At some point in this process, Big Bill's leg was broken and he had to be put down. He did, however, enjoy some posthumous fame. Chappell arranged to have him stuffed, and the hog was later purchased by the taxidermist's family, who charged people ten cents a visit. Later still, he was sold to a carnival, after which his trail goes cold.

Big Bill's breed, the Poland China pig, was developed in the United States in the early nineteenth century and has never achieved any notable success outside its country of origin. A

British breed, the Yorkshire, proved to be more of a trendsetter. It was bred from pale Danish pigs imported by the British in the eighteenth century. Once the breed was established in England, it was exported back to Denmark in its new form, paving the way for further development of what would become known as the Danish "bacon pig," or the Landrace breed. This was the pig that would become the catalyst for breeding programs worldwide during the twentieth century.

PART OF THE REASON for the Danish success story plays out before my eyes as the pigs enter the piggery: the sows, which amble one after another down the narrow passage between the pigpens, are too big to walk two abreast. That's why there's such a commotion when the leader opts to do an about-face as they reach a gap where there's a bit more space. Suddenly, she ends up on a collision course with the sows behind her. Incapable of backing off, the sows stand snout to snout, tossing their heads, only to discover that it's impossible to turn. Even so, the sow that is facing the wrong way tries her best to do just that. Twisting her head, she shoves her snout against the wall behind her with all her might as her rear end remains jammed against the other side of the corridor. At the point where her body has formed an almost perfect U, she becomes completely stuck. Her forelegs and hind legs scrabble against the floor and she squeals in desperation. She can't move.

And that, precisely, illustrates the genius of the Danes: through targeted breeding, they managed to give the pigs a few extra vertebrae and ribs. This yields more side pork and bacon, as well as more chops. We get more out of the animal, as they say.

I lean my body weight against the sow's shoulder and shove as hard as I can. Gradually, I work her free from the walls and shift her back around until she's facing in the right direction. It strikes me that what her long, short-legged body most reminds me of is an outsized, hairless dachshund.

UNTIL THE MID-1850S, Norway had no preferences when it came to how pigs should look. They came in all shapes, sizes, and colors. Eighteenth-century sources refer to everything from purebred Chinese to West Indian breeds. But one variant was more dominant than the rest. This one is considered the original Norwegian Landrace breed, prior to the launch of breeding in the late nineteenth century. It had long legs, steel-gray bristles, and a long, narrow head.[6] In other words, it wasn't all that different from a wild boar.

When the first purely Norwegian pig breed was developed in 1895, the Danish example was followed: Norwegians also cross-bred pigs with Britain's Yorkshire breed. They, too, bred animals with extra-long spines, big litters, and plenty of fat. But at some point or another, they diverged from the practices of their southern neighbors: they weren't so concerned about skin color. Thanks to the Chinese genes, it wasn't all that unusual for Norwegian breeding pigs to be black all over in the first half of the twentieth century, or to have large dark patches. This would never have passed muster in Denmark, where rind with dark pigment was seen as unappetizing.[7] The Danes selected only the palest pigs for breeding stock. And since the Danes produced so much and were so far advanced in their breeding efforts, they also set the standard when it came to skin color.

I follow the sows into the pigpen where they will live together while they await the arrival of estrus. The moment they're inside the pen, the atmosphere becomes agitated. One of the sows launches an abrupt attack on another. Even though their tusks have been removed, the victim ends up with a seeping wound on her side. The blood oozes out of the scratch and trickles slowly down the naked, exposed skin.

Why, in fact, did the pig end up almost naked?

Throughout most of history, hog bristle has been an important raw material for us humans, especially for the production of various kinds of brooms and brushes. But as new materials saw the light of day in the twentieth century, there was no longer any need to breed pigs for their bristles. That was handy, really, because once the pig was imprisoned in temperate buildings, most of its bristles vanished of their own accord.

Since the pig has no sweat glands, it is sensitive to high temperatures. Consequently, a pig without bristles is a pig that is adapted to life in an environment where it is no longer exposed to cold. This is easy enough to see if we compare the bristly European wild boar with the naked boar found in Southeast Asia (babirusa) or Africa (warthogs). The same, by the way, is true of elephants and rhinoceroses, which today exist only in their hairless variants, since the fur-clad types that lived in the cold north long ago became extinct.

UP UNTIL THE FIRST WORLD WAR, pig breeding would remain an insignificant source of supplementary income for farmers in Europe. But at the beginning of the interwar period, there was a change of pace, with enormous growth in pig production during the 1920s, which continued through the 1930s: in Norway's case, pig production more than doubled over a twenty-year period.[8] But this was nothing compared to what happened in the postwar era, especially after 1960.

The number of farms and the proportion of the population employed in Norwegian agriculture currently stand at three-quarters of the levels seen in 1960. Paradoxically, though, only 13,500 tons of animals were sent to slaughter in Norway in 1960, compared with 325,000 tons in 2018.[9] A similar pattern is evident in the United States. While the number of hog farms has fallen steadily from 1,057,570 in 1965 to roughly 60,000 in 2021, pork production has risen from 13,905 million pounds in 1960 to 27,673 million pounds in 2021.[10] It hardly seems to add up. But it was during the 1960s that the foundations of a technological revolution in the agricultural sector were laid, with horses replaced by tractors and manual labor by combine harvesters and mowing machines. Haymaking and stacking, which could take weeks in the 1950s, was doable within days by the 1960s. And the changes didn't just take place out in the fields; what happened indoors was just as significant.

Given the reduction in farmers and farms, there was only one way meat production could increase: through a dramatic increase in the size of herds. And the consequences for the remaining farmers were evident—they would have to become more specialized. Grain, vegetables, cattle, sheep, chickens, or pigs? A choice had to be made. It was no longer possible to combine them all and use the pig as a waste-disposal unit. From now on, vast, specialized units would be developed. The days of subsistence farming were numbered.

And the tradition that was being abandoned was hardly insignificant: the subsistence farm is probably the oldest economic unit to have existed on earth since humans made the transition from hunter-gatherer societies. But with increasing urbanization, ever greater numbers of people came to depend on farmers to produce food *for* them. So much for tradition and nostalgia. From the pigs' point of view, the new business model meant that they could no longer be fed on the waste that was produced by a nonspecialized farm. Instead, the practice adopted in Ancient Rome was reintroduced: the pigs started to eat food that could just as well be eaten by people. In this case, tailor-made feed concentrate made up of grain, fat, proteins, and vitamins. And of course the introduction of feed concentrate didn't just solve the problem of organic waste shortage; it also improved the animals' health and growth rate. It served to streamline the animal itself.

WITH THE RESTORATION of social democracy after the Second World War, efforts became focused on new livestock breeding programs. In the United States, the Regional Swine Breeding Laboratory had already been studying the effect of inbreeding on various swine traits since 1937, and in 1960, the Farmer's Hybrid Company developed new hybrid lines that would be crossed in rotation.[11] In Norway, cattle, sheep, and pigs were all assigned research groups mandated to develop the ideal animal. The pig-breeding team focused on the Norwegian Landrace, ultimately devoting its efforts to breeding animals that produced lean pork, to bolster Norwegian public health and nutrition. Because the increased appetite for meat in the interwar period turned out to have a worrying result: a wave of cardiovascular disease had swept the Western world. From the 1970s onward, a continuous stream of research results showed that animal fat was bad for us. "Healthy" became synonymous with "lean"—and suddenly "fat" went from being a culinary honorific to a metaphorical swear word. The aim of the new breeding programs was clear: the pig must be slimmed down.

As early as 1958, ultrasound machines were used to check that a pig's fat layer wasn't too thick. This was technically groundbreaking stuff considering that such equipment hadn't even found its way into some hospitals yet. The result was that from the 1970s until the mid-1990s, the pig lost as much as 30 percent of its fat layer. Along with the Danish and Swedish Landraces, the Norwegian pig ended up among the leanest in the world. And not only had its pork become "healthy"; the new, intensive business model meant that the meat was increasingly cheaper. The dinner tables of postwar nuclear families were kept amply supplied with sausages, pork chops, ham hocks, and bacon, and more and more people were able to treat themselves to the more lavish dishes on high days and holidays: roast pork, pork loin, and pork belly. The Norwegian Landrace breeding program had become an agricultural and commercial success story. Similar achievements were being made elsewhere—such as in the United Kingdom, where the Pig Improvement Company was set up in 1962 by a group of pig farmers intent on correcting the lag between pig breeding in Britain and the rest of Europe; it later made inroads into the American market. Pigs were not just the backbone of European meat production; they had become a bedrock of the European diet.

But something got lost along the way.

Without the intermuscular fat—or marbling, as it's known in cooking circles—the pork became dry, tough, and tasteless. That was fine in products like sandwich fillings, sausages, and other processed food, but by the beginning of the 2000s, pork as pure meat in the form of chops and fillets had become a gray symbol of dull everyday cuisine. So it came like a gift from the gods for both the pork industry and consumers when nutrition researchers around precisely that time began to question whether saturated fats really were as bad for us as previous research had concluded. In the United States in particular, it had become clear that dietary advice about reducing fat intake had made little impact.[12] Obesity and type 2 diabetes had become veritable American plagues, which just kept escalating—despite the fact that the market was flooded with "light" products and McDonald's had stopped cooking its French fries in animal fat.

Between 1970 and 2000, more and more calories from fat in the Western diet had been replaced by carbohydrates in the form of huge amounts of white bread, pasta, and refined sugar. The new processed and semi-processed products that started to fill the shelves and freed up time that people would otherwise have spent in the kitchen were certainly low in saturated fat but contained massive amounts of added salt and refined sugar. No problem, people thought. Because, as a report from the UN Food and Agriculture Organization claimed as recently as 1997, "Sugar is not bad for health."[13] Sugar could not, at any rate, be converted into dangerous fat when it entered our bodies. Or so people thought.

Since the end of the 1990s, research has shown that carbohydrates are, in fact, extremely good at converting into fat.[14] This opened up a new direction in food research, and it wasn't long before further studies revealed that carbohydrates were as much of a threat to public health as fat, if not more. Sugar evidently was converted into fat, whether it came from candy or corn products. On top of that, it became clear that high and continuous consumption of refined sugar hindered the functioning of the mechanisms that regulate blood sugar levels. As a result, people developed type 2 diabetes.

In 2003, just six years after the FAO had claimed that sugar was harmless, the research was unambiguous enough for the World Health Organization to issue an official recommendation to reduce sugar intake.[15]

Even though no one had yet concluded that animal fat was actually healthy, everything appeared to have been turned on its head. Bookstores were flooded with books about the Atkins Diet, which exhorted people to say "no to carbohydrates, yes to fat and proteins." And no matter how uninterested you were in dietary advice, you'd have to have been a hermit not to have heard of the new concept of "low-carb" living. Fat had a renaissance, and at around the same time as the cover of Time magazine was exhorting people to "eat butter"[16] (subtext: "eat animal fat"), this change in the nutritional climate convinced the Norwegian breeding facility Norsvin that it could give pork back its flavor.

The pig was fattened up again.

Attempts to increase the marbling in the meat had admittedly started a long time previously. But it wasn't until 2013 that the new, juicier "edelgris" (noble pig) which owed 50 percent of its genetic material to the American Duroc pig, was ready to invade herds nationwide. This breed, which originated from the fat Spanish Ibérico pigs, was prized for the high quality of its meat. Not that it was terribly fatty—the Duroc, too, had been put on a diet after the Americans had imported their pigs from Spain. No, the quality of the meat was largely down to how the

Duroc's fat was *stored*. Like the cattle that produce Japan's exclusive Kobe beef, a large share of the Duroc pig's fat is stored in the musculature itself. The "dry" Landraces, by contrast, store almost all their fat in the outer layer of fatty tissue.

The intramuscular fat made the meat more tender, juicier, and tastier. Not only did the new slaughter pig taste a little different, it *looked* different. Like the original Iberian pigs, the Duroc pig is brown all over. Introducing these Duroc hogs into the breeding line tends to produce slaughter pigs that are still pale pink, courtesy of their Norwegian Landrace mothers, but generally with large brown patches. However, this pigmentation does not go deep enough to affect the color of the rind. And this has enabled us indifferent consumers to remain blissfully ignorant of the fact that the animal we eat has altered its appearance over recent years.

ALTHOUGH MANY WOULD SAY that the Norwegian slaughter pig, now known as "Noroc," is still not fatty enough, the breeding industry itself claims that it has developed a more or less "perfect animal." Because the truth is that the quality of meat from the Duroc sperm donor, combined with the health, growth, and fertility of the new Norwegian sow that goes by the prosaic name of TN70, has transformed Norway into something of a star of the global breeding market. Since Norsvin in Norway and Topigs in the Netherlands merged to form a single breeding company in 2014, Topigs Norsvin has been the world's second-largest swine genetics supplier in the world, beaten only by the British-American Pig Improvement Company.

The pig is not what it used to be.

Against
Nature

A PACKAGE HAS ARRIVED at the farm. It contains semen—and plenty of it: around three pints of fresh boar semen diluted with saline solution to improve the flow, sent by the Norwegian breeding facility Norsvin. Twenty-three sows in estrus are ready for a new round of insemination. The product came by express delivery because it has a short shelf life. Unlike cows, horses, and sheep, which are often inseminated with frozen product, pigs need fresh semen: it makes for larger litters.

Among the crowd, I find the sow from pigpen thirteen, shuffling around in the muck by the wall of the pen. Just seven weeks have passed since she last gave birth, but there's no rest for a breeding sow. Two weeks ago, she was separated from her young and placed in this enclosure with the other breeding sows. In just over three years, she has farrowed six litters. With a gestation period of three months, three weeks, and three days, that's the best performance possible. But breeding animals don't earn medals for long and loyal service: if she doesn't come through this time too, she'll be ground into mincemeat.

There's not much more mercy on display among the sows, either. Matriarchal rule applies here, but number thirteen is no matriarch—you can tell by the scratches she acquired during the inevitable struggle for hierarchy that takes place whenever sows are housed together like this.

CONVENIENTLY ENOUGH, sows' cycles become coordinated, meaning that all twenty-three sows ovulate almost simultaneously. This phenomenon, which is purported to occur among humans too and is known as the McClintock Effect in this context, is probably familiar to anyone who lived in an all-woman dorm in their college days. It was first discovered by the American psychologist Martha McClintock in the 1970s, when she conducted a study of female students at Wellesley College, Massachusetts. As the months went by, McClintock noticed that the menstrual cycles of the women living together on campus altered. To start off with, each had her individual cycle, but gradually their cycles started to move closer together, becoming fully synchronized after several months.[1] According to McClintock, the phenomenon was caused by the pheromones secreted by all mammals. Although we're not aware of their smell, they apparently affect us in social groupings—like a subconscious, scent-based form of sexual communication. And there was nothing random about *who* controlled the synchronization in the dorms at Wellesley: the most extroverted and socially dominant women—the ones who, in a piggery, would be called the matriarchs.[2]

Menstrual synchrony has been detected in many species, but its evolutionary function remains unclear. Some have suggested that it may be an advantage for herd animals to give birth simultaneously, as this makes it easier for the young of any of the mothers that die to be adopted. McClintock herself suggested it was simply an epiphenomenon—a nonfunctional by-product of a separate process in the body. This, along with the fact that follow-up studies have been unable to confirm McClintock's findings, has cast doubt on whether the phenomenon exists at all among humans. For pigs, however, pheromones play such a crucial role that Leiv keeps a spray bottle of the boar pheromone androstenol in the back room in case synchronization fails to occur. A quick squirt is all it takes to get the sows going.

Androstenol is also found in celery, by the way—and truffles, which explains why sows in estrus are particularly good at sniffing out these delicacies in the deciduous forests of Southern Europe. It may well be that this scent of boar is precisely why we humans have such a rich tradition of using truffles and celery as aphrodisiacs.

"THERE! DID YOU SEE THAT?"

We've moved into a space occupied by a herd of young sows, or gilts. Leiv points at one of them excitedly. The animals have just reached sexual maturity and are due for their first insemination a week from now. Life moves fast for them: they're only eight months old.

"Is it something to do with her gait?" I ask.

"Watch."

Leiv shoves his way through the crowd and grabs her hips. Then he stands astride her, sits lightly on her rump, and starts to bounce up and down, a bit like a rodeo rider.

"She's ready," he says with a smile, slapping her on the backside.

Leiv's peculiar behavior has demonstrated one of the countless tiny miracles of evolution: the standing reflex. During estrus—when imminent ovulation increases the animals' sexual receptivity—the joints in the hind legs of sows, cows, and other female mammals lock, bracing their rump area. Their hindquarters become slightly elevated, too, easing the journey of the aimless sperm cells from the cervix to the fallopian tubes, where fertilization takes place. The bracing of the sow's joints also helps her bear the weight of the massive boar during mating. But this is only useful in a natural environment. The closest the sows at this piggery will get to anything resembling mating is the procedure Leiv and I are about to embark upon.

We go into the back room and organize our equipment: tubes of semen the size of tubes of toothpaste and a flexible plastic hose somewhere between the thickness of a drinking straw and a garden hose. At one end of the hose is an ovoid front section that appears to mimic the head of a penis. But that's where the resemblance ends, because a boar's penis looks like a screwdriver.

I pick up one of the transparent tubes of semen and hold it up against a strip of light that falls through the dirty window. The contents are runny and cloudy, like a mixture of milk and water.

HUMANITY'S TEN-THOUSAND-YEAR HISTORY of animal husbandry is predicated on our ability to control the fertilization of animals. Pigs or cows, dogs or cats—none of these would exist in their current form if it weren't for the fact that humanity has tirelessly selected the species we've kept imprisoned. Chihuahuas would still be big gray beasts that hunted in packs; horses would tramp freely over the steppes; and pigs would live deep in the forests and be classified as wild boars.

The procedure used to be relatively uncomplicated: a male and a female animal with desirable traits would be brought together, and then the humans would simply stand back and wait for the animals to work things out for themselves. But some fifty years ago, a shift took place. Farmers went from being facilitators of animal reproduction to virtually performing the act on the animals' behalf. It was a long and winding road that took us from Antonie van Leeuwenhoek of the

Netherlands, who discovered sperm cells in his own semen in the 1670s, to the pig farmers of Jæren, who decided to jettison boars in favor of plastic hoses and tubes of semen in the 1980s.

IT WAS LEEUWENHOEK'S technological innovation—the practical compact microscope—that paved the way for his discovery. Leeuwenhoek started out not as a scientist but a cloth merchant with an eye for detail, and he built his device primarily to study textiles. But when at last it was in working order and he placed a scrap of fabric beneath the lens, he unwittingly laid the foundations of modern medicine—by discovering bacteria in his fabric sample.[3]

After this first happy accident, we can only imagine what Leeuwenhoek didn't put under his microscope. In those days, most people already knew that semen played a significant role in the fertilization of women and female animals. What they didn't know was how or why. When, a few months later, Leeuwenhoek peered through the lens at his own ejaculate, he set eyes on the solution to the problem that had kept people scratching their heads for millennia. There, swarming upon the surface of the glass, he saw the minute origins of life.

Like the Enlightenment man he was in the process of becoming, Leeuwenhoek at once felt compelled to conduct further investigations and comparisons. But the seventeenth century was no time to go around asking people if he could examine samples of their semen. Instead he sought donors among the animals around him, starting off with his own dog and rabbit. He described the activity in the various semen samples and made detailed sketches of the intricate heads of the cells. Over the decades that followed, he worked his way through most of the animal kingdom: vertebrates, invertebrates, fish, amphibians, birds, and mammals—all were made to ejaculate for Leeuwenhoek's microscope.[4]

Thanks to the haze of testosterone that hung over society back then, no one realized just how far away they still were from fully solving the mystery of the birds and the bees. The most prevalent theory in Leeuwenhoek's era was that the microscopic head of the sperm cell contained a fully developed embryo that simply needed a little nutrition from a placenta in order to grow. A further two hundred years would pass before the female's role in conception was fully recognized and science reached consensus on the matter.

A similar length of time passed before successful artificial insemination was achieved. Despite his ignorance of the inner workings of a uterus, Lazzaro Spallanzani of Italy managed to fertilize a female dog via artificial insemination in 1784. Sixty-two days later, she gave birth to three healthy pups that would grow up to become the first documented donor offspring. But artificial insemination of animals would remain a cumbersome, time-consuming, and messy business of little interest to agriculture long after Spallanzani's days. It would remain so until the Soviet Union entered the stage, along with a determined researcher whose criminal record in the name of science is so hair-raising that he is surpassed only by the Nazi doctor Mengele. His name was Ilya Ivanovich Ivanov.

Ivanov was a middle-class boy from Imperial Russia who studied biology at Kharkiv University in the 1890s. Early on, he became interested in the study of reproduction and the mysterious field of hybridization. After playing an active role in the October Revolution of 1917, he obtained a key post at a research center somewhat ominously named the State Experimental Veterinary Institute. It was here that Ivanov would eventually go totally off the rails.

In the late 1890s, when he first embarked on his work, the only way to disseminate good genetic material among livestock was to transport prize males to the different local herds, where they would be mated with as many females as possible. Ivanov saw the limitations of this method, which failed to exploit the full potential of the genetic material in herds across the empire. As Ivanov saw it, there was only one way to achieve optimal dissemination of the very finest genes: artificial insemination. But there was a catch. The technology didn't yet exist.

So far, the procedure had only been possible in the form of isolated experiments, which required insemination to occur immediately after ejaculation because the sperm could only survive for a short time away from the warmth and humidity of the testicles. If they didn't immediately find their way into a similar environment in a uterus, they would rapidly lose their ability to swim, then dry out and die. If Ivanov's vision were to be achieved, a method would have to be developed for storing and protecting the sperm cells during the critical phase between ejaculation and insemination.

One of the first stages in the research process was to amputate the testicles of oxen, then study them at different temperatures and under different environmental conditions. Ivanov rapidly discovered that sperm cells remained viable as long as the testicles were kept cool. But the truly critical question remained unanswered: How could they keep the sperm alive *outside* the testicles? Ivanov set to work diligently, mixing sperm with different combinations of fluids, and eventually discovered that a sterile saline solution was the environment needed to keep the little swimmers alive. He was soon ready to inseminate animals in locations far removed from the semen's place of origin. Yet a feeling of disquiet hung over the whole project.

At that point, insemination was still largely untested. No one knew whether large-scale artificial insemination would lead to deformities or other abnormalities. If it did, that would be the nail in the coffin of Ivanov's ambitions. Nonetheless, he and the research community that grew up around him had no choice but to continue their work and await the outcome. They developed apparatuses to brace the female livestock, keeping them still and correctly positioned during insemination. They also invented devices for holding the vagina open during the procedure, as well as artificial vaginas that completely revolutionized the harvesting of semen.

As the practice of artificial insemination became more widespread, especially in horses, Ivanov saw that the resulting offspring were largely healthy and viable. When, at a certain point, he managed to inseminate five hundred mares with the sperm of a single stallion, it was nothing short of a sensation. After the Russian Revolution in 1917, it rapidly became clear that Ivanov's work was well aligned with the new Soviet state's ambitious plans for agriculture. In a country where the climate was often brutal and it wasn't uncommon for livestock to succumb to the harsh conditions, his methods paved the way for a more effective breeding program that could help make animals more resistant to disease and extreme weather.

But Ivanov wasn't satisfied with breeding conventional livestock such as horses, cows, sheep, and pigs. He also saw that his new methods offered opportunities to breed entirely new species with new—and unknown—traits. Without the technology he had developed in the preceding years, such experiments would have been well-nigh impossible. But now, Ivanov set painstakingly to work, crossing European wild horses with African zebras and dairy cows with bison. To his disappointment, none of these projects got beyond the experimental stage, but they reinforced his fascination with the art of hybridization.

Ivanov knew his Darwin and was well aware of the links between humans and apes, but the motivation for his next project isn't entirely clear. Perhaps he was driven by sheer scientific curiosity, or perhaps the aim was to create a new, harder-working human species to implement Stalin's next five-year plan. Lavish state financing of his experiments might seem to suggest the latter.[5] Whatever the case, the project involved trips to Africa, transplanting a human ovary into a chimpanzee, and attempting to inseminate women with orangutan sperm.

Ivanov's experiments came to an abrupt halt in 1930, when he was purged along with many other scientists and exiled to Kazakhstan, where he ended his days in 1932.[6] Nonetheless, Ivanov—dubbed the "Red Frankenstein"—left a legacy of pioneering work on livestock breeding and artificial insemination that his Soviet students would further develop and perfect over the years to come, laying the foundations for much of what we now think of as industrial animal husbandry. The insemination technology they developed for livestock breeding has also proven helpful for humans, and modern hospitals still use methods in human medicine that are broadly based on those developed by Ivanov.[7]

IF WE ARE TO BELIEVE feminist theorist Kate Millett, the fact that *men* have been largely responsible for livestock breeding throughout history has had consequences that are far from insignificant. Millett has pointed out that women, like animals, enjoyed far higher status in hunter-gatherer societies than they did once humans had gained control of animals' reproductive processes.[8]

The archaeological record for the Neolithic age is teeming with tiny Venus sculptures, images of naked, fertile goddesses. Back then, women represented fertility and creativity through the children they bore. Thus womanhood came to embody the wider natural cycle of growth and decay, life and death. Men were left on the sidelines, constantly hauling home huge and powerful prey in an attempt to make up for their shortcomings. As the anthropologist Henry S. Sharp put it after studying

Indigenous peoples in Africa: "To be female is to be power, to be male is to acquire power."[9]

Livestock breeding upended these gender roles, according to Millett. Because once men gained control over breeding, female fertility was demystified. What's more, livestock husbandry placed men in possession of the powers of fertility and creativity that had previously been the preserve of women.[10] Womanhood was diminished, manhood expanded. And with that, the early agricultural societies created a model of government for the great civilizations where the king ruled over the people just as the "good shepherd" ruled over the herd and the family.

The patriarchy had arrived.[11]

BACK IN JÆREN, Leiv has made a start on the foreplay. That is to say, he has filled a bucket with feed concentrate and emptied it into the trough. As the sows cluster around it, their backsides are exposed to us.

"So now it's just a matter of getting down to business," he says as he enters the pen. He crouches behind the sows with a calm offhandedness that can probably only come from a lifetime in a piggery. As for me, I find myself trying to shake off some uncomfortable associations and a general sense of emotional ambiguity. Because inseminating pigs turns out to be just as hands-on as you might imagine.

The swollen pink vaginal opening poking out beneath the tail is full of wood shavings and dirt that must be wiped away with a little cloth. Leiv takes care of the penetration itself: with a practiced gesture, he guides the ovoid-headed hose as far into the sow as it can go. Next comes my job: snipping off the tip of the tube of sperm and attaching it to the other end of the hose. Then it's just a matter of squeezing away.

We could, if we wished to optimize the entire business, follow the advice of agricultural researchers and pretend to be boars. Supposedly this will increase the sows' arousal and fertility levels. The recommendation is to slap their flanks, tug at their groin, and pummel them directly below the vaginal opening.[12] Perhaps it's just as well that we opted to skip that bit.

FOR LEIV, INSEMINATION is a trivial task. I can't say I feel the same. At one point when I'm fully occupied with tubes of semen in both hands, inseminating two sows simultaneously, it suddenly starts to feel as if the temperature in the barn is rising. The T-shirt beneath my overalls clings to my back, and I start to wonder what the hell I've gotten myself mixed up in. It's the synapses in my brain sending a physical message to my back and limbs about where the boundaries are meant to lie in contact between humans and animals. I peek at Leiv. Can he tell what I'm feeling?

When you come into contact with animals in this way for the first time (and somewhat unprepared, I'd say), there's no avoiding thoughts of the darker taboos in Western sexual culture. Perhaps it's hardly surprising I'm so hyperaware of the discomfort of this situation: if there's one thing people have worked diligently to achieve in Europe over the centuries, it's been to deter humans from unduly intimate relations with their animals. England offers an example that illustrates just how high a priority this was: the country introduced capital punishment for intercourse with animals in 1534, but took until the twentieth century to impose a general prohibition on incest.[13]

It was a hard-fought struggle for churches and governments, because the phenomenon of human-animal abuse goes back a long way. Petroglyphs and cave paintings that date back millennia offer us the oldest documentation of it, and the phenomenon can be found in a variety of ancient cultures—from the Babylonians and Egyptians to the Greeks and Romans. In certain cultures and tribes cut off from Christian cultural influence, the practice has even been socially acceptable.[14] It's also described in lively fashion in Norse literature. In the bloody *Story of Burnt Njål*, swords are drawn for the first time when Skarphedin teases Torkjell over an incident with his horse: "There are still some scraps of muck between your teeth from your mare's asshole. Those who saw it said it was a repulsive sight."[15]

During the Middle Ages and the Renaissance, the struggle to eradicate bestiality became a matter of existential importance to the church. For the early Christian thinkers, the distinction between humans and animals was the very foundation stone of their faith. If it were erased, if animals and humans merged into one, the entire religious structure would be in danger of collapse. Consequently, efforts to keep the animal and human worlds apart and to suppress what Plato had called "the wild beast within us" rapidly became one of the Church Fathers' most fundamental struggles.

Saint Augustine, who lived in the fourth and fifth centuries, was among those worked most assiduously on the matter. However, even he had to admit that there was something strikingly animal or bestial about the act of sex, during which, he said, "there is an almost total extinction of mental alertness." Saint Augustine and many of his peers considered this to clash with the distinction Christianity had established between people as rational and animals as irrational. For Augustine, the irrational and bestial aspect of sexuality was most apparent in male erections, which he called "bestial movements," because they are driven by lust and desire rather than rational will.[16]

Although humans might be reminiscent of animals during sexual intercourse, even the Church Fathers realized that they couldn't ban the act of reproduction entirely. Instead, it became crucial to impose certain dogmas about how to perform it. But this meant studying what the animals did: it was the only way to ensure that humans avoided the most obviously animal aspects of the act.

Few creatures better illustrated the bestial nature of sexuality than the pig. In antiquity, pigs—and especially gilts—were a living symbol of sexuality and fertility. In Ancient Greece, young pigs were called khoiros or delphax, terms that could also be applied to female genitals, as could the Latin name for pigs—porcus.[17] The pig was also sexualized in Scandinavia. In Norse mythology, the fertility gods Frey and Freya were both associated with boars. Frey, who is depicted with a prominent phallus, was accompanied by a boar called Gullinbursti, while Freya often rode on a boar called Hildisvíni.

The descriptions of animal behavior formulated by the second-century Greco-Roman poet Oppian are among the classical texts that influenced medieval thinking. Of the boar, he writes:

> Unceasingly he roams in pursuit of the female and is greatly excited by the frenzy of desire… He drops foam upon the ground and gnashes the white hedge of his teeth, panting hotly; and there is much more rage about his mating than modesty. If the female abides his advances, she quenches all his rage and lulls to rest his passion. But if she refuses intercourse and flees, straightway stirred by the hot and fiery goad of passion he either overcomes her and mates with her by force or he attacks her with his jaws and lays her dead in the dust.[18]

In the Middle Ages, the boar was frequently used as a symbol of male sexuality and virtues associated with masculinity, such as power and dominance. The boar, with its prominent testicles, was both depicted and hunted by men who wished to be imbued with the same virile power the animal represented. This status may well have been bolstered by the fact that the boar's ejaculation is among the most prolonged and voluminous in the animal kingdom.

The Church Fathers were, of course, repulsed by all this and condemned any sexual undertones in human dealings with animals. At the same time, knowledge of how the animals functioned and of their sexual behavior was useful when it came to establishing how *not* to have sex: penetration from behind was quite out of the question—that was the animals' position. Likewise, grunts and groans were banned because those sounds also belonged to the animal kingdom. It didn't help matters that such practices were assumed to increase people's lust, since lust and desire were bestial qualities too. No, for Saint Augustine and his peers, the ideal act of sexual intercourse was silent and absolutely devoid of lust, emotion, or anything else suggestive of devotion. It should be carried out as only humans could do it: face to face, like a conversation with God.[19]

CONSIDERING HOW MUCH intellectual effort had gone into these efforts to prevent people from resembling pigs or other animals, it isn't hard to imagine how seriously the matter was taken when people engaged in sexual intercourse *with* them.

Unsurprisingly *crimen bestialis*, as the crime became known in Norway, was considered one of the most monstrous forms of sodomy the church could imagine. Not just because animals were a different life form, which God had given into humanity's stewardship, or because the act dragged humans down to the level of animals, performing an act that was "against nature," as Thomas Aquinas put it in the thirteenth century. On the threshold of the darker and more bewildered centuries of the Middle Ages, people were also becoming increasingly aware that animals could represent a demonic darkness against which humans should be on guard. The association between animal and devil naturally helped to foster some wild flights of fantasy about the possible results of intercourse with animals—producing some of the most bizarre writings of the Middle Ages.

In *The History and Topography of Ireland*, from the late twelfth century, Gerald of Wales tells of the Irish people, whom he considered so remote from civilization as to be almost animals. The author claimed this was also reflected in their sexual habits, which frequently involved animals. His account becomes particularly fascinating when he writes about the outcome of such sexual encounters, which resulted in a constant stream of half-human, half-animal monsters. On one occasion a man even managed to squeeze a calf out of his gut after being impregnated by an ox. At around the same time as Gerald of Wales was writing his fantastical nonfiction, a monk in Evesham, England, had a revelation about how such sins would be punished in the hereafter:

> All who were punished there had been guilty of a wickedness in life that is unmentionable by a Christian... those therefore were continually attacked by huge fiery monsters, horrible beyond description. Despite their opposition, these committed upon them the same damnable crimes that they had been guilty of on earth.[20]

As these demonic notions became more widespread, the penalties for *crimen bestialis* became increasingly harsher, resulting in the introduction of the first genuinely punitive law addressing bestiality. New Christian legislation that found its way into Norway's Gulathing's Law in the eleventh century stated: "We may have no carnal dealings with cattle. And if a man is accused and convicted of it... he shall be castrated... and he shall depart from the king's dominions as a malefactor and never return."[21]

The centuries passed, but even the threat of castration and banishment was never penalty enough to keep people away from animals. So when Christian V's Norwegian Code came into force in 1688, it tersely stated: "Intercourse that is against nature shall be punished with flames and fire."[22]

By this point, capital punishment had long been the European norm for bestiality. Yet despite this fearsome deterrent and other gruesome punishments visited on offenders across the continent, it was still so common for boys to have sex with the cattle and sheep in their care that the Catholic Church tried to prevent youths from being employed as shepherds.[23] As the Swedish historian Jonas Liliequist has documented, Swedish farm boys in the seventeenth and eighteenth century often experienced their sexual awakening with farm animals. The boys would learn techniques from each other and often engaged in such activities in groups, as a game or pastime.[24] Something similar occurred in Norway, where a review of eighty trials between the seventeenth and nineteenth century reveals that the defendants were exclusively male, often very young, and employed on farms.[25] The crime would cost many of them their lives. This was especially true in Sweden, where between six and seven hundred people were executed for bestiality between 1635 and 1754.

Norway's last execution for *crimen bestialis* took place in 1757. And at around this point it would seem that the Dano-Norwegian authorities opted for a new strategy in their desperate battle against bestiality. The merciless punishments had never had the hoped-for deterrent effect, so from then on, they settled on a time-honored technique for dealing with anything that's too painful to talk about: silence.[26]

IN NORWAY, the prohibition on bestiality was lifted in 1972, an unintended consequence of the battle for gay liberation. Back then, paragraph 213 of the Penal Code, also known as the "sodomy paragraph"—which placed gay people and zoophiles on an equal footing—was seen as a legal relic of an outmoded biblical morality. But rather than taking the opportunity to establish a legal distinction between the two practices, it was as if a slightly perverse wind of tolerance and scorn of prejudice wafted in through the windows of Parliament. Moralistic obstacles of all kinds should now be a thing of the past. So why not just liberate both groups?

Once paragraph 213 was repealed, it would take a surprisingly long time for Parliament to realize that there was at least one essential difference between the two practices. Under pressure from animal welfare organizations, the Norwegian public gradually became aware that the liberation of zoophiles had failed to take into account a fundamental aspect of any sexual act: consent. What's more, vets were increasingly seeing signs of gross sexual abuse of animals. In 2007, prior to a parliamentary debate about reintroducing the ban on bestiality in Norway—this time as a provision under the animal welfare act—a survey was conducted among 650 veterinarians. One in five responded that they had noticed or strongly suspected the sexual abuse of animals under their care. And this was only where there were visible injuries. The number of undetected cases was assumed to be enormous.[27]

At the point when the new Norwegian ban on "having sexual intercourse with or undertaking sexual activity with animals" came into force in 2010, Norway was something of a laggard in the European context. Almost all the animal welfare laws that had been introduced in other countries already contained a prohibition on sex with animals.[28]

In the United Kingdom, the modern prohibition was introduced in 2003. And it was this law that would add an extra layer to former prime minister David Cameron's embarrassment in 2015 when an unauthorized biography claimed that he had performed a sex act on a pig's head.[29] This bizarre incident, said to have taken place during his student days at Oxford, was even allegedly documented in a photograph. Most greeted the revelation with blushes and revulsion, but the *Independent* gleefully embarked on an investigation of whether Cameron had broken laws prohibiting sex with animals and necrophilia. Since the alleged penetration had involved the head, the newspaper found him not guilty on the first count. He was also absolved of the second because the law on necrophilia only applies to humans. Whether or not the newspaper's interest in the matter was strictly legal in nature is, of course, a matter for debate.

ALTHOUGH NORWAY WAS a late starter compared with most of Europe, it led the way in Scandinavia. In 2010, all the other Scandinavian countries had repealed the old prohibition against bestiality but had yet to introduce new legislation under animal welfare laws. In the interim, business boomed at Danish animal brothels as zoophile sex tourists arrived in their hordes from Norway and other countries where prohibitions were already in place.[30] Under the pretense of running regular farms, some Danish farmers were pimping out their animals. Visiting customers could choose from pig, sheep, cow, or horse—they could just help themselves. For a fee, of course. But in 2015, Denmark brought a halt to bestiality too, on the same grounds as those given by Live Kleveland of the Animal Welfare Alliance when the new Norwegian prohibition came into force: "This is abuse, not sex. An animal cannot consent to this treatment."[31]

At the time of writing, the Danish ban on bestiality was the most recent legislation enacted in Scandinavia (only Finland has yet to produce legislation in the field); and, like the Norwegian law, the Danish prohibition is not restricted to assaults that cause physical injury. As the then Danish minister for food, Dan Jørgensen, said in 2015, "In all circumstances, any doubt must be settled in favor of the animals."[32] Because, as Kleveland has said in Norway: "We have every reason to believe that they also suffer psychological pain, since sexual intercourse with a human being is a totally unnatural act for animals."[33]

UNNATURAL ACTIVITIES? I squeeze the final drops out of the tube and discover that the semen has suddenly started to trickle *out* of the vaginal opening. Confused, I tug off the tube, leaving the hose inside the sow. The negative pressure in the hose sends the liquid spraying back out at me; it mostly lands on my hands and overalls, but a few drops hit me in the face.

The act is over, the tube is empty. I pull out the hose and sling it over the pigpen.

AS WE NOW KNOW, there was never any real danger that animals and humans would merge, resulting in the monstrous offspring imagined by some in the Middle Ages. The laws of biology have since established that humans are incapable of reproducing with pigs or other animals to produce half-animal, half-human issue. It is curious, then, that no field has done more to challenge this law of nature than the biosciences.

The Human Model

SCISSORS, SCALPELS, AND CLAMPS clatter against brushed steel surfaces. The green-clad figures in hairnets and latex gloves weave their way among machines and clusters of cables. Here, up on the fourth floor of Haukeland University Hospital, there's more shouting than talking going on:

"We have a patient with extensive stab wounds!"

"Heart's stable at 150 but the patient is shaking severely!"

They refer to her simply as "the patient" and I very much doubt she has another name. Very few pigs do.

The patient is deeply anesthetized now. An oxygen tube has been inserted into her throat to supply her with the oxygen she needs, and the anesthesiologist is monitoring her heart, blood pressure, and oxygen saturation on a large plasma screen on the wall. Her snout and trotters are half hidden beneath a blue cloth. Only her chest and belly are exposed to the sharp light of the surgical lamp. If it weren't for the trail of small teats running down either side of her belly, you could easily mistake her for a person. And that, of course, is the point for the doctors who travel here to Bergen from local hospitals all across Norway to take a course in emergency medical surgery.

I've taken a break from the piggery to come and observe work in the operating room. As if this simulation on the operating table weren't human enough already, the pig's immediate family is also nearby. Admittedly, two of them are lying on their own operating tables with similar injuries in another wing of the department, but the rest are hale and hearty—for now; I just met them in a little cubicle down the hall. They had everything they needed: food, water, and plenty of hay to root around in. These conditions are probably an improvement on those in the conventional piggery they came from. And they'll remain in this relative comfort until the course leader inflicts the injuries the course participants will be required to repair. But one thing's for sure: they won't be getting out of here alive. That's never an option when pigs are used in medical research.

IF THERE'S ONE PERSON who can take the credit for identifying the pig as a model for the human body, it's the Greco-Roman physician Claudius Galenus, who plied his trade in the second century CE. Galen, as he is usually known, started his career tending gladiators at the arena in his hometown of Pergamon before becoming personal physician to Emperor Marcus Aurelius. He went on to become one of the greatest names in the history of science.

Unlike most physicians before him, who treated their patients based on external symptoms and sheer guesswork about what was going on inside their bodies, Galen realized he would never understand a thing unless he could observe the workings of the organs within. The only trouble was that it was strictly taboo to tamper with human bodies in those days, living or dead. Dissecting human bodies was prohibited. This may seem paradoxical in a society as fixated on violence as Ancient

Rome, which made spectacular entertainment out of gladiators battling to the death and prisoners being torn to shreds by wild animals. But the taboo against mutilating the human body had deep roots that went back to prehistoric times.

Galen got the idea of substituting animals for humans from Aristotle, who had been the first to observe the striking anatomical resemblance between people and animals. The similarities were so great, indeed, that he believed humans should be classified as part of the animal kingdom. And it was Aristotle who became the first person to dissect animals as a means of understanding humans. But it's debatable how successful his efforts were, because when Galen embarked on his own practice, Aristotle was precisely the person he started to prove wrong. Without ever getting under the skin of a single person—living or dead—Galen achieved an insight into the human body that would remain unparalleled until almost 1,500 years after his era.[1] And the animal he had to thank for almost all his feats was the pig.

Galen didn't favor pigs just because they were so readily available in Ancient Rome. His preference also stemmed from an observation to which doctors can still attest to this very day: apart from the great apes, no animal's anatomy is more akin to that of the human body than the pig's. No modern medical student can avoid encountering pigs' organs when taking an anatomy course, or pig skin when learning how to suture; and no surgeon-to-be will ever learn to operate without first rehearsing on living pigs. Because, as Galen discovered, the pig's skin, subcutaneous fat, musculature, and organs are remarkably like our own.

Galen didn't keep this discovery to himself. His dissections and vivisections (dissections of living animals) were conducted as public anatomy lectures, and he soon became famous for his spectacular demonstrations. Among the most famous was "the screaming pig," which brought philosophers, aristocrats, and the political elite flocking to his lectures. While the pig lay squealing on the dissection table, Galen would run his scalpel across a nerve close to the larynx. As if by magic, the pig fell silent, but continued to strain desperately against the ropes that bound it to the table. Galen had discovered what is known as the "recurrent laryngeal nerve," which causes the vocal cords to open. This demonstration, which was intended to show how the nerves transported information between body and brain, may well have been the first experimental evidence of the brain's influence on our behavior.[2] Similarly significant was Galen's discovery of the function of arteries. Before his era, the prevailing theory was that arteries were air channels, and only veins contained blood. In the presence of an audience, Galen pulled a large artery out of a living pig, clamped it at either end, and then cut through it, enabling the spectators to see that the arteries contained blood and not air.[3]

Although Galen was interested in all physical functions, the nervous system was the area he worked hardest to understand. On repeated occasions, he cut a pig's spinal cord, leaving it paralyzed, to his audience's astonishment. He would then open up the cranium and stimulate different areas of the brain, noting the effects this had on the animal's behavior.

In his writings, Galen describes his experiments in such forthright detail that it's hard to imagine he felt any qualms about his treatment of these animals. On the contrary, in On the Usefulness of the Parts of the Body, Galen expressed his frustration over how troublesome vivisections could be for *him*, especially when he was trying to access the beating heart: the blood had an annoying tendency to spray everywhere, which risked ruining the entire demonstration. When an animal had its thorax cut open, he noticed, it would often stop crying out and sometimes stop breathing. But this could easily be reversed: if the incision was covered briefly, both breathing and squeals would resume.[4]

In neither Aristotle's nor Galen's era did people view animals as machines entirely devoid of feeling, as later thinkers would. If they had, this kind of mistreatment might be easier to grasp from a modern perspective. It's difficult to surmise from the sources just what Galen thought about the animals on his dissection table. Unlike Aristotle, who pointed out that vivisection could be unpleasant, Galen never commented on how he felt about dissecting living animals. However, these vivisections rarely failed to make an impression on those who came to watch him in action: Galen found it necessary to write down instructions for his students that included the injunction to set aside all "compassion" in their encounters with the animal on the dissection table.[5]

WHEN GALEN DIED, in around 200 CE, classical science died with him. Yet the common perception that the people of the Middle Ages had almost no interest in the physiological aspects of the body is not strictly true—as evidenced, among others, by a twelfth-century work called *Anatomia porci* (The anatomy of the pig). The influence of Galen is clear as early as the introduction: "Although some animals, such as monkeys, are found to resemble ourselves in external form, there are none so like us internally as the pig."[6] Still, Galen's old feats were not fully rediscovered until the seventeenth century.

The first person to achieve new insights based on Galen's work was the physiologist William Harvey. Harvey trained at the University of Padua, then the epicenter of anatomical study in Europe, and his greatest scientific achievement was a direct continuation of Galen's pig studies: the discovery of the circulatory system. Harvey found that blood vessels didn't simply store blood, as Galen had shown; they transported it around the body. Admittedly he discovered this without recourse to Galen's favored animal. Instead Harvey dissected what he had on hand: his wife's parrot and his own late father.[7]

In Harvey's day, it was no longer taboo to dissect humans. Nonetheless, he concentrated mainly on animals because corpses were hard to come by. The idea of donating one's body to science was not yet widely understood. Nor were prisons able to supply enough executed prisoners to satisfy demand. The chronic shortage of female research subjects was also a problem. That was what prompted another Paduan pathologist, Andreas Vesalius, to visit graveyards by night with his students to dig up female corpses for their laboratory. But even grave-robbing didn't help: the cadavers they dug up were usually too decomposed for their purposes. As a result, Vesalius had only one corpse at his disposal for his study of the female genitalia. So, like Galen, he resorted to using animals, preferably alive. He and his students don't appear to have been very choosy about which animals they worked on. As a rule, they used those that were most readily on hand—dogs, rabbits, sheep, goats, and pigs.

THE ENLIGHTENMENT WASN'T just the age of new, hard knowledge; it was also an era in which abstract ideas flourished. And among the most important were those of the philosopher René Descartes.

Whereas Aristotle considered body and soul to be inseparably connected, Descartes turned this idea on its head in the seventeenth century. He believed them to be totally separate entities: the soul came from above, and the body was simply a mechanical frame that transported the soul around on earth. If people felt pain or experienced other emotional states, it was a reaction of the soul and not the body, according to Descartes. This led to the conclusion that animals, being without souls, were incapable of pain, feelings, or thought. If animals on the dissection table squealed and trembled as they were dissected, it was simply because the dissector was fiddling with the machinery of their bodies—like brushing the strings of a musical instrument.[8]

For people today, this worldview explains how people back then were able to set themselves above animals and torture them with vivisection. But the picture is a bit more complicated than that. First of all, Galen, Vesalius, and Harvey conducted their experiments well before Descartes had a chance to think anything whatsoever. Second, Descartes's ideas didn't catch on immediately. Indeed, it was in his era that a new sensitivity toward nature also emerged, which took the opposite view of animals. Michel de Montaigne, for example, believed spiders' webs and beehives showed that nature could surpass human intelligence. Montaigne was also the man who was unsure whether he was playing with his cat or his cat was playing with him.[9] Pierre Charron, a contemporary of Descartes and near-contemporary of Montaigne, wouldn't rule out the possibility that animals might even have souls like those of humans. For many people in the Age of Enlightenment in the seventeenth and eighteenth century, Descartes's ideas about nature as a machine were taken to be a metaphorical rather than a literal description. And although Descartes's ideas may have helped legitimize the later treatment of animals—and some people swallowed them hook, line, and sinker—very few truly believed that animals felt no kind of pain.[10]

Some modern thinkers, such as Peter Singer, have held up Descartes and the seventeenth century as examples of how bad things can get when people have a warped worldview. Yet the history of vivisection is mostly a tale of how easy it has always been to mistreat and mutilate animals, regardless of how we perceive the victim's experience of such abuse. The rise in vivisections over the course of the eighteenth century did not necessarily stem from increasing acceptance of Descartes's ideas. It was as much to do with the fact that the West had entered a period of scientific advance, and the need to study animal physiology was becoming more urgent.

Although pigs continued to be dissected, dogs were the ones that suffered most frequently from the seventeenth century onward. And perhaps the fact that dogs were the victims was what eventually provoked so much indignation from observers that vivisections ceased to be public events in the eighteenth century. The nineteenth century, meanwhile, was the age of new anesthetic preparations, such as ether, chloroform, and morphine. That also made it the century when people gradually abandoned the two-thousand-year-old tradition of dissecting conscious animals.

REGARDLESS OF WHAT WE THINK about animal experiments, there is little doubt that the world would be a different place without them. Nor is there any reason to think that a world without them would have been a better place—at least for us humans.

Although pigs have a long history as research animals, they are not the most frequently used species—far from it. That honor goes to small rodents, particularly mice and rats. The main reason for this isn't simply that they, like us and pigs, are omnivores and therefore share anatomical traits with us. The most important factor is their size, and the fact that they live short lives that are easy to study. If anatomy were the sole criteria, pretty much all medical research would be done on our closest relative, the chimpanzee. But although the chimpanzee has been used in medical research—and continues to be in some places—it poses several key challenges: it takes up a lot of space, reproduces inefficiently, and grows slowly. In addition, chimpanzee research is a source of such ethical concern that it has been banned in the West other than for strictly behavioral studies. Small rodents, on the other hand, are seen as so insignificant that they barely prompt any ethical qualms at all.

That's why it's so interesting that the pig has risen up the ranks as an ever more frequently used research animal in various areas of clinical specialization over recent decades. Several factors account for this, one of which is anatomy. But there's something else, too: conveniently, pigs also rank pretty low on the list of animals that we humans are inclined to pity. Given that we already hide them away in industrial facilities where they're bred to be eaten, why should we have any misgivings about using them as research animals?

There is something almost paradoxical about this considering that the many similarities between pigs and humans have prompted some people to speculate that we may be more closely related than evolutionary theory has hitherto suggested. Among them is the American geneticist Eugene McCarthy, who proposed a hypothesis in 2012 that was startling—to put it mildly.

Humans, claims McCarthy, did not result from an evolutionary process as linear as the one suggested by Darwin, which involved gradual evolution from apes. He does accept that apes played a key role in events—but at some point in the remote past, he thinks, something else was thrown into the mix: the pig. According to McCarthy, the human race is the result of a pairing between prehistoric versions of a chimpanzee and a pig.[11] He believes this probably involved a male pig and a female chimpanzee, whose offspring were then raised among the chimpanzees and mated with them, in line with the theory of evolution.[12]

This kind of hybridization is not unknown in the animal kingdom. Typical examples from our own world are crosses between lions and tigers (ligers) or horses and donkeys (mules). As long as one presumes that the cross between pig and chimpanzee happened many millions of years ago, when the two species were much closer to each other on the evolutionary family tree, such a cross is not inconceivable, McCarthy claims.

One immediate objection to this theory is that hybrids are born sterile, but McCarthy notes that some hybrids are fully capable of reproduction—especially among bird species. Another is that there would be clearer traces of pig in our genes if this theory were correct. But here, too, McCarthy believes he is on solid ground. He points out that genes become diluted over time. If the cross happened several million years ago, that's far enough back for the genetic traces to have vanished.

McCarthy, whose entire career has been devoted to hybridization, sees more anatomical similarities between pigs and humans than can be listed here. However, the key factors are the traits that humans share with pigs but *not* chimpanzees: subcutaneous fat, local hair growth, the absence of a penis bone, and certain microstructures in our organs. For McCarthy, this simply cannot be explained without factoring pigs into the equation.

Unsurprisingly, perhaps, almost nobody has taken this theory seriously. McCarthy has largely been ignored or accused of dealing in pseudoscience. At the same time, though, established theories have yet to satisfactorily explain the anatomical traits that distinguish us from the apes but link us to the pigs. However, as so many have pointed out, you sometimes just have to accept that the world is full of coincidences.

REGARDLESS OF WHETHER it's down to coincidence or kinship, the pig serves as a good model for us humans. Cancer research benefits greatly from working with pigs rather than the far more commonly used mice: cancer in humans often follows a course more like that seen in pigs than in small rodents.[13] And one form of the disease that's particularly interesting in pigs is skin cancer. That isn't just because pigs—being hairless and prone to sunburn—develop skin cancer like humans. It's also because many pigs have an unusual capacity to recover unaided. This is true of the Vietnamese potbellied pig, which needs no assistance to rid itself of melanoma, the highly aggressive form of skin cancer. If scientists can find out what triggers the potbellied pig's immune response, this could be a giant step toward curing future human cancer patients.[14]

Pigs are also rapidly becoming a favored research animal in the study of incurable neurological diseases such as Alzheimer's and Parkinson's. This has prompted a team of researchers at Denmark's Aarhus University to breed cloned pigs with an added gene that causes them to develop neurological diseases in the same way as humans do.[15] In thirty years' time, the proportion of the human population that succumbs to Alzheimer's may have increased as much as fourfold. Perhaps pigs will be the key to finding a much-needed cure.

OF ALL THE ROLES the pig plays in human medicine, none is better known than its role as organ donor. And this goes back a long way: as early as 1838, a person in England was given a new cornea taken from a pig—a whole sixty-five years before the first human-to-human corneal transplant took place.[16] Between 1920 and the 1980s, the pig's pancreas was the main source of insulin for the world's diabetics, and from 1965, surgeons began to transplant heart valves from pigs to humans. But the biggest breakthrough has been a long time coming: transplanting an entire organ from an animal to a human.

Since there are more patients in need of new organs at any given time than there are donors, medical science has long pondered the possibility of using animals. Indeed, human-to-animal transplants—xenotransplants—have been attempted several times in the past, with chimpanzees, unsurprisingly, seen as the species best suited to the purpose. Between 1960 and the 1990s, American researchers made many attempts to transplant kidneys, livers, and hearts from monkeys to humans, but none of them ended well.[17]

Fresh progress has been made more recently. In October 2021, surgeons in New York successfully transplanted a pig's kidney into a human recipient—admittedly one who was brain-dead and therefore had no chance of recovering. Then, in January 2022, the University of Maryland Medical Center in Baltimore transplanted the heart of a genetically modified pig into a patient with terminal heart disease. The patient was ineligible for a human transplant on grounds of ill health, and the hospital had to seek special dispensation to carry out this experimental procedure, which was seen as the last chance of saving his life. As the patient, David Bennett, put it himself: "I know it's a shot in the dark, but it's my last choice."[18] Unfortunately, he survived for only two months after the operation; at the time of writing, doctors were still trying to determine the reason the transplanted heart failed.[19]

The reason xenotransplants are so hard to achieve is that it's difficult to prevent the body's immune system from rejecting a foreign organ. Even in human-to-human transplants, patients must undergo intensive immunosuppressive therapy. This problem is the motivation behind a research project that marks a watershed in the relationship between humans and animals; and since chimpanzees are protected by animal welfare legislation on ethical grounds, the pig is the best alternative.

At labs around the world, scientists are laying the groundwork for what could be seen as Version 2.0 of the pig-human relationship. One of the leaders in the field is California's Salk Institute, which is developing an entirely new animal. They have dubbed it the "chimera," after a hybrid animal from Greek mythology—a lion with a goat's head protruding from its back and a snake as a tail. The original chimera was a terrifying monster that breathed fire, like a dragon, and was said to terrorize the people of Lycia (now Anatolia in Turkey). And while its modern-day namesake may be less spectacular, it is groundbreaking nonetheless, because this research pushes the boundaries between humans and animals in ways the world has never seen before.

The work involves injecting human stem cells into a pig embryo at an early stage of development. The resulting animal will therefore not just be a pig; it will also be part human.[20] Here's how the scientists envisage that this process will work: A sow is inseminated in the usual way. When the fetuses have developed in the uterus, they are processed in two ways: using CRISPR gene-editing technology, the genes that are programmed to produce a particular organ—a heart, say—are "switched off." At the same time, human cells are injected. The idea is that the fetus will use the human cells to compensate for the deactivated genes, enabling the pigs to develop fully functioning human organs. In a world with a chronic deficit of organ donors, chimeras could save thousands of human lives every year. But progress is slow.

Scientists first succeeded in transferring stem cells from humans to pigs in 2017, but no pig-human hybrid has yet been born. There are several reasons for this: What if the human cells do not remain isolated in the organ that is to be produced but spread around the body, affecting its development in unintended ways? What if the human cells affect the pig's central nervous system? Will that influence the pig's brain, making it behave like a human? Is a pig that thinks and feels like a human still an animal, or has it crossed a line? And if so, how will that affect the way we treat it? These dilemmas compel the research

communities to confront a question that has haunted humanity throughout the history of animal husbandry: Where exactly
does the boundary between humans and animals lie? The
response from scientists so far has been to avoid taking a stance
on the issue. Instead, they have terminated gestation after four
weeks to analyze the fetal development.

To date, there is nothing to suggest that these fetuses are
developing into humans in pigs' bodies. And although most
scientists view that outcome as highly improbable, it's still possible enough to prevent any chimera pregnancies from being
brought to term.[21] One of the scientists in California, Juan Car-
los Izpisúa Belmonte, found his patience so sorely tested by
the caution of his colleagues that he left for China, where medical ethics are lower on the agenda than in the West—to put it
mildly. And there, in 2019, he successfully produced a monkey-
human hybrid, although it's debatable how much further that
took him, because that chimera was also terminated at the
embryonic stage. Still, Izpisúa Belmonte's main intention was
for this knowledge from China to help Western research on
pig-human hybrids take another step forward.[22]

These groundbreaking research projects involving pigs have
undoubtedly raised new ethical questions, ones that don't just
apply to chimeras, either. In 2017, a research group at Yale University managed to resuscitate the brains of dead pigs, keeping
them alive outside the animals' bodies for more than thirty-six
hours.[23] While the scientists could confirm that the brains
never achieved consciousness, they had more difficulty answer-
ing questions of a deeper and more existential nature: What if
these were human brains? Would they have the same legal pro-
tections as people? Would it be possible for the brains to regain
consciousness, with the same memories and cognitive abilities
they had possessed when they were still safely tucked away in
a cranium? And what does this mean for the boundary between

life and death? One of the people asking questions like this is psychiatric researcher Steven Hyman, who has commented: "It may come to the point that instead of people saying 'Freeze my brain,' they say 'Hook me up and find me a body.'"[24] In 2018, *Nature* published a comment by a number of scientists pointing out that the brain and chimera experiments both raise new issues on which the medical science community will rapidly need to take a stance.[25]

While ethical and legal guidelines are in the pipeline, there's little to suggest that the distinction between humans and animals is about to be erased anytime soon. And this means that we can, for the time being, continue to define animals as *ours* and use them for our own benefit, whether as food, medical models, or military research animals. As a medic with the U.S. Marine Corps told the *New York Times* about the pigs they used in training for trauma treatment on the battlefield:

> "My pig?" he said. "They shot him twice in the face with a 9-millimeter pistol, and then six times with an AK-47 and then twice with a 12-gauge shotgun. And then he was set on fire. I kept him alive for 15 hours," he said. "That was my pig."[26]

"WE HAVE FIBRILLATION!" shouts the course leader at the hospital.

The young sow has endured a great deal, and now her heart is clearly signaling that she's running on empty. A tangled mass of intestines lies glistening outside her body. Her stomach has been punctured and sewn back together, her thorax has been broken open and her heart pierced with a scalpel so that the doctors can learn to suture it in a beating state.

A fibrillating heart is a heart that has switched from beating to vibrating. If it doesn't recover its sinus rhythm, the blood will start to pool and the heart will collapse. This requires rapid treatment, but rather than concentrating on the heart, the course leader turns to another doctor and asks him to take the cell phone out of his pocket. Then he pulls off one of his latex gloves, and after a few keystrokes the sound of the Bee Gees' "Stayin' Alive" streams out into the operating room.

Ah, ha, ha, ha…

He reaches his hands deep into the sow's thorax and gently lifts out the quivering heart. In time with the music, he squeezes it firmly between his flattened palms.

Ah, ha, ha, ha…

Several of the other doctors get to try, but none of them can return the heart to its regular rhythm.

"Okay, this isn't working," he says. "We'll need to bring out the defibrillator. Where's the defibrillator?"

I'm standing with my back to the wall observing all of this intently when I suddenly become aware that all the green-clad figures are facing *me*. What do they want?

"You!" the surgeon nods at me. "You have clean hands. Can you get it ready?"

"Er…"

"You're standing right next to it," he says impatiently.

I look to one side and confirm that there is an apparatus on a trolley there. I assume this is what he's referring to, but I haven't got a clue what to do with it. The anesthesiologist comes toward me with bloody hands.

"I'll give you a hand. You've got this!" he says, without a trace of irony in his voice.

I follow his instructions like a little kid.

As the electrodes are laid against the heart, which has now been replaced in the thorax, I stand with my hand on the shock button, awaiting the command.

"Clear!" shouts the course leader.

"Shock!"

I press. The pig jerks.

Status? Still fibrillating. Another round:

"Clear!"

"Shock!"

Her chest heaves. Still fibrillating.

As we prepare for another round, a steady flat *beeeeeeeeeeeeep* pierces the room.

That was our pig.

Ugly Mug

IT'S AN EARLY MORNING in October, and the road is in darkness. I yawn over the wheel as I steer the car, guided by the reflective markers on the sides of the road. I think that I need more sleep; I think about my children, who've had to go to preschool earlier than is strictly necessary. I think about the smell. I'm *dreading* the smell; I dread starting my day mucking out the pigpens that are getting too small for the fast-growing pigs. The morning chores have started to bother me.

The truth is, there's nothing to stop me from simply turning around. The pigs don't really need me—Leiv is there, after all. But what if I were the only person responsible? What if I followed through on this idea and decided not to bother mucking out the pigs, just this once? Is that how animal tragedies start?

We've all heard about him: the lone farmer whose life hits a rocky patch; he puts off mucking out the animals, first once, then twice, and in the end it gets to be a habit and the animals are left unsupervised, unfed, and untended. The animal tragedy is always preceded by the personal tragedy. Leiv and Eirik are well equipped in this respect—they have plenty of people around them on the farm: partners, children, grandchildren. People who can keep track of things, give them a hand, fetch help. But not everyone is that lucky.

I PARK OUTSIDE THE BARN and walk across the dark farmyard to the piggery. In the back room, I shut off my nostrils and breathe through my mouth. I can tell by the number of boots lining the wall that Leiv hasn't come over from his house yet. I step into the pant legs of my overalls and pull them up over my shoulders. As soon as I'm all zipped up, though, I realize I've accidentally picked up a pair of overalls that's too small. I usually wear a different pair. The seam cuts into my groin, but I can't be bothered to change. This is a day for getting things over and done with. Quick in, quick out. Carefully, I open the door into the piggery.

The hall is lit but still has a nighttime air. It's totally silent apart from the noise of the ventilation fan in the roof and an occasional snort. The parentless siblings huddle together for body warmth and social contact. The atmosphere reminds me of that calm you get in many workplaces early in the morning before the working day has officially started. When the first batch of coffee is gurgling through the percolator and concentration is at its peak. It's that moment you want to last *just a little bit longer*, but which mercilessly slips away as the daylight seeps in and colleagues arrive, one by one.

I grab the scraper, which is leaning up against the wall, and gently place a hand on the spring-bolt latch on the gate of the first pigpen. I try to do everything as quietly and calmly as I can to avoid alarming the pigs and disturbing the peace. But the second I push the gate open, the silence is broken by the dry, metallic squeal of the hinges.

All is lost.

Waking with a start, the pigs lunge desperately, spinning around and bumping into one another, squealing and whining in aimless panic. The shock wave spreads from pen to pen until the whole piggery is alive with the frantic commotion.

The day has started.

THEY'VE GROWN BIG NOW: many of them weigh well over four hundred pounds. Their slaughter date can't be more than a few weeks off.

The pigs in pen one quickly recover and come toward me. Not to say hello but to try and push their way out. I shove them away with my knees as I push the gate closed. There's always been something odd about the bunch in pen one, something I've never liked, which sets them apart from the rest. For a start, they don't look great; they're completely smeared in excrement. In principle, this isn't really something you should hold against a pig, but I do all the same. How come the other pigs look freshly showered compared with this lot?

The short answer is that the pigs in pen number one have developed bad habits. Or rather they've failed to develop the good habit of excreting over the grate at one end of the pen the way the other pigs do. Instead they crap everywhere—on the floor, on the walls, on each other—and then they roll around in it, of course. But their lack of cleanliness isn't the thing I hold against them most.

Their main problem is their personality: pushy and sometimes aggressive, which doesn't scare me but does make my job much more difficult than it needs to be. The pigs in the other pens are easily rattled and run away as soon as I come in. Sometimes that's been irritating too, especially when they were small and I was trying to get close to them to give them a pat. I can't count the number of times I've been left looking like an idiot—on all fours in the middle of the pen, hand outstretched, making noises intended to be enticing. It's a while now since I gave up the struggle to get to know the animals. Instead, their frayed nerves have become useful to me: they stay out of my way, and that means I can get my job done. In pen one, though, the pigs are always under my feet. I constantly worry that I might accidentally thrust the scraper blade into their trotters and injure them. So far, I've been able to hold them at bay by force. But something has happened. The pigs can't be budged any more. And it isn't just difficult to move them; there's hardly a spot in the whole pen that isn't occupied by their massive bodies. I'm starting to lose hope of getting any cleaning done at all.

I try to shove and slap them gently. It's hopeless. No sooner have I gotten one of them out of the way than another takes its place. I bang the scraper on the floor to try to scare them, but it has the opposite effect. It seems to wind them up, and they press up against me even harder than before.

And now they start to bite me too. Especially my feet. It doesn't hurt much, but it stresses me out, and the only solution that occurs to me is to give up on this pen. Maybe Leiv will have some tips for me when he arrives. He can't be far off.

I'VE MADE A BAD START. And now my irritation increases as the mucking-out progresses. As always, my job is to scrape the feces and damp wood shavings down into the shaft beneath the excrement grate and then strew the pen with fresh straw. But the work has become distinctly more difficult, and not just in pen one. The pens are all too cramped, even though they're a bit larger than regulation size.

The pigs are also crapping more than they used to. Although the pens are cleaned out twice a day, the muck is so trampled down in some places that you almost have to chisel it off. "That's just how it gets toward the end," Leiv told me. Still, though, I worry about not doing a thorough enough job. Not just for the pigs' sake, but also for Leiv, who is painstaking in his own work and scrutinizes everything I do. And another thought often occupies my mind while I'm working: to my own surprise, the idea that the Food Safety Authority might turn up unannounced for an inspection has had a motivating effect on me. If that happens, I want the inspector to praise us for the job we're doing and comment on how well looked after our pigs seem to be. "You're an example to the rest," I imagine this inspector saying. That's what keeps me standing there, hacking and chipping away, scraping and shoveling until my face is boiling hot and the sweat rolls off me.

My arms and hands are starting to go numb. It feels like an effort to scrape the muck off even where it *hasn't* hardened. The scraper doesn't seem to be working properly. I can't get into the flow, and it snags on the concrete, jerking and butting. In my haste to finish, I don't notice Leiv coming in.

"Turn the scraper around," I hear a voice say.

"What?"

"You're holding it the wrong way," he says. "Turn the blade around so it hits the ground from the opposite angle."

I do as he says, wipe the sweat from my brow, and attack the floor again.

Well, what do you know…

I'm worn out and bored stiff. As I put more and more pigpens behind me, I stop seeing the pigs. All I can see is a great pink mass that's obstructing my work. On the few occasions I have any dealings with individual animals, it strikes me for the first time that the pig's snout really *is* an appropriate symbol of the repulsive. I can tell I'm starting to get demoralized, and that gets me down even more.

EVER SINCE PEOPLE started philosophizing several millennia ago, they have pointed out that beauty is relative. But relativity aside: What is it about the pig—in sheerly objective terms—that makes it as ugly as our language and culture suggest? In William Golding's *Lord of the Flies*, a pig's head on a stake symbolizes the evil and violence in us all. The Norwegian writer Dag Solstad also chose the pig's snout to describe one of the ugliest things he could imagine—the United States. In Solstad's novel *Armand V*, we follow the fortunes of the eponymous Norwegian diplomat. Armand starts out as a young, anti-American radical but ends up joining the Norwegian Ministry of Foreign Affairs; there he is gradually indoctrinated into the game of global politics, in which the United States sets the premises for all Norway's actions on the international stage. But one day, when Armand happens to bump into the American ambassador in a urinal, his past catches up with him: Armand looks up at the ambassador and finds himself gazing at a pig's snout.

The main challenge in trying to understand what makes the pig ugly is that so few people have tried to get to the bottom of what ugliness really is. Philosophers have toiled over the concept of beauty, while biologists have been more interested in attraction. But the ugly or hideous has been left more or less unexamined.

Admittedly, a few people have touched on it. One of them is Umberto Eco, although it's true that his book *On Ugliness* doesn't actually deal much with pigs: Eco's area of interest is how the ugly has been expressed in art and literature. Nonetheless, he points out something that's absolutely key for anyone with an interest in the concept: although the opposite of beauty is ugliness, the absence of beauty is not synonymous with the presence of ugliness. In the absence of beauty, a thing or person may be anonymous or ordinary—or at worst, boring. But to be ugly requires a very particular presence of *ugliness*.

Eco thinks ugliness is expressed in different ways: ethically, emotionally, or morally. Even so, his conclusion may still be useful. The cultural history of ugliness reflects what Eco calls "deformity as a human tragedy."[1] By this he means that the experience of ugliness often involves a violation of our expectations about how something should look or be. Consequently, things that strike us as repulsive are often inharmonious, disproportionate, or deformed.

And isn't this precisely the key to the pig's ugliness? The fact that its most striking feature is also the one unique to it as a species, which distinguishes it from so many other creatures and *violates our expectations about the way an animal is supposed to look*? We are, of course, talking about its snout.

With most species in the animal kingdom, the first features we encounter are the eyes, whereas the nose is a rounded and unobtrusive part of their face. The opposite is true in the pig's case. The naked, moist surface of its snout is the first thing that catches our attention, and prevents us from meeting those tiny, tucked-away eyes. In popular culture, the pig may, at best, be charming, funny, and likeable. But it will definitely never be a beauty. Some have also been interested in the negative impression the snout can create in us humans—including the Walt Disney Company, which has been fine-tuning and optimizing the audience appeal of its cartoon characters for a century. The most obvious example of this is the pioneer: Mickey Mouse.

When Mickey Mouse first appeared on the silver screen in 1928, he was far from the sweet, loveable character we know today. In his essay "A Biological Homage to Mickey Mouse,"[2] Stephen Jay Gould analyzes the gradual change, or "evolution," of Mickey Mouse in the fifty years between 1928 and 1978. When he studied sketches from different periods, Gould found that Mickey Mouse had gone from being a sly, ratlike creature to possessing features that became increasingly like those of a small child: high forehead, big eyes, and a small nose. All the features that the pig doesn't possess, in other words. Disney may not have based all these changes on scientific insight, but it might just as well have done. Because what it was trying to achieve was what biologists call the "cute response." This is an evolutionary mechanism that makes humans and animals devote extra attention to their offspring.[3] And how do we experience this mechanism? We find children cute and can't take our eyes off them. This theory was formulated by Konrad Lorenz, one of the founders of the biological behavioral science known as ethology. In a 1950 study, Lorenz showed how similar childish features occur throughout the animal kingdom.[4] According to Lorenz, we humans can be fooled by this mechanism, which can also influence our response to other species— and, as Gould suggested, even to cartoon characters. The Walt Disney Company found the key to its success in this phenomenon, never more evident than when the adorable Bambi made his screen debut in 1942, with his high forehead, big eyes, and tiny snout.

While little piglets may undoubtedly be cute because they share traits common to all young animals, there's little doubt that the fully grown pig's snout fails to fit into Lorenz's scheme. And it's no accident that the species traditionally championed by the conservation and animal welfare movements are the ones with the childish features that trigger our evolved nurturing reflex—the panda and the harp seal, to name two of the most obvious examples. Only in recent years has a dawning awareness begun to emerge of creatures with less attractive features. But our responses are so deep-seated that it took the greatest mass extinction since the age of the dinosaurs to stoke our engagement.

FOR NOW, THERE'S little indication that any nurturing mechanisms are at work in me. Indeed, if there's one thing that defines my attitude, it's the distinct decline in my concern for the animals here. But before I can give up and leave, I need to have another go at pen one. I ask Leiv if he has any tips, but his answer mostly boils down to phrases like: "It's a matter of not giving in" and "You're the boss." I feel as if I have no choice but to listen to what he says. So I go back in.

You're the boss.

I stomp up and rattle the gate extra hard when I open it. Initially, my new approach seems to work. I lower the scraper, make sure it hits the floor at the right angle, and manage a few strokes before any of the pigs get in my way. The same tactic: *I'm the boss.* I shove their bodies, holler and shush, and carry on that way until the first third of the pen is clean.

Then the mood changes. My authority is diminishing and before I know it, I can't get the pigs to budge anymore. They crowd around me and start biting me again. I slap them lightly on their necks and rumps, but I might as well not have bothered: they don't seem to feel a thing.

More forcefully now, I shove them aside with my knees, and at last I open up a space on the floor. Quickly I take aim, preparing to scrape up the muck in front of me, but as I jerk the shaft of the scraper back to increase the momentum of my downward stroke, I smash one of my hands against the edge of a hatch that stands open outside the pen and gash three knuckles. The bandages will have to wait, I think, and carry on. Before long, I feel the blood sticking my fingers to the shaft. And that's about when it happens.

One of the pigs sits down on the scraper blade, making the handle slip out of my hands and land on the floor with a crack. I bend down to pick it up, but the pigs squeeze up against me, like a coordinated muscle, and I'm trapped. I lose my balance and fall to my knees.

They tug at my overalls and I'm sure I feel one of them licking the blood off my hand. Instinctively, I pull my hands toward me and press them to my body, as if to protect my vital organs. My heart is hammering, my head is seething, and it feels as if everything is unraveling.

In Tarjei Vesaas's novel *The Seed*, pigs are responsible for destroying the life of Andreas, a simple character who has recently arrived in a small island community on the Norwegian coast. When Andreas visits one of the farms on the island, he witnesses a chaotic series of events that will make him lose his mind. One of the pigs gets loose and is chased around the farm-yard before falling into the well and breaking its neck. Back in the pigpen, a sow becomes so stressed by the commotion that she attacks and eats her piglets. Shortly after the tragedy on the farm, Andreas murders a girl. The inhabitants of the island are seized by a lynch-mob mentality and Andreas is killed. As so often with Vesaas—one of the great Norwegian writers of the twentieth century—the text is an allegory, this time for a civilization in a state of collapse. "Who better to initiate something like this than pigs?" Vesaas must have thought.

I try to push away the snouts. But since pigs are allegedly capable of breaking down asphalt and concrete with this part of their anatomy, I could *sit* on their snouts to equally little effect.[5] So I'm stuck kneeling there and rocking from side to side as I hear Leiv's voice in the back of my head: "If you start feeling bad when you're in the pen, you have to get out. If you fall over, you risk getting eaten." He was perfectly serious. He's seen for himself how bloodthirsty pigs can be. When a slaughter pig has to be put down on health grounds, they do it in the center of the pen, among the other pigs. The bolt pistol is placed against the animal's forehead, its throat is cut, and its siblings slurp up the blood.

Is it *my* blood they're after now? That thought brings to mind something I read recently. The story of a fifty-six-year-old Russian farmer's wife who popped out to the pigsty to feed the animals one evening after her husband had gone to bed. Next morning, when he found she wasn't in bed, he went out to look for her. What are you supposed to do when you find the half-eaten corpse of your spouse on the floor of a pigsty?[6]

This isn't working. I throw out my arms and eventually manage to raise one of my knees, and that enables me to get to my feet. Leaning on the pigs' backs, I stand up as the snouts follow me, snapping at my groin.

That's when I punch. A bit too hard, right on the snout. I drive my knee into the throat of another and kick a third on the flank with my heel. At last I manage to grab the wall of the pigpen and hurl myself over it.

IN THE BACK ROOM I rinse my knuckles in the sink as my adrenaline levels subside and my body cools down. I can hear Leiv rummaging around with something out in the corridor. I stay where I am, watching the red water swirl down the drain in a pattern that reminds me of a wild rose.

What just happened out there?

After drying my hands, I meet Leiv by the fodder machine.

"Where's your first aid kit?"

He looks at my hand, which is still bleeding.

"Have they been eating you?"

"Nah, I just cut myself," I say. "I'm not very happy with the cleaning job I've done today, by the way. Especially in pen one."

Leiv grins.

"A pig farmer never gives in, you know."

"I don't expect he does," I say, as I accept a bandage.

BEFORE CLIMBING INTO my car to drive home, I stand out in the farmyard for a while filling my lungs with sea air. My eyes rest on the wind turbines standing on the bare ridge far to the south like spindly candles on a cake.

It's been a strange day. I've experienced repulsion, I've kicked and punched. Was that an overreaction? I'm not sure. The only thing I do know is that at some level or another, I'm starting to become morally stunted. The pigs have become objects rather than individuals—much less sensitive beings. And that has affected the way I relate to them, the way I treat them. Isn't that an animal tragedy too?

The animals will soon be sent to slaughter. Something has to be retrieved, before it's too late.

14

Is Anybody Home?

SHE STILL DOESN'T HAVE A NAME. I call her number thirteen, after the pigpen she was assigned to the first time I was at the piggery. Her new piglets are well fed, it seems; they lie intertwined in a pink bundle beneath a flap in the corner of the pigsty. She herself lies on her side, because it's hard for her to hold up all 650 pounds of her body weight for long. I sit on my haunches and stroke her neck. Suddenly she lifts her head and looks me in the eye. Not in that vague way a sheep or a cow tends to, where the mental presence of the animal never seems quite real. It's different with number thirteen: she looks me in the eye as a human would. Or at least that's the impression I get. Perhaps I'm projecting my own imaginings onto her. At the same time there's something about this gaze that makes such imaginings seem inevitable, because I have never seen animal eyes that remind me more of my own. Encased in naked folds of skin, with long pale eyelashes, her eyes have white eyeballs, clear, defined irises, and within them, distinct black pupils. The concentric circles of her eyes seem to draw me to her; to something that lies behind them—to a sense of... *soul*?

The eye contact doesn't last more than a few seconds before her gaze wanders off to the side and she lets her head fall back onto the concrete. Soul or not—judging by her body language, she is utterly consumed by apathy.

But who am I to judge the body language of a pig? It would be so much easier if she could talk.

PERHAPS IT'S RIDICULOUS to imagine something like this. The philosopher Ludwig Wittgenstein was the one who said, "If a lion could talk, we could not understand him."[1] He did not mean by this that the lion would probably speak a different language from us. Wittgenstein's point was that, regardless of how close it was to our own mother tongue, the language itself would have no meaning for us humans. The mental world of animals is so starkly distinct from our own that it will never be possible to establish a shared conceptual apparatus capable of conveying the different experiences and worldviews we possess as human and animal, respectively. There is a hopelessness to Wittgenstein that can be difficult to take for anyone wishing to understand an animal. But we're not much better off listening to another philosopher—Thomas Nagel—who, in a 1974 essay, posed the question "What is it like to be a bat?"[2] We can never know, he concluded. First of all, bats move by flying. Second, bats navigate principally using echolocation instead of sight. And as if this weren't difficult enough to imagine in itself, things are complicated even further by the need to factor in the unique way bats process or perceive their sensory impressions. No: the inner life of animals will always be beyond human understanding, Nagel writes.

Still, the fact that philosophers find it difficult to get inside the mental world of animals has never stopped humans from longing to do precisely that. Few have expressed this more clearly than Stephen Jay Gould, who wrote the following lines toward the end of his long career: "Give me one minute—just one minute—inside the skin of this creature. Hook me for just sixty seconds to the perceptual and conceptual apparatus of this other being—and then I will know what natural historians have sought through the ages."[3]

For Gould, it didn't go beyond yearning, but British philosopher and lawyer Charles Foster didn't give up until he had gone the whole hog. In his book *Being a Beast*, Foster tells us of his attempts to live like various animals, including a badger on a hillside in Wales, with all that this entailed: living in a set, crawling around on all fours, and eating insects, worms, and carrion. I inspect the floor of the pigsty: wood shavings, urine, feces. It isn't very tempting to follow Foster's example. And perhaps that's just as well, because even he had to accept in the end that the experiment had failed. We can all play make believe, but it's hardly likely that we'll ever be capable of comprehending bats' echolocation, elephants' ultrasonic hearing, insects' capacity to perceive flowers' ultraviolet light, or certain species' ability to sense the earth's geomagnetism. As a friend says to Foster, "It's like trying to live in a fifth dimension. You can describe it mathematically, but you can't give any account of what it would be like to live in it."[4]

The notion that it's possible to adopt the perspective of animals is probably as old as the human mind itself. And perhaps this was part of what inspired Homer, when he wrote his epic poem about the warrior king Odysseus in around 720 BCE. The work, which depicts Odysseus's journey home to the island of Ithaca after the Trojan War, is today regarded as the classic of classics in the Western literary canon. Few, if any, literary works have been subjected to such penetrating analyses and interpretations. But there's something striking about the *Odyssey* that's rarely pointed out: it contains a lot of pigs.

Pigs and wild boars turn up in brief mentions throughout the work, but it all comes to a head when Odysseus and his crew pay a visit to the goddess of sorcery, Circe, who has prepared a welcome drink the men will wish they had never allowed to pass their lips. When they've downed the witch's brew, they undergo a metamorphosis that transforms the entire crew into a grunting herd of swine. Then, with a slap on the rump, they are driven into the pigsty.[5]

If there's one thing Homer's depiction of the bewitched crew can teach us about a pig's life, it's that this is an unhappy existence: the crew, now in the guise of "nine-year-old hogs," weep in their pigsty but cannot speak. When at last Odysseus rescues his men from the enchantment by going to bed with Circe, their sobs of joy are so piteous that even the goddess is moved.

Not all thinkers of antiquity shared the view that a pig's life is as dismal as Homer would have us believe. The Greek historian Plutarch, who lived in the first century CE, saw things differently. Inspired by the same scene from the *Odyssey*, Plutarch composed a dialogue between Odysseus and the pig Gryllus, in which it's unclear who is worse off—man or pig.[6] In Plutarch's version, Odysseus sleeping with Circe is not enough to make her release his crew from the enchantment. Instead she asks him how he can be so sure that his crew truly want to become men again. Odysseus answers that of course he can't prove it, since pigs can't talk. But it seems self-evident to him that his crew would wish to escape their "piteous and shameful" existence as swine. Circe parries by giving one of the pigs the power of speech, and it becomes clear to Odysseus at once that he was wrong. Gryllus, as the pig calls himself, doesn't want to return. After just a few hours as a pig, human life strikes him as objectionable and immoral. Odysseus tries to convince him of the contrary, but in the ensuing discussion, the pig always has the upper hand. In the end, Gryllus comes out of the dialogue as having both greater eloquence and higher moral standing than Odysseus can display. And that's saying a lot.

Although Gryllus doesn't tell us much about what life as a pig is like in itself, Plutarch's dialogue nonetheless demonstrates a long-held view: pigs are intelligent. So it's hardly an accident that they were assigned the role of strategists, ideologues, and teachers in George Orwell's allegorical fable *Animal Farm*. As Orwell writes, "The work of teaching and organizing the others fell naturally upon the pigs, who were generally recognized as being the cleverest of the animals."[7] The farm in the story represents Tsarist Russia, which is shaken by a popular revolt, represented by the animals. The power that falls into the hands of the revolutionary leaders—represented by the pigs—gradually corrupts them, and the farm that was supposed to abandon the neglectful management of humans, in favor of a system controlled by and for animals, ultimately ends in a piggy dictatorship as ruthless as the rule of the farmers. "The creatures...looked from pig to man, and from man to pig, and from pig to man again; but already it was impossible to say which was which."[8]

IN THE PIGGERY at Jæren, where sow number thirteen lies heavily slumped upon the concrete floor, there is little to indicate any grassroots rebellion or other conspiratorial intent on the animals' part. In the eyes of number thirteen, apathy still reigns. Or is it perhaps resignation? My human capacity for projection also enables me to conjure up a trapped "Help!" inside there. But why should she say that? Number thirteen knows no other life. She has never seen the sky, or birds, or any other animals, for that matter. She has never set foot outside the door of the piggery either, and nor will she. Only when her duty as a breeding pig is done and she is herded up the ramp into the slaughter truck will she catch a glimpse of a world other than this. For me, her life brings to mind Plato's allegory of the cave, or *The Matrix*. But I guess epistemology isn't for pigs either.

Is there really anyone at home there behind those seemingly human eyes of hers?

WHEN BIOLOGISTS STARTED to study animal behavior in the 1800s, the inner life of animals was an irrelevance. In a world where knowledge of nature was limited, biology continued to pursue the old tradition of gaining an overview of nature's diversity and dividing it into categories. This task, started in earnest by Aristotle in the fourth century BCE, was more or less completed in the mid-eighteenth century by the Swedish botanist Carl Linnaeus in his towering work *Systema Naturae*. Here, Linnaeus classified all known plant and animal species, simultaneously assigning them Latin names.

As the biologists of the nineteenth century continued to gather species into Linnaeus's taxonomic system, a new branch of biology emerged, with a similar mania for collecting: zoology. The zoologists' niche was collecting behaviors, so-called species-specific behaviors: "dogs do this," "pigs do that"—end of story. If the pig grunts and roots in the soil with its snout, it does so simply because it is a representative of the species *Sus scrofa domesticus*, for which this is a species-specific trait. The factors underlying the behavior and the circumstances in which it arose still lay outside the scientists' field of interest. There was no room for the notion that animals—like humans—were individuals with a flexible range of behavior patterns, depending on the situation in which they found themselves. In this way, science became an expression for what's known as biological determinism—the perception that the behavior patterns and destinies of different individuals are completely fixed by the biological mechanisms in their bodies.

At the same time as zoologists were going to the forests and lying behind rocks and anthills to note how animals behaved, something else started happening in a much larger segment of the population. And this would present a stark contrast to the zoologists' work. In ever-increasing numbers, ordinary people started taking animals into their homes to coddle and pamper them. And for ordinary people, of course, the animals that waltzed into their parlors and made themselves at home on rugs and sofas were not taxonomic categories. They were autonomous, named individuals—even family members. More importantly, the owners didn't perceive their pets as fixed biological machines; they were creatures with feelings, intelligence, and complex personalities. Ever since those days, there has been an awkward conflict between popular wisdom and scientific theory, because scientists have always had trouble demonstrating the very thing that seems self-evident to any pet owner.

ONE OF THE MOST DIFFICULT barriers to overcome for those wishing to defend animals' mental powers to science is a fundamental philosophical premise that we find again in Wittgenstein and Nagel, among others. It's about language and the way we categorize our inner life. All experiences, feelings, states of mind, and sensory perceptions have been assigned terms and labels based on a mental register that originates from us. Consequently, any attempt to attach the same labels to other species will simply demonstrate that we are viewing animals through the prism of humanity and ascribing qualities to them that we can't be certain they possess. If, for example, you perceive your dog as being happy when you come home after a long day at work, you will be unable to document this in a satisfactory fashion. The only thing you have to offer is that it appears to be happy, since it does things you associate with the concept of "happiness." The trouble is that you can't know whether what you associate with happiness is what the dog is actually experiencing, or indeed whether the dog possesses the psychological apparatus required to experience this feeling. If you choose to overlook these objections—as most ordinary people do when it comes to their pets—and insist on believing that your dog is happy, you are indulging in what is known as anthropomorphism, or the humanization of animals.

This concept has long been a major taboo in all animal research because it fails to satisfy science's requirement that a phenomenon must be objectively observable. It is therefore something of a paradox that one of the greatest scientific authorities of them all, Charles Darwin, considered it perfectly natural to attribute feelings and frames of mind familiar to us from our own emotional lives to animals. The reason was simple: Darwin was a dog person.

For Darwin, it wasn't just natural to perceive his own dog in this way. He went so far as to use this assumption as a building block of his evolutionary theory. In his 1872 book *The Expression of the Emotions in Man and Animals*, he expanded his evolutionary theory to include brain function as well. According to his theory, all physical functions in mammals had key similarities as a result of their shared evolutionary origin. He saw no reason this shouldn't apply to the brain as well. A comparison between the human brain and that of other mammals showed only degrees of difference between us, not essential differences, according to Darwin.[9] Based on the time spent with his dogs, Darwin argued that animals have many of the same senses as humans: they can remember and learn, and they can experience emotional states such as pleasure, fear, joy, or despondency. In short, his views appear to coincide nicely with traditional folk wisdom but not with later science.

Throughout the twentieth century, Darwin's *On the Origin of Species* and *The Descent of Man* were almost bibles for biologists, yet his book on brain function remained virtually unread. The reasons for this are complicated, but if we are to place the blame on any individuals, there are two prime candidates.

The first is Darwin's assistant and successor, George Romanes, who swallowed his master's ideas a little too greedily. For Romanes, it was the most self-evident thing in the world that animals had a mental life akin to that of humans. He got so hung up on this idea that he eventually went completely off the rails, attributing highly advanced states of consciousness to animals and even going so far as to claim that they had consciences and lofty morals. On one occasion, he described how a monkey that was shot by a hunter smeared its hand with blood from its wound and held it up in front of the hunter to make him feel guilty.[10] Today, even the most fervent advocate of animals' mental powers would think that such a description was taking things too far.

The other culprit is the biologist and psychologist C. Lloyd Morgan, who reacted forcefully to what he perceived as Romanes's fabrications. In an apparently sensible response, Morgan proposed toning down the anthropomorphism and ended up formulating the principle that animals' behavior should never be "interpreted in terms of higher psychological processes if it can be fairly interpreted in terms of processes which stand lower in the scale of psychological evolution and development."[11] "Morgan's canon," as the principle was called, rapidly became a mantra for almost all studies of animals and still holds sway to this day.

The consequences have been significant. As Morgan's idea caught on, it sparked a profound skepticism about animals' mental faculties. And the skeptics would become virtually unassailable. After all, how are we to deal with the skeptic who considers it suspect to assume that a dog is expressing the joy of reunion when it comes, tail wagging, to meet its owner after a lengthy absence? For a doubter, the behavior could just as easily mean that the dog is simply hungry. Or what about the dairy cow whose calf has been taken away, which stops eating and lows for days on end without stopping? Could this be an expression of grief or loss? Not as long as there's a possibility that it is merely a primitive expression of confusion unconnected to any emotional register.

In the face of a scientific hegemony in which instinct always trumps mental faculties, the motivation to demonstrate anything at all about animals' inner lives swiftly dissipated. Instead, two towering—and often competing—fields of behavioral science emerged in the 1930s, each of which, on either side of the Atlantic, achieved the feat of revealing complex aspects of animal behavior without attributing any higher mental powers at all to those same animals. One emerged from the field of psychology in the United States and was known as behaviorism. The other grew out of biology in Germany and was called ethology.

AT THE SAME TIME as the inner lives of animals were being swept aside by science, something else was happening: the industrialization and intensification of agriculture. Small farms were replaced by industrial farms, and domestic animals were transferred from open fields to cramped sheds and stalls, where they were subjected to extensive breeding programs that drastically altered their physiologies. If the scientific hegemony surrounding the understanding of animals' inner life that prevailed in the 1900s didn't directly cause the intensification of livestock farming that took off in the 1960s, it nonetheless created a climate that helped legitimize the new organization of animal husbandry. As long as the agricultural industry—backed up by science—has been able to choose between interpreting a pig's howl from its concrete stall as an expression of pain and desperation on the one hand, or a need to create sound without any particular intent on the other, the choice has been pretty simple. After all, who wants to suffer pangs of conscience when they can just as easily avoid it?

The practical result of the scientific consensus of the twentieth century has proved suspiciously similar to that of René Descartes's view of animals as machines in the seventeenth century, when the heartrending screams of animals on the dissection table were never a cause for any concern. It's still common to meet skeptics who call animals' emotional lives and cognitive powers into question by arguing that, after all, we can never know. But thanks to breakthroughs in neurology, psychology, and biological behavioral research over the past two decades, overwhelming numbers of scientists have come to the fairly unsurprising realization that traditional folk wisdom and Darwin's ideas had some merit all along.

Among Neurons
and
Neural Pathways

ONE CURIOUS CONSEQUENCE of our newly acquired knowledge about animals' emotions and cognitive abilities is those endless lists of the world's ten smartest animals. While cows, sheep, and chickens never find their way onto these top ten lists, pigs do. What exactly is it that makes them so smart?

Among those we can turn to for answers are Hamlet and Omelette. These two highly unusual pigs reached their prime in the latter half of the 1990s, when Nintendo consoles had already found their ways into most kids' rooms and science was starting to realize that animals' heads might contain more than automaton-like instincts. This was when Stanley Curtis of Pennsylvania State University had the idea of bringing pigs into his lab and placing them in front of computer screens, with modified joysticks. It may at first sound like a foolish whim, but Curtis was deadly serious: he thought it was time for pigs to have a go at gaming too, and his scientific reputation was on the line.

The game was a far cry from *Super Mario*—more along the lines of primitive early computer games like *Pong* or *Snake* (for any gaming history mavens out there). It involved dragging a highly pixelated dot to a colored field at the edge of the screen. When the task was completed, the pigs were rewarded with M&M's. Banal, you might think. But the task requires much more thought and concentration than we can often expect from small children. First the animal has to perceive what's displayed on the screen, then it has to understand that the graphic on the screen is relevant and something it must focus on. Next it must grasp that what happens on the screen can be influenced and manipulated through a console that isn't directly connected to what the animal is seeing. Finally, the animal must understand the task itself.

For Curtis and his team, the experiment was the result of much pondering about animals' mental faculties, and how to investigate and document them without making a laughing-stock of themselves or being accused of reading too much into the results. Curtis was well aware of the climate in scientific circles. He also knew what the pioneers in this field had gone through in the 1960s and 1970s when they had tried to demon-strate that animals possessed traits until then ascribed exclu-sively to humans. One of these pioneers was Jane Goodall, who was sent to Tanzania—without any formal training—to study wild chimpanzees on behalf of a scientist who didn't want to do the job himself. When she returned home with results that challenged fundamental notions about the differences between humans and animals, she was rebuffed, ridiculed, and accused of getting publicity on the strength of having nice legs.[1] It's no acci-dent that the first established scientist who attempted to argue in earnest for the existence of cognitive abilities and awareness in animals did so only after he had turned sixty and no longer had to worry whether or not his research would further his career. Donald Griffin was the one-time wunderkind who had discov-ered bats' echolocation in the 1930s while still a student. When

he published his 1976 essay "The Question of Animal Awareness,"[2] in which he argued that animals may possess advanced
forms of consciousness, most were dismissive. Yet some people
were convinced by his ideas, and thus Griffin launched a brand-
new branch of biological behavioral science known as cognitive
ethology. This was the field in which Curtis worked.

At the time when Curtis set up his experiment, his discipline
was mostly interested in studying primates, because of their
resemblance to humans. But if skeptics were already dispar-
aging about research involving apes, Curtis thought, how on
earth would they react to an experiment that aimed to demon-
strate higher cognitive abilities in pigs? He absolutely had to
find a method whose results would speak for themselves, or the
entire attempt would collapse into yet another debate about
interpretations and subjectivity.[3]

Using something as tangible as the results of a game probably enabled Curtis to cover his back. Another crucial factor
was that the game had already been tested on other species too,
which provided a fruitful basis for comparison. At the Yerkes
National Primate Research Center in Atlanta, it had previously
been tried out on chimpanzees and other primates, which had
showed an impressive ability to perform the task. Before starting work with pigs, Curtis also tested the game on a Jack Russell terrier, but even after a year of training the dog was still
struggling to master the task.

At last it was Hamlet and Omelette's turn. Curtis suspected
that they might be able to outperform the dog, but what he
hadn't foreseen was that they would totally crush it. And that
was only in the first round. The real surprise came when the
pigs started to rival the primates. Curtis gradually increased the
game's difficulty level, but the pigs kept up, displaying a totally
unexpected capacity to learn new techniques and follow the
progression of the game.[4]

And something else became clear to Curtis and his team: the pigs weren't just doing it for the treats—they were interested in the game itself. When the animals had completed the tasks they were set, his team usually had to terminate the session: "Otherwise they may play all day."[5] In other words, it became clear that the pigs not only possessed complex mental faculties but also had an innate need to use them.

This showed Curtis that animal welfare was not just a matter of physical considerations, such as pain and injury. All at once, mental health also became an issue, but no one yet had any idea how to address animals' psychological needs in agriculture. Scientist that he was, Curtis thought that a great deal more research would be needed before any conclusions could be drawn. Nonetheless, he was convinced that computer games would become a natural component of all industrial piggeries within a matter of years.

You can't fault his optimism. However, as soon as the results were published, his funding from the U.S. meat industry dried up. Not only did his backers withdraw the financing on the grounds that the research had no relevance for them; they took active steps to block publications.[6] Nor did Curtis's dream of transforming piggeries into piggy gaming arcades materialize. Or at least not in the United States. In the Netherlands, however, a research group took up the baton. In 2011, they developed technology that enabled humans to play online with slaughter pigs. People sitting in cafés or their own living rooms could operate light effects projected onto the wall of the pigpen using a tablet, while the pigs followed them with their snouts.[7] Curtis, who died in 2010, never had the pleasure of seeing this project from the Netherlands. In any case, there is little to suggest that this system will find its way into the swine industry in either the Netherlands or elsewhere. The project was shelved before it was properly launched.

But research into pigs' cognitive abilities hasn't ended with Stanley Curtis. Since the glory days of Hamlet and Omelette, a wealth of further studies have been conducted. And it seems that pigs never fail to surprise us.

FEW ANIMAL INTELLIGENCE TESTS are better known than the mirror test developed by the psychologist Gordon Gallup Jr. in the 1970s.[8] He got the idea for it after hearing how a visit to London Zoo in 1838 had set Charles Darwin thinking about the possibility that animals might possess mental faculties akin to those of humans. His inspiration was an orangutan by the name of Jenny whom he saw gazing long and lingeringly at her reflection in a mirror in her enclosure.[9] A hundred and thirty-two years later, Gallup picked up the thread: What was it Jenny saw in the mirror that day in 1838? Did she recognize herself? Or, to put it another way: Did Jenny genuinely experience being a distinct, autonomous individual separate from her surroundings and other beings? Was Jenny self-aware?

Gallup thought the only way to find out was by using mirrors. And since the 1970s, when he conducted his first tests on chimpanzees, countless species have been brought face to face with their own reflections. A handful of species have passed the test, but the vast majority have not. Dogs and cats, for example, have never come close to passing, although—surprisingly enough—ants have.[10] Yet there is much to suggest that the mirror test isn't a fair test for all species. Some have poor eyesight and others—like gorillas—avoid eye contact.

In humans, the mirror test has been shown to have a cultural dimension: the age at which children succeed in performing the task varies dramatically in different countries and regions. In the West, almost all children pass the test at around the age of two, whereas those in other places may not do so until they're closer to six years old.[11]

The traditional method involves placing a mark on the forehead of the animal. If, after repeated testing, the subject touches the mark when it is standing in front of the mirror but stops doing so when the mirror is absent, it has passed the test. Chimpanzees, for example, are quick to scratch the mark on their forehead as soon as they're placed in front of a mirror. The same goes for elephants, which reach up and touch the mark with their trunks. And ants do the same with their flexible forelegs.

But how can the mirror test be performed on an animal like the pig, which lacks hands, a trunk, or flexible legs? Donald Broom of Cambridge University came up with a bright idea: What if, instead of having the pig touch itself, he presented it with a mystery that it could only solve if it understood how a mirror worked?

Before the pigs were set the task, Broom and his team allowed them to spend time in front of a mirror, so they could get used to their reflections. And even at this early stage, the scientists discovered something interesting: the pigs stood looking at themselves for a remarkably long time, moving around and gazing at the mirror from different angles. This is a behavior pattern scientists have typically observed in animals that pass the test.

Once the pigs had gotten used to the mirror, the team set up the room: in addition to the mirror, they also sat up partitions and hid a bowl of treats behind one of them. The key point was this: the bowl would not be directly visible to the pigs, who would only be able to see it as a reflection in the mirror. If they didn't understand how a mirror worked, they would probably look for the treats behind the mirror—not ignore the reflection, turn around, and go all the way to the other side of the partition where the treats were hidden.

Then they got started. The experiment was a success from the very first pig. It almost immediately ignored its reflection in the mirror, turned around, and ran to the place where the treats were hidden. Four out of five other pigs did the same. But the task proved too difficult for one pig, which searched in vain behind the mirror, just as Broom had expected the pigs to do if they didn't understand the task.[12]

The pigs' performance made such an impression in research circles that two scientists at the University of Bristol decided to test whether pigs also had the capacity to grasp the perspective of other individuals. This is a trait that is closely linked to the concept of "theory of mind." Among humans this kicks in at the age of three to five, and self-awareness is assumed to be a prerequisite for its development.[13]

In humans, possessing a theory of mind means understanding that other people have thoughts, emotions, knowledge, or experiences that differ from our own. Much of the defiance displayed by children of three can be ascribed to the absence of a theory of mind, for example. When children lie kicking and screaming on the floor because their food has been cut up wrong, this may simply be because they're unable to understand that their parents don't automatically perceive exactly what they do. The same goes for children who put their hands in front of their eyes when they're supposed to hide: as long as they can't see anything, they assume no one else can either. Most three-year-olds perceive the mind as a shared platform of emotions, experiences, and desires, to which everyone has access—not as individual closed systems that that need language in order to communicate with one another. Human language is therefore assumed to play a key role in the development of this trait. Notably, deaf children with hearing parents perform more poorly on theory of mind tests, but those who are raised by deaf parents and learn sign language early perform similarly to hearing children.[14] Some people with autism also have more difficulty with theory of mind tasks, though abilities can range widely.[15]

One way of testing theory of mind in children is to present them with two boxes. The first is unmarked and the other has a sticker on the outside. If the children are asked which box they think contains stickers, most will naturally choose the one with the sticker on the outside. This is, after all, the logical answer. But this turns out to be a trick question: the unmarked box is revealed as the one containing stickers. And now comes the critical point. The children are asked: Which box do you think other people would choose if they were given the same task as you? If the children have developed a theory of mind, they answer that the others will choose the wrong box too, since those people can't know that it's a trick question. But children who haven't developed a theory of mind will answer that the other person would choose the correct, unmarked box, because now they assume everyone knows where the stickers are.

And so to animals: How are we supposed to go about confirming or disproving theory of mind in creatures that lack speech? The first people to attempt this were the American psychologists David Premack and Guy Woodruff, who developed a test for chimpanzees in 1978, based on the same method that the scientists in Bristol used on pigs.[16] Pigs, like chimpanzees, are social animals with a clear hierarchy, and the interaction between different-ranking animals is precisely what scientists must exploit to assess whether animals have these capabilities.

The experiment went like this: A low-ranking pig was placed in an enclosure where there were several buckets. All were empty except for one that contained food. The pig sniffed around and eventually tracked down the bucket with food in it. But before it had a chance to start eating, it was removed from the enclosure. After a brief period outside, it was put back in, this time accompanied by a larger and more dominant pig. The smaller pig remembered where the food was and sauntered straight over to the bucket to eat from it. As soon as the dominant pig became aware that the smaller one had found some food, it ran over, shoved the smaller pig out of the way, and ate up all the food itself. As the experiment was repeated with more pigs, a pattern emerged: the dominant pigs realized that the smaller pigs knew something they didn't. Instead of searching themselves, they stood there passively and waited for the smaller pig to find food *for* them. But the smaller animals couldn't be tricked for long. After a few unhappy outcomes, where the dominant pigs chased them away, they opted for a different strategy. Instead of running straight to the food, they wandered around the enclosure, feigning ignorance. After a while, the dominant pigs lost patience and started looking around for food on their own. The tables were turned: now the smaller pigs were the ones observing the larger ones. And when the dominant pigs were far enough away, the smaller ones would dash over to the right bucket and gobble up the food before the dominant animal had time to think things over.[17]

The main thing this test demonstrates is that pigs have what is known as Machiavellian intelligence—the ability to understand the perspective of other individuals and engage strategically with social power structures. But many animal behaviorists are very cautious about applying terms such as "theory of mind" and "self-awareness" to animals: although the two tests may *indicate* that pigs have such abilities, it's still debatable whether they can be considered *proof*. What the tests *do* show, however, is that pigs are cognitively flexible creatures and share many of the same traits as animals we tend to view as highly intelligent—chimpanzees, dolphins, ravens, or elephants.

IF PIGS GENUINELY are as intelligent as many tests suggest, shouldn't it be possible to see traces of this in the porcine brain? After all, we live in a neurocentric age—an age of seemingly endless optimism about the discoveries we can make by studying the brain. It is this murky realm we are now entering in our quest to find out who pigs really are. And if you thought the human brain was mysterious—just wait until you find out about the pig's!

The best entry point is the snout, because the nose is the origin of the brain. In all vertebrate embryos, the brain develops from the olfactory organ. In other words, if one removed an embryo's optical system or inner ear, the brain would develop very differently, but in the absence of the olfactory apparatus, it would not develop at all.[18]

One common way of simplifying a mammal's brain is to split it into three levels: the reptilian brain, the mammalian brain (or the limbic system), and the primate or human brain (also called the cerebrum).[19] This also gives us an image of how the brain has evolved over the millions of years that have passed since we were all reptiles.

The reptilian brain consists of the brain stem and the cerebellum, and I can surely be forgiven for calling it the most boring part, since it handles the automatic, robot-like survival mechanisms. The main function of the brain stem is to keep us alive by regulating our breathing, heart rate, and blood pressure. The cerebellum, meanwhile, mostly handles motor functions such as movement, balance, and physical coordination. So far, all of us are more or less alike, from reptiles to humans. But after this, we part ways with the reptiles.

Above the reptilian brain lies the mammalian brain or limbic system, which shows us that humans are nothing but simple animals at heart. The limbic system consists of different core regions—the hypothalamus, the amygdala, the hippocampus, and the thalamus—all of which perform fundamental functions, most easily summed up as the four Fs: "Fight, Flight, Feed, and Fuck." These are the primal drives that prompt us to do our evolutionary duty: to survive long enough to reproduce.

Fundamental emotional states such as fear, anxiety, anger, arousal, and concern all originate here. And the fact that all mammals have a fairly highly developed limbic system tells us how fundamental emotions are to the existence of both pigs and humans. Fear motivates us to stay alive by avoiding danger; anger motivates us to defend ourselves against enemies; arousal motivates us to reproduce; and concern motivates us to care for our offspring and other individuals who are important to our own survival and reproduction. It's more difficult to establish similarly straightforward evolutionary functions for states such as anxiety and happiness, but various techniques for monitoring brain activity and behavior enable us to track anxiety in animals as well as humans.[20] Admittedly, it's more difficult to prove an emotional state such as happiness, but since animals are capable of experiencing anxiety, it's reasonable to assume that they can experience its opposite.[21] All mammals are controlled by the same reward system in the brain. Whether it's us humans getting a "like" on Instagram or pigs listening to the gurgle of the liquid feed concentrate splashing into the trough, the same thing happens to both of us: a shot of dopamine rushes out into our brain.

It's more controversial to claim that animals experience more complex emotions such as grief or empathy—not to mention shame—since it's almost impossible to work out whether these emotions are natural or cultural in origin. Not that this has prevented some of the world's most influential ethologists from ascribing such emotions to animals.[22] One thing is certain, though: these emotions do not arise in the limbic system alone, but involve advanced cognitive processes that play out in the crown jewel of the brain: the cerebral cortex.

And this brings us to the "human brain" or cerebrum, which is what, in practice, we picture when we think of a brain. The cerebral cortex, the outer layer of the cerebrum, is a thin layer densely packed with neurons and synapses. The middle and rear sections control fine motor functions and sensory impressions, while the front section, known as the frontal lobe, handles advanced cognitive functions such as thought, analysis, imagination, sense of time, and language. In other words, this small area is the origin of all the human accomplishments that can be summed up in the concept of civilization. It's therefore interesting that humans are not the only species with a cerebral cortex or frontal lobe. All mammals possess them.

So how can we *see* whether a brain is intelligent or not? How can we *see* that humans are smarter than pigs and pigs are smarter than, say, sheep?

THE THING THAT first strikes us when we compare different brains is their relative size. And for a long time, this was the clearest indicator available for estimating how advanced a brain was. I should point out right away that pigs don't come out well on this measure: the porcine brain weighs between four and six ounces. That's roughly the same size as a sheep's brain and roughly a third of the size of a cow's.

Luckily for the pig, though, general brain volume is a fairly hopeless measure of a brain's complexity. The human brain, which weighs around forty-seven ounces, is admittedly enormous compared with the pig's, but hardly measures up to those of the elephant and the blue whale, which weigh in at around eleven pounds and eighteen pounds, respectively. Measuring the brain relative to body weight may get us a bit closer, however. The trouble is that humans are beaten by shrews on that measure—and there is plenty to suggest that this can't possibly be right.

Several factors can muddy the waters here, since the enormous variety of body shapes and sizes in the animal kingdom makes it impossible to establish an absolutely direct relationship between brain and body. Neuroscientists soon realized this, and psychology researcher Harry J. Jerison decided to do something about it. Early in the 1970s, he developed a model known as the encephalization quotient, or EQ. Put briefly, EQ is a mathematical formula that calculates the ratio between observed and expected brain volume based on body size. If the brain of a species has the same volume one might expect for its body size, it is assigned a value of 1. If it has a larger brain than one might expect, it is assigned a number greater than 1, and if the brain is smaller than expected, the number is less than 1. In this way, Jerison created an effective model for comparing brain volumes across the animal kingdom. He also created a simple— if very approximate—way of ranking animals by their presumed intelligence levels.[23] Since this is a frequently used scale, it may come as no surprise that humans are on top, with an EQ of 7.5 points. We are followed by dolphins, with an impressive 5 points, while chimpanzees and ravens are a bit lower down the scale with a score of 2.4 points. Dogs have a score of 1.2 points, while the blue whale comes in well below 1 with a score of 0.4.[24]

And then there's the pig. Things still don't look good. On EQ, its brain is downgraded even further, ranking the pig as one of the dimmest creatures in the entire animal kingdom. It has managed to end up at the very bottom of the scale with a measly 0.3 points. This doesn't make sense.

Or does it?

Italian veterinarian Serena Minervini was the person responsible for revealing the pig's unimpressive EQ score in her 2016 study. It was based on *Sus scrofa domesticus*, the domestic pig, rather than the original pig, *Sus scrofa*—the wild boar.[25] It seemed like a natural starting point for Minervini to select two of the commonest pig breeds in the world: the Danish Landrace and the British Yorkshire. However, both have been subjected to some of the most intensive breeding programs in modern agriculture, which have utterly transformed the animals' physiology. And this brings us to a key objection to the EQ scale.

Our livestock—particularly the species used exclusively for meat production—have been bred in such a way that their physical build is no longer in proportion to their organs.[26] This is not just evident among pigs; we see the same phenomenon in Belgian Blue cows, whose muscles bulge so much that they seem in danger of bursting out of their skins. The Ross 308 broiler chicken is another example: its breast muscles have become so enormous that it has a tendency to tip over onto its front.[27]

The most striking thing about Minervini's study was not that the pig brain was small; more striking was the fact that the pig brain, in isolation, has shrunk by comparison with earlier measures. And not only has it shrunk: in some pigs, the volume has diminished by as much as 34 percent. Minervini doesn't offer any conclusive explanation for this, but suggests that it may be linked to several factors, such as feed, and other social or environmental adaptations to the pigs' cramped and passive indoor life.

At the same time, the history of evolution has taught us this: if an animal is going to take the trouble to maintain a large, energy-intensive brain, the advanced brain function must be crucial to its survival.[28] But the passive industrial pigs barely need a brain at all. In fact you could simply hook these outsized beasts up to a drip and leave them to live lives akin to those of coma patients. The modern breeding programs that created today's industrial swine were a high-speed evolutionary process, with humans at the controls instead of nature. None of the programs to date have intentionally set out to alter domestic animals' brains, but all the physiological benefits breeding has brought us humans have also had unintended anatomical costs for the animals. In the pigs' case, diminishing brain volume has definitely been among them.

And now we are face to face with a paradox. How is it possible for pigs to continue performing so well on tests of higher cognitive ability? For Minervini, it's clear that neither EQ nor brain volume in general are satisfactory indicators of an animal's cognitive abilities.[29] But what are we to look for instead?

EVEN THOUGH THE PIG'S BRAIN is small and shrunken, we still have to consider its cerebral cortex, identifiable as the characteristic ripples on the outer surface of the brain. These ripples are evolution's way of optimizing the space available in a cramped skull for the important cognitive and sensory regions of the brain. A dense and complex pattern of folds is therefore a typical indicator of a complex brain.

When the German veterinarian and neuroscientist Verena Schmidt decided to map the entire structure of the pig brain in 2015, she sent several miniature pigs through an fMRI scanner. But the resulting images revealed a sad fact—at least for anyone on the lookout for intelligence. Pigs' brains proved to have a less complex structure than those of any other ungulate. And their cerebrum constituted a much smaller part of the brain as a whole than it did in cattle. Nor was the frontal lobe, which houses the key cognitive functions such as problem-solving and thinking, especially prominent. In short, nothing in Schmidt's study indicates that pigs have the prerequisites for unusually high mental abilities—at least by comparison with other large domestic animals.[30]

IT'S STARTING TO LOOK as if we're reaching a dead end in our quest for the pig's intelligence. But there's still hope. When it comes down to it, all that thinking and feeling is not done by the brain mass itself but by tiny brain cells, or neurons.

If you took a brain out of a tank of formaldehyde, put it on the kitchen counter, and sliced straight through it, all you would see would be a featureless, pallid mass with a few gaps here and there. This is what Camillo Golgi of Italy did to a human brain in the late nineteenth century, and he was greatly troubled by this pitiful sight. Golgi, who worked at the University of Pavia, was the very model of the distinguished scientist. So obsessed was he with the brain that he set up a little lab in his own kitchen, where he could devote evenings and nights to the study of this mysterious gray matter undisturbed. Into the small hours, he carved slice after slice of brain and placed them under the microscope. But all he saw was pallid grayness. The brain was apparently nothing but bland soft tissue. And so it went on, until one day he had one of those happy accidents that so often lead to new scientific insights.

The story goes that he happened to drop a slice of brain into a dish of dye containing silver nitrate. He can't have realized it was missing, either, because the days went by and the slice remained where it was until he found it again by chance. The sight must have filled him with elation, because now, for the first time, he could see what he had striven so long to find: an intricate pattern of spiraling lines interspersed with tiny dots had appeared on the surface of the slice of brain. Golgi had accidentally revolutionized the study of the nervous system by finding a method for staining neurons that made them visible under the microscope.

In what must have been a bitter blow to Golgi, his archrival, the equally distinguished Spanish scientist Santiago Ramón y Cajal, was the one to spot something about Golgi's discovery that he himself had failed to notice. The accident in Golgi's kitchen enabled Cajal to formulate what is now known as the "neuron doctrine," which marked the birth of modern neuroscience: "The nerve cell is the anatomical, physiological, metabolic and genetic unit of the nervous system," he wrote. By the time Golgi and Cajal were named joint winners of the Nobel Prize in 1906, their relationship was so poisonous that they apparently had to stand facing away from each other during the award ceremony.[31] Ultimately, Cajal was the one to win the accolade of "father of modern neuroscience," a fact that Golgi should be grateful he never lived to see.

THANKS TO THE PIONEERING EFFORTS of Golgi and Cajal, we now know that the human brain contains no fewer than 86 billion neurons. And each of them again is connected to between ten thousand and twenty thousand others via synapses. This barely conceivable range of potential brain connections provides the starting point for our every action, from movement to abstract thought.

Nowadays, there is much to suggest that the number of neurons in the brain—especially in the cerebral cortex—may be the factor that determines a species' cognitive abilities.[32] The neurologist Suzana Herculano-Houzel has used this assumption to hazard the answer to a familiar question about our family pets: Which is smarter—cat or dog? Since dogs turn out to have twice as many neurons in their cerebral cortex as cats, Herculano-Houzel doesn't rule out the possibility that dogs may be twice as smart.[33]

The 16 billion neurons in the human cerebral cortex leave most other species looking pretty dim. At the same time, we can see that the number of neurons an animal has corresponds fairly well with how intelligent we judge the species to be, based on its behavior. For example, the dolphin is right behind us, with an impressive 12 billion neurons. Then come gorillas with 9.1 billion, chimpanzees with 6.2 billion, macaws with 1.9 billion, and horses with 1.2 billion neurons, while dogs are well below that, with just 530 million.[34]

Is this where the pig brain will at last come into its own? Is this where it will make up for all the limitations it has so far displayed?

Far from it.

Pigs have only 430 million neurons, meaning that they are beaten not only by dogs, but by everything from lions and hyenas to owls and magpies.[35] It's impossible to say whether pigs beat cows and sheep on this metric since no one has bothered to measure those animals. As a consolation to pigs, I should point out that there is also—surprisingly enough—one species that towers above us humans in the neuron stakes. It's an animal we know very little about, which has almost never been kept in captivity and is almost impossible to observe in the wild. Our super-being is the pilot whale. The few things we do know about it include the fact that it's not actually a whale but a dolphin, and that it's a victim of a bloody annual hunt in the Faroe Islands known as the *grindadráp*. But we also know this: the pilot whale has 37 billion neurons in its cerebral cortex alone.[36] That's more than twice as many as us humans. What on earth does it use this brain for?

IT'S A FULL 2,400 YEARS since Hippocrates wrote: "From the brain, and from the brain only, arise our pleasures, joys... our sorrows, pains, grief and tears... It is the same thing which makes us mad or delirious, inspires us with dread and fear... brings sleeplessness... and aimless anxieties."[37] There is little doubt that the brain is the most impressive, complex, and intricate organ that has ever evolved. It is, perhaps, also the organ scientists have spent the most time attempting to understand. But no matter how hard and often it's hammered home to us that neuroscience has made vast strides in recent years, this fact remains: the brain is the organ we understand the least. That is true for both human and pig brains. There's a certain irony to it, really; our brains are not advanced enough to understand the brain.

Doubt and uncertainty about what thoughts and feelings may be housed in an animal's brain will persist for the foreseeable future. But whereas this doubt spelled trouble for animals in the twentieth century, a more empathetic tendency now prevails, and our doubts increasingly serve to benefit the animals. In the end, does it even matter how smart pigs are? Not according to the eighteenth-century thinker Jeremy Bentham: "The question is not, Can they reason?, nor Can they talk? but, Can they suffer?"[38]

What We Talk About When We Talk About Suffering

JUST WHAT HAPPENED in the piggery last night, no one can tell, but when Leiv came in this morning, there was blood: blood on a tail and everything it had touched. It probably happened the way it often does when slaughter pigs start to bite each other: one of the pigs gets a bit too curious about a sibling's tail. And then it strikes.

It's impossible to know what provoked this, of course, but once blood has been shed, the other pigs get wind of it too. The victim attempts to parry by swishing its tail, but that only attracts more attention. In the end, it finds itself chased not just by one pig but by an entire mob—and there's no way out.

Although most of the pigs here undoubtedly appear to be adapted to their passive indoor life, they still retain many of the drives inherited from the time when they lived in forests and swampland. From the time when the world was open and boundless; when the expectation of finding a tasty tuber beneath the soil released just enough dopamine in their brains to keep them wandering around on an endless quest. A quest that also set the synapses in their frontal lobes sparking as they scanned their surroundings for food and danger. A time when estrus was a hazy hunt for scent signals, a drive that provided direction, motivation, and perhaps even an experience akin to what we humans would call *meaning*. The pigs have been robbed of all this. But the "yearning" for it persists—perhaps in the form of an undefined, nagging sensation in the breast or belly.

So what do pigs do when they live indoors on a concrete floor, with three square feet of space at their disposal, fed on a soup that splashes down into their trough once a day?

They bite each other's tails.

ACCORDING TO THE Norwegian Food Safety Authority, tail biting is one of the most serious and widespread animal welfare problems in the Norwegian swine industry. (In many other countries, the tails are docked to prevent this.) The fear and pain the victim suffers as it is chased around the cramped pen is not the only problem. Above all, this is a sign that all is not well with the pigs that bite. Ethologists define the phenomenon as "destructive behavior" triggered by the environment the pigs inhabit. In this sense, the bloody tail stumps are an indictment of the way the whole industry is organized.

I try to catch a glimpse of the injuries suffered by the victim, who has now been placed in the piggy sick bay—a little stall screened off from the other animals. But the pig is lying with its rump to the wall, so I hear about it from Leiv instead.

"The tail's intact and won't need amputating."

AS STANLEY CURTIS SHOWED in the 1990s, good animal welfare is about a lot more than the absence of physical pain; it's also a matter of mental health. But how are we to ensure that the pigs have healthy minds? After the events of last night, I have every reason to doubt my own—and most other people's—capacity to grasp the subtle codes of animal behavior. Many of us find it difficult enough to read other people. So it would be quite a feat to work in a piggery and pick up on much more than the signs of physical pain we can see with the naked eye: a bloody tail, a limp, an inflamed eye, or an umbilical hernia dragging on the floor. Even so, it's a bit alarming to hear who bit the pig: Leiv tells me it was those notorious brutes in pen one.

Of course the pig was from pen one. There's a reason those pigs I hit and kicked in fear have been aggressive. Perhaps it's even wrong to call it "aggression"; it's probably more accurate to call it desperation—a cry for help. But none of us saw the signals they were sending us. Now a question I've been pushing aside for more than long enough catches up with me: Can I eat these pigs with a clear conscience?

AS LONG AS I CAN TAKE Leiv's word for it when he tells me that his business follows the legislation to the letter, I can at least content myself with the idea that these particular industrial pigs enjoy world-class animal welfare. No country has stricter legislation in the field than Norway. But what difference does that make if the animals are still suffering?

For anyone assuming that conditions in pen one are representative of the well-being of the rest of the animals here, I must stress that all the other pens are largely calm and clean, and their inhabitants show no signs of aggression—or desperation, if you prefer. Some animals do suffer injuries, of course, just as wild animals do. But instead of enduring prolonged physical suffering before becoming weak and ultimately starving, or else being caught by a predator that tears them to pieces (while their hearts still hammer and their minds remain conscious), these pigs are either killed "humanely" or nursed back to health.

In nature, suffering is such a fundamental part of existence that the concept almost loses any meaning. For modern, affluent

Westerners, this can be difficult to grasp, because we have made such strides toward mitigating suffering. We may have passing aches or pains, but brutal, prolonged physical suffering has largely been eradicated. The resulting vacuum has been filled with new, vaguer concepts, fostered by a mostly pain-free life. We may experience "discomfort" or "anxiety," feel "off-color" or be "unwell." But these states are also generally weeded out. And so we've reached a place where many of us aren't satisfied until we have achieved a more or less complete experience of well-being. This is often a thoroughly unnatural or artificial state enabled by the inventions of medical science and the pharmaceutical industry. In the meantime, our awareness that suffering continues to exist in the outside world has made it grow and expand into a terrifying beast in our heads. Our fear of suffering and our efforts to achieve well-being are the prism through which we encounter the animal world. How appropriate is that?

ALTHOUGH PIGS HAVE emotions and basic thought processes, there is little evidence that they have a conceptual apparatus capable of defining states such as "suffering" and "well-being." A pig may suffer terrible pain—unbearable pain, if you like— and may in such cases be better off dying. But when pigs suffer in silence, when they limp a bit or aren't sufficiently stimulated, they aren't capable of longing for a different existence, one that is pain-free or happier. They will be in the suffering and probably become accustomed to it in a way that may be hard to grasp for a thinking, comfort-loving species like our own. One helpful human parallel may be people afflicted with tinnitus. The condition rarely causes physical pain, but the sufferer is plagued by an irritating noise that never goes away and can't be cured by conventional medicine. Tinnitus comes in different levels of intensity, but two people who are equally afflicted may respond differently—one copes fine while the other is destroyed by it. There's a simple factor that may explain the difference: how much the afflicted person longs for a life free of the ringing in their ears. This is why the most successful tinnitus treatment is cognitive therapy, which trains patients to live with the noise by learning, among other things, *not to wish it away*.[1] This brings the patients closer to an animal state, in that they relinquish the idea of a different, tinnitus-free existence. After treatment, the noise often ceases to bother them altogether.[2]

In case anyone is in any doubt: this is not a defense of animal neglect, but rather an attempt to home in on what we're talking about when we talk about suffering in a pig. The pigs in pen one are not suffering from tinnitus, as far as I know. Based on the tail biting, though, we *can* say that they are displaying "destructive behavior," which may be an external sign of an underlying problem. But is destructive behavior in a pig an indication of actual suffering?

To take another human example, picked more or less at random: Some children and young people have so much energy, so little impulse control, and find it so hard to sit still and concentrate on something that doesn't interest them to start off with that they may have trouble following ordinary (old-fashioned, if you like) classroom teaching without some kind of adaptation or medication. The cartoon cliché is the rowdy lad dangling from the striplights on the ceiling, carving penises into a desk with a compass, or otherwise sabotaging the teacher's lesson plan. A teacher might well define this as "destructive behavior." The pupil is clearly suffering, in the sense that he has no outlet for his natural drives—perhaps the need for some kind of meaningful physical exercise. But is it correct to say that the boy hanging from the striplight is having a subjective experience of suffering at these moments when he is detached from any thought of what he really wants to be doing, when he is simply living in the "now" (which is a pig's permanent state)? Of course we can't say for sure. Similarly, we can't take it for granted that what we think of when we think about suffering in an animal is always as bad as it might initially sound.

BUT LET'S NOT BE TOO CYNICAL. When two of the most influential thinkers of our age—Australian philosopher Peter Singer and Israeli historian Yuval Noah Harari—say that our treatment of domestic animals is the greatest crime in human history, we don't have to agree with them, of course.[3] Yet there's little question that they have a point.

Our livestock currently accounts for 60 percent of all mammals on earth. We humans account for 36 percent of the biomass, and wild animals are at risk of vanishing entirely, accounting for a mere 4 percent of all mammals.[4] First and foremost, perhaps, this unbelievable statistic is a warning about the ecological imbalance we have created for ourselves. But let's take the issue of animal welfare first: since we know that our domestic animals are sensitive beings and that the overwhelming majority of them live in conditions that make those in Norway look like a romantic, bucolic dream, it's hard to deny that humanity is on a morally dubious course. No matter how much we flirt with the idea that our livestock have better lives than wild animals, there is a crucial difference between the two: animals in nature are not our responsibility, whereas domestic animals are. As long as the quality of an animal's existence depends solely on how we treat it, the natural conclusion must be that we have assumed a moral obligation to take the best possible care of it.

But we do not do so—either in Norway's conventional swine industry or elsewhere in the world. As Leiv has pointed out several times while I've been working in the piggery: "The animals should live a good life, but we have to be able to make a living out of it too. So there's a limit to how many animal welfare regulations we can take on board."

In other words, Leiv thinks that a world in which all pigs lived the way free-range pigs do—a more expensive business model, in which the animals have more freedom to develop their natural drives—would not yield a livelihood. Of course he's right, unless this change also involves him getting a better price for the animals he sends to slaughter. But surely we can count on that happening. Or can we?

Never before have we spent a smaller share of our income on pork than we do today. This situation is predicated on the production conditions that enable Leiv and his colleagues in the industry to keep large numbers of animals in a small area, with automated feeding systems and a building design that makes it easy to tend the pigs and muck out the pens quickly and efficiently. It's a development that is universal throughout the Western world. In Norway's case, it has allowed pork production to triple between 1960 and the present day even while the number of pig farmers has fallen from around fifty thousand to just over two thousand. Something else happened too: while the annual production of Norwegian pork has tripled between 1960 and 2020, the value of the total volume of meat has remained more or less unchanged. This means that Leiv's father was paid more than double the amount per pound for the animals he sent to slaughter than Leiv receives today.[5] Even after the introduction of regulations aimed at improving pig welfare in the early 2000s, which were costly for farmers, prices continued to fall. In other words, history has shown Leiv that improvements in animal welfare are rarely reflected in the price he is paid for the animals. That has left many farmers feeling under pressure to make their businesses even more intensive—which leaves us no better off than we were to start with.

So what are we to do?

One obvious suggestion is that anyone who feels moved to do so should exercise their consumer power by buying meat from free-range "happy pigs." Presumably this will reduce the sum of suffering in agriculture and slightly diminish green-house gas emissions. At the same time, it will send a clear signal that people can cope with higher meat prices. Obviously, there's nothing to stop anyone from doing this. However, as long as the free-range share of the total pork market continues to decline—and it currently accounts for no more than 0.1 percent in the United States[6]—there is little reason for much optimism on the pig's behalf.

What's more, many will detect a bitter whiff of cultural classism in this approach. Not everyone is highly paid or keen on cooking, and not everyone has the energy or motivation to think through lengthy, lofty arguments about animal ethics. Many people just want to enjoy a pork chop or two before mowing the lawn, and who can blame them? Still, those who can face it may find it useful to turn to one of the people who *has* given the matter long and lofty thought.

IF THERE'S ONE TEXT that can claim the honor of having defined the modern, ethical conversation about the relationship between people and animals, it's Peter Singer's *Animal Liberation*, first published in 1975. Singer, now a professor of philosophy at Princeton University, is considered one of the most influential, and controversial, moral philosophers of our age. This alone is reason enough to listen to what he has to say.

Even today, nearly fifty years after its publication, the title *Animal Liberation* can seem almost parodic—or at least naive—in its reference to earlier human liberation movements. But that was part of Singer's intention—to write in the tradition of Mary Wollstonecraft, who faced scorn and humiliation when she published A *Vindication of the Rights of Woman* in 1792. And just as Wollstonecraft has become a saint in the church of women's liberation, Singer is on his way to gaining similar status among a growing group of people who are passionate about animal welfare.

Of course, Singer was far from the first person to write a book about animal rights. However, he adopted a new approach: rather than concerning himself with the physical mistreatment of individual animals—tortured cats or whipped horses—he addressed the new system for organizing animal husbandry that came about in the 1960s, when farms started to resemble factories and the animals, mass-produced goods. With *Animal Liberation*, Singer became one of the first people to point out that the entire concept of industrial livestock farming was one vast, structural assault. At the same time, his reasoning was a more general critique of humanity's long tradition of believing we have the right to exploit and slowly torture other sensitive and biologically equal beings on the trivial grounds that they "taste good."

So, how relevant is it to read *Animal Liberation* today?

This may be a daring claim, but if the state of global animal husbandry in 1975 had been similar to current conditions in Norway, we can't be sure that Singer's book would have been written in the first place. It's at least conceivable that it wouldn't have made as much of an impact. The book's arguments are shored up by lengthy descriptions of grotesque livestock farms in Australia and the United States, which it would be problematic to compare with conditions in the Norwegian livestock business today. Reading *Animal Liberation* in Norway in 2020 can sometimes feel like reading a historical war report from a foreign country: it may be thought-provoking and informative, but the text need not be read as an appeal to Norwegians to rise up and call for freedom in their own country. We *have* peace. And—thanks to Peter Singer and the movement he helped start—we also have relatively good animal welfare.

But it's worth noting that Nordic countries outperform most other places in the world on animal welfare standards; the United States and Canada, for instance, both have a rating of "D" on the World Animal Protection Index.[7] And even where there have been improvements, we run the risk of seeing history bite us on the tail: if there's one thing we've learned from other liberation movements—such as feminism—it's that the war isn't won just because conditions are better than they used to be.

This is about as far as we can get in our attempts to formulate an objective explanation of the ethically correct thing to do—unless we're willing to write an entire thesis on it. But Singer has already done that for us. And here is his conclusion: We should totally abolish livestock farming—no matter how "humanely" the animals live before they die.

Peter Singer is probably one of the most ethical people alive today. He lives by a utilitarian philosophy involving an attitude to others that appears to be thoroughly self-sacrificing. In brief, his every action is guided by the principle that it must aim to achieve the greatest happiness for the greatest number of people. This does not mean that the actions must always *benefit* all involved, but that we should choose the option that involves the least possible harm or suffering. In Singer's view, as long as we can assume that it is in animals' interests to live and as long as humans don't need to eat meat to live a good and healthy life, there is no truly compelling reason to imprison and then kill our livestock. This contrasts with his position on the use of animals in some research experiments: here, Singer is open to the idea that if the exploitation of animals can cure enough suffering, the reduction in the sum of suffering may justify the practice.

It's hard to fault Singer for the ethical position he proposes. But what we *can* fault him for is his belief in human willpower and humans' capacity to analyze their own choices. Most of us would find it hopelessly difficult to navigate a world where our every action must be guided by rational argument. Admittedly, more and more people are starting to ask enlightened questions at the supermarket (Is this good for the environment? Is this good for animals? Is this good for the workers who produced the goods? Does this product represent something I otherwise despise on cultural or ideological grounds?). But no matter how many of these questions we've asked ourselves in the course of a day, all of us will realize when evening comes that most of our actions have been decided by that intuitive moral compass we call "gut feeling."

So what is my own gut feeling after almost six months in a piggery?

Slaughter

IT'S EARLY NOVEMBER. The tractor ruts in the soil have frozen and a bitter gale blasts across the gravel of the farmyard. We shiver as we scowl up the road. It's approaching midday and the end is nigh: the slaughter truck could be here any second.

"Do you think he's far off?" I tug my hood down over my head and thrust my hands in my jacket pockets.

"The timing's always a bit vague," Leiv replies. "We can't stay out here, at any rate."

I follow him into the warmth of the piggery. We settle on the aging furniture in the dusty back-room office and there we sit, chatting as we flip through old issues of *Pig News*, until his phone rings. I hear Eirik's voice on the other end.

"I've just heard he'll be there any minute."

"Better get moving, then," Leiv says, getting up from the sofa.

He goes in to the pigs while I stay sitting in the back room. It'll just be father and son today. From now on, I'm no longer a pig tender. I've been reduced to an observer, a gawker, the way I was when the pigs were born five months ago. Today, I'll be leaving with the slaughter truck instead.

223

Before, I'd imagined that this day would feel melancholy; that I'd be connected to the pigs in some way. But my role as a pig tender has left no room for that kind of intimacy, so the seeds of sentimentality were never sown. Indeed, if there's one thing that defines me as I sit here alone in the back room listening to the first squeals through the wall, it's indifference, in the sense that I'm close to agreeing with Leiv's remark that "pigs are industrial animals. They're not for cuddling."

Does this mean I've become indoctrinated or emotionally stunted? Or could it simply be that life in a regular piggery isn't as grim as some would have us believe? I think it's probably a bit of both.

THE SQUEALS INCREASE in volume, lending a dramatic undertone to the entire situation. Yet I know how little it takes to provoke the pigs into making that racket. Often, it's enough to catch them a bit off guard or refuse to let them go in the direction they want to. And after all, getting a hundred or so pigs out of the building at the same time is bound to cause a bit of a commotion. Isn't it?

However much we might wish to romanticize the relationship between people and livestock in times gone by, we can't be certain that slaughter day was much better back then than it is now. In the early modern period, the recommended slaughtering method was to stab the pigs in the flank with a knife and leave them to run around with it until they collapsed.[1] Things don't appear to have been much more humane in the nineteenth century, either, if we're to believe Arabella in Thomas Hardy's *Jude the Obscure*, from 1895. "The meat must be well bled, and to do that he must die slow… I was brought up to it, and I know. Every good butcher keeps un bleeding long. He ought to be eight or ten minutes dying, at least."[2] Not that a pig's life was especially happy before then. As an observer in Elizabethan

England once commented: "They feed in pain, lie in pain and sleep in pain."[3]

THE SLAUGHTER TRUCK roars past the window. I walk out into the gale and watch the trailer back up to the door where the pigs will be let out.

And then it's underway: the truck's tailgate is lowered, the door of the piggery opens, and the pigs in the front of the group see the light of day and smell fresh air for the very first time. It's an egalitarian moment. From this point onward, the pigs' provenance becomes irrelevant—whether they're from an industrial farm where they've been neglected or are ethically raised animals that have spent their entire life out in the open: without special dispensations and agreements, they're all sent to the same place in the same way. The aim of centralized slaughterhouses is to ensure hygiene and animal welfare. Closed industrial slaughtering facilities are supposed to offer a clinical, sterile environment that protects us against disease and parasites. At the same time, supervisory authorities are empowered to observe procedures, to ensure that the animals are handled and slaughtered in line with regulations. Mind you, it doesn't look as if there'll be any slaughtering done at all right now, because the line has backed up: the pigs refuse to go out.

They lurch around, sit down, and start to squeal. It's sometimes said that pigs know what's going to happen when they're sent to slaughter, but we all know that can't be true. At least not this soon. A more likely explanation for their reluctance is the icy wind and the low November sun shining in their eyes.

Eirik stands behind them pushing, shoving, nudging, and tugging until the bottleneck eases and the first pigs tumble out in one great mass.

"That's enough," the driver shouts. There's a limit to how many animals he can let into the trailer at a time.

Once the pigs are outside, they lumber calmly up the ramp all by themselves. The truck has six chambers on two levels. When the innermost one is full, the floor is raised, freeing up a new stall beneath.

That's roughly when it starts.

The squeals, screams, and desperation inside the slaughter truck are beyond anything I've ever heard. The sounds are urgent, piercing, distressing, and they don't stop. I try to exchange a few words with the driver; I want to ask him what's happening, whether this is normal, but he can't hear what I'm saying. Of course he can't. Nothing could penetrate the racket echoing across the farmyard. I see the bodies pressing up against the gaps in the air vents. One of the pigs appears to be lying on the others' backs. It tumbles around, rolling like a barrel before it finds an open space and is absorbed into the pink mass. It's impossible to say how many of them are squealing, but one of the noises is especially affecting: A sad, hooting wail that sounds just like weeping. I try and fail to ignore it, and for the first time I truly catch myself thinking: What on earth are we doing?

After a few minutes, the squeals subside, but the discomfort of the experience sits in my belly as I watch more pigs board the truck. It doesn't last all that long, though. Suddenly, I find myself feeling remarkably relaxed about the situation again, as if the entire episode had been some vague dream. Is that hypocritical? It probably depends who you ask. Me? I'm inclined to say yes.

After forty minutes, eighty-three pigs have boarded the truck. I wave goodbye to Leiv and Eirik and climb up into the driver's cab. And with the pigs grunting behind us, we set off.

WE DRIVE OVER the Jæren uplands, a rolling agricultural landscape scattered with hilltops and rocky outcrops. The air is crisp and cold, and the naked birches cast long distorted shadows over the pale hillsides where the sheep are still out, grazing on the last green tufts of grass. The driver nods at one of the herds.

"You know, pigs would enjoy a life like that too. Living outside, wandering around in the fresh air. They'd root around in the earth, make mudholes, and get dirty, but that's what they like best. You can tell when they board the trailer. The second they're out of the piggery, they poke their snouts in the soil, snuffle away, and chew everything in sight. They're inquisitive animals," he says. He doesn't want to be identified. Slaughter truck drivers aren't so popular these days.

"Sometimes people shout 'murderer' at me when I'm out driving. But mostly people just don't understand how I can cope with the work, driving animals to slaughterhouses where they'll be killed. 'How can you do a job like that?' they ask."

He shakes his head.

"It happened by accident. I took my trucking license, the slaughter company was hiring, and that was that."

WE PASS MANY FARMS where, the driver tells me, he often picks up animals. All of them piggeries. But the landscape also contains other livestock buildings, and after a while we make a game out of my attempts to guess which animals are hidden in them. The cowsheds are easy to identify: they're those high-ceilinged cathedrals with open walls where you feel almost as if you're outside even though you're indoors. Spotting the difference between a poultry farm and a piggery requires a different expertise. Both structures are oblong, with fairly low roofs. The general rule is that piggeries have small square windows on the long side, whereas the walls of poultry farms have ventilation hatches. The challenge is that piggeries are increasingly adopting the same architectural model as the poultry facilities, and when that's the case, I'm lost.

AFTER THIRTY-FIVE MINUTES on the road, we arrive in Forus, between Sandnes and Stavanger. The slaughterhouse is almost invisible from the road, hidden in a dip in the landscape. It's surrounded by housing developments, schools, and stores. We stop and wait for a gate to open. Activists often stand here holding up placards with messages for the drivers—usually "Stop and think it over." But there are none today. Perhaps they've given up. At any rate, none of the drivers have ever lowered the tailgate of their trailer and set the animals free.

The activists view this complex as the scene of a heinous crime. While many would disagree with the worldview and rhetoric of the most radical of them, it's an undeniable fact that around a thousand four-legged animals meet their end here every single day, without most outsiders ever realizing it.

It's been a long time since ordinary people have been allowed to witness the death of a domestic animal.

New York City was already moving slaughterhouses out of central locations as early as 1676, and by the end of the eighteenth century, meat was being sold through city-owned marketplaces and licensed slaughterhouses.[4] However, in much of the Western world, slaughtering happened in open booths in the city centers until the late eighteenth and early nineteenth century. In the Norwegian capital, then called Kristiania, the central street of Dronningens gate was long the place where slaughtering and butchering were done. The blood flowed into the muddy streets, where the butchers would also toss the guts and other useless cuts, to the delight of stray pigs, which happily gobbled up the waste.[5] The same was true elsewhere in Europe: up until the eighteenth century, the Parisian quarter now known as Châtelet and Les Halles was a hub of slaughtering and butchery. A contemporary source cited by French anthropologist Noëlie Vialles complains that the butchers' shops "corrupt the atmosphere" and sniffs: "What could be more revolting, more disgusting than to slit animals' throats and cut them up in public?"[6]

In many cities across Europe, covered bazaars were established in the second half of the nineteenth century to improve sanitary conditions and make the slaughtering process more rational and efficient. But customers could still handle the meat a stone's throw from the spot where the slaughtering was done. This doesn't mean that slaughtering was centralized, though. In the 1890s, even a modest-sized European city might have had multiple different locations where animals were slaughtered and butchered.[7] In most of the world, animals and death were everywhere.

As urban citizens became increasingly remote from animal husbandry and the rural way of life, they were less keen to deal with the grim and indelicate aspects of meat production. Slaughtering had become an indecent—even repulsive—profession, which did not just disturb the general aesthetic of the streets, but was also seen as a threat to civility in the cities.[8] In the early twentieth century, slaughterhouses were expelled from city centers throughout Europe and banished to closed complexes in more rural locations. According to Vialles, the strategy of eradicating this activity in the cities also had an underlying aim: to hide death away "in order not to give people ideas," she writes.[9] Many viewed slaughterhouses as morally dangerous enterprises, which risked spreading decadence and breeding a more violent society. A committee investigating the impact of London's Smithfield Market in 1849, for example, was told that the violence against animals "educate[d] the men in the practice of violence and cruelty, so that they seem to have no restraint on the use of it."[10] Or as Tolstoy is said to have put it: "As long as there are slaughterhouses, there will be battlefields."

With the actual slaughtering out of sight, the meat industry had a cleaner and more appealing product to offer to an ever-more-discriminating body of consumers. Instead of "slaughterhouses," the cities saw growth in butcher's shops, which totally altered the perception of who butchers were. Once seen as bloody, slovenly, and often morally dubious figures, they became connoisseurs behind spotless counters, who presented delicate, ready-prepared cuts of meat to an expanding group of urban buyers. As if by magic, farmers' and butchers' hands were washed clean of blood and death. In the meantime, the hidden slaughterhouses could take care of the dirty end of business—killing, gutting, and butchering—without any customers standing there wrinkling their noses. And the job became increasingly dirtier because, as the population grew, so did demand. The process had to be streamlined.

Unsurprisingly, perhaps, American slaughterhouses were the first to adopt an industrial approach to the business. So great was the need for streamlining that the Chicago slaughterhouses that emerged in the late nineteenth century are viewed as the first businesses in the world to have used production lines.[11] In other words, the widespread belief that Henry Ford was the first person to adopt this technique in the early twentieth century for mass production of the first popular car, the Ford Model T, is simply false. As Ford himself wrote in his 1922 autobiography: "The idea [for the conveyor belt] came in a general way from the overhead trolley that the Chicago packers use in dressing beef."[12]

This link between Henry Ford and the slaughtering trade led historian and animal welfare activist Charles Patterson to write one of the most macabre—some would say far-fetched—books ever written about the modern slaughter industry. *Eternal Treblinka* has become required reading and a reference work for animal rights activists worldwide. Patterson explains that there is a clear link between the American meat industry, Henry Ford, and the genocide of Jewish people in the Second World War.[13] His reasoning is based on the historical fact that Henry Ford was ferociously anti-Semitic and much admired by Hitler for both his opinions and his significance to German industry. Since the Germans applied the industrial logistics developed by Henry Ford to carry out the Holocaust, and since Ford himself had sought inspiration in the slaughterhouses, Patterson believes that the slaughter industry ultimately paved the way for the Holocaust. Or as Nobel Prize–winning author J. M. Coetzee has one of his characters put it in *The Lives of Animals*: "It was from the Chicago stockyards that the Nazis learned how to process bodies."[14] Patterson's analysis is rooted in this philosophical conclusion: "The exploitation and slaughter of animals provides the precedent for the mass murder of people and makes it more likely because it conditions us to withhold empathy, compassion, and respect from others who are different."[15]

No reasonable person could deny some of the logic in the grotesque analogy between the Holocaust and the industrial slaughter of animals. At the same time, many would claim that the comparison trivializes one of the most appalling crimes against humanity in the history of the world while assigning an unduly high value to animals. That said, the analogy is legitimate as a rhetorical and philosophical point for those who consider animals and humans to be of equal worth. What's more, recent research has shown a link between killing people and slaughtering animals. For one thing, there is a well-documented correlation between violence against animals and domestic violence. Even more startling are the studies revealing that slaughterhouse workers share a suspiciously large number of traits with soldiers returning home from war.

One of these is post-traumatic stress disorder (PTSD), which is widespread among many social groups. A subcategory known as perpetration-induced traumatic stress (PITS) is common among veterans, executioners in U.S. jails, convicted murderers, people who have collaborated in genocides, and, last but not least, slaughterhouse employees. Whereas PTSD affects people who have been subjected to a traumatic event and is constantly triggered by new experiences associated with the trauma, PITS affects those who have subjected others to trauma.[16] It is assumed that many slaughterhouse employees who have experienced prolonged exposure to and participation in the slaughtering process eventually reach breaking point and can no longer function properly in their everyday lives. Studies show that slaughterhouse employees often have a history of criminality, alcohol and drug abuse, and domestic violence.[17] On top of that, working in a slaughterhouse is one of the most physically dangerous professions, with a high rate of serious injuries, and the crowded environment creates favorable conditions for the spread of communicable diseases: throughout the COVID-19 pandemic, large outbreaks in a number of countries have been traced to slaughterhouses and meatpacking plants.[18]

WE HAVE NOW passed through two barriers on our way into the slaughterhouse, the second of which was a massive iron gate with orange warning lights topped by a wreath of barbed wire.

I clamber down from the driver's cab and get the driver to point the way toward the animal reception area. While the trailer backs in through the gate, I go inside. The hall is the size of a small soccer field. The floor is covered in a labyrinthine system of partitions that reminds me of the way airport lines are organized. There's a sharp metallic smell in the air, but it's hard to tell whether it's caused by the industrial construction of iron and concrete or whether the whole complex has become impregnated with the steam from all the meat and blood.

I meet an NFSA inspector wearing a face mask, ear protectors, and outsized overalls. It's her first day at the slaughterhouse, where she'll be monitoring the animals that arrive.

"I'm pleasantly surprised, really," she says. "I'd been expecting a lot more stress and squealing from the animals. But as you see, it's very calm here."

After a few minutes in the hall, I'm able to agree. It is remarkably calm here. For one thing, there aren't all that many animals. For another, the few that are here clearly aren't troubled by their new surroundings. But I have yet to see how Leiv's animals will react.

The NFSA's job is to check that the animals arrive here in good health. Are there any dead animals left in the trailer? Do the animals have any injuries or hernias? Are they limping or suspiciously dirty? The inspector hasn't noticed a single irregularity all day.

THE TRAILER HAS backed into the hall, the tailgate has been lowered, and out amble the pigs, sniffing the air. I wonder what they make of the scents here. But whatever they feel about the matter, it doesn't appear to stress them out. A slaughterhouse employee walks behind the pigs, slapping them gently on the rumps with a long plastic rod. At one end is a container that rattles when he shakes the rod. The noise is supposed to make the animals move, but it doesn't seem to be especially effective.

It isn't long before all the pigs are out of the trailer. None of them managed to sneak away, as other pigs have done before them. Among the most famous are two British pigs nicknamed Butch Cassidy and the Sundance Pig. The drama took place in 1998, when the herd they belonged to was sent to slaughter in the small British town of Malmesbury. Everything went to plan until the pigs were gathered outside the entrance to the slaughterhouse. That was when two pigs found a hole in the fence and managed to squeeze their way through. Before anyone knew it, the pair were in full flight from the slaughterhouse. It was as if they knew what lay ahead. They sped down to the banks of the River Avon, which ran just below the slaughter-house, hurled themselves into the icy water, and swam straight across. Once on the other side, they slipped into a copse and vanished. It was perfect British tabloid fodder. Once the Daily Mail got wind of the story, it wasn't long before the entire British press corps was on the case. The piggy escape artists became world famous almost overnight. Not that this persuaded their owner to have a change of heart: he insisted that the pigs must be tracked down and returned to the slaughterhouse. After all, they were his livelihood. However, after he received an undis-closed sum from the Daily Mail, the pigs were given a reprieve. In return, the newspaper acquired exclusive rights to tell their life story as the quest to find them continued.[19] After seven days on the run, the pigs were found in the garden of a local couple. Butch Cassidy and the Sundance Pig, originally destined to end their days in a slaughterhouse at the tender age of five months, ended up instead at a local rare breeds center, where they lived for thirteen and fourteen years, respectively. In 2009, the Daily Mail's coverage of their great escape was voted one of the best journalistic scoops in the history of the British press.[20]

BEFORE I KNOW IT, my own pigs have already made it a long way down the hall. I realize I need to find the executioner before he finds the pigs. Not to save them, of course; I just want to be there to witness the moment of their death.

At the end of the hall, the line of animals stops at a barrier beyond which lies something resembling an elevator. It's a gas chamber that lowers the animals beneath the floor and is then filled with concentrated CO_2. It's intended to stun the animals, but if the gas concentration is high enough, they'll die at that point. The screen outside the elevator shows that the concen-tration is currently set at 99 percent.

Behind the elevator, I catch a glimpse of the bloodbath that awaits them afterward. A man in orange oilskins wields a large knife. His oilskins are covered in blood. I feel relieved that none of the animals can see what's happening there. At the same time, I'm a bit stumped: Who's actually going to kill the pig? The man operating the gas chamber or the man with the knife?

It turns out that they don't even know themselves. The responsibility is hazy, fragmented, pulverized. As is any sense of guilt they might experience at the end of their working day. The principle is suspiciously reminiscent of a well-known practice when conducting executions. Who actually killed Norway's notorious wartime traitor Vidkun Quisling in 1945, for example? The firing squad was formed of ten soldiers who all fired simultaneously. But no one could possibly know which bullet proved fatal, so none of the soldiers had to leave the execution ground weighed down by the knowledge that "it was me." Similarly, in some U.S. states, multiple executioners are used to administer lethal injections, so no one knows who delivered the lethal dose.[21]

Slaughter, like war, mostly involves middlemen.

THE PIGS HAVE reached the elevator. They look fine. Nothing about their behavior suggests that they are scared, or "stressed" as we call it when speaking of livestock. No trembling, no squeals, no escape attempts.

"Are they yours?" asks a man who operates an electric gate that pushes the animals into the elevator. I nod in confirmation and watch the first five shove their way into the cubicle together. The door shuts, the elevator descends.

From here I can't see what happens, but beneath the ground, the pigs are hurled around in a net so that they lose their sense of direction at the same time as they lose consciousness. There is little time for reflection. I go around the back to the other side, where they are supposed to come out when the elevator returns to ground level. After three minutes, the gate opens and the floppy naked bodies tumble out, slapping down onto the conveyor belt in contorted poses. This is the beginning of the slaughter line.

The process is so streamlined, mechanical, and sterile, and the different stations so detached from the animals' lives, that I have difficulty imagining either animals or employees can experience this as trauma. And the fact is that practices in Norwegian slaughterhouses are different from those reportedly seen in the United States, Britain, Russia, or China. Here, the animals are not stunned senseless with a steel bolt before having their throats cut. Here, they are not driven into the reception area with electric prods. Here, there is no constant squealing and howling of desperate animals. Not these days, at any rate, although there's no doubt that the welfare of people and animals was more poorly safeguarded in the past. In 2004, the European Free Trade Association's Surveillance Authority, the ESA, published a highly critical report on the Norwegian slaughtering industry.[22] Some pigs were stunned with electrodes applied directly to the eye, some were scalded alive, while others were stabbed in the neck while still conscious. There must have been a thorough overhaul since that time. The most traumatic aspect of the slaughtering profession, as observed here, must be the extreme monotony of the work. The first man—yes, the slaughter line employees are all men—has just one task: to fasten a chain around one of the hind legs so that the pig can be hoisted toward the ceiling. The next man— the one in orange oilskins—also has a single task: to cut the animal's throat with his knife. He repeats this same movement hour after hour, day after day, for an entire week before switching stations to avoid repetitive strain injury. With a practiced gesture, he grabs a shoulder to hold the animal steady. Then he stabs it—a controlled, brief movement—straight in the throat. The blood gushes at once. It doesn't spray, it *falls*, as if from an upended bucket. Most of it ends up in the runnels in the floor, but a lot of it oozes out across the white tiles like a dark delta. The man in oilskins has a job like no other: profoundly macabre and totally legitimate at one and the same time.

LIFE IS DEFINITELY OVER for the first pig. I was there at its birth—perhaps it was even the one that reminded me of my own newborn son when I held it in my arms on my first visit to the farm. But this attempt to prod myself into sentimentality fails. I haven't got a clue which pig this is. They look the same, all of them, and I know that it doesn't really make any difference. They have remained remote from me even when I've tried to get close.

If life is over, the butchering process has only just begun. Now Leiv's pigs come sailing along, one after another, and all have their throats cut with an identical gesture. It takes only seconds for each animal to bleed out. After that they vanish—one by one—into a steam chamber, which scalds their outer skin, and are then placed in a drum that hurls their bodies around to flay off the last scraps of skin. Next the blood and muck is sprayed off the pigs before they're sent through a fiery furnace, where the rest of their bristle and loose skin is singed off.

So far, all these processes have merely served to prepare the carcasses. Now the butchering proper starts. On a long bridge just beneath the ceiling, the butchers stand in line, dressed in white clothing and blue plastic aprons. They receive the carcasses and each in turn performs his specialized task. The first makes a circular incision around the animal's anus. Hour after hour, day after day, he does nothing but make this circular movement that loosens the rectum from the rest of the carcass. That prepares the ground for the next person, who splits open the belly. The glistening mass of intestines and bladder oozes out almost by itself. The weight of the offal makes the job of dealing with it the most arduous part of the whole butchering process. When the belly is empty, it's time to move on to the organs. The next person cuts out lungs, heart, and liver in a single bundle, while another cuts out the kidneys. The livers will be made into pâté, while the other organs will be used in the fur industry as fodder for foxes and minks. After this, the pigs are sent through a mechanical saw that splits their carcasses lengthwise, from tail to snout. The split skulls are separated from the carcass and thrown into trays on the floor, where three people strip them of ears, tongues, and cheek muscles. The brains are left. Next the headless carcasses pass on to two inspectors from the NFSA, who inspect them for injuries, tumors, and parasites. After that, the long cadavers are dispatched to an enormous cold-storage facility, where they will be left to hang for a day or two before undergoing a final physical and conceptual deconstruction that will spare any of us from having to think about the animal as we eat it. The carcasses are quartered, sawn, and trimmed before being stripped of muscle mass and fat. Anything that doesn't end up as ham, chops, ham hocks, fillets, rib sirloin, and bacon is ground and kneaded into minced meat and forcemeat for use in sausages and pâté. The trotters are boiled down for gelatin while other bones are ground into meal. Finally, the last unusable offcuts of fiber, bone, and soft tissue are sent to a protein company, which will wring out the last remaining drops of fat and mix them into a fresh batch of feed concentrate, thereby closing the circle. This liquid feed will slosh down into the troughs of a new generation of slaughter pigs, which will be fattened up using the residual fat of their forebears.

SOMETHING HAPPENS as I follow the split carcasses through the enormous hall, where hundreds of animals already hang. The steam that swirls around the hall, saturated with the smell of freshly butchered pork, seems to erase my sense of myself as a pig tender. And just like that, a mindset that has lain dormant for months is reactivated. Only as I regard these body parts that are now defined as meat rather than animals do I begin to wonder what purpose their wretched lives have really served, as if gaining distance from the animals and the work has made the situation clearer. And that provokes a disturbing thought that would be unwelcome to many in this industry: a dimly lit piggery is (unfortunately) not the place to see the great connections. As with so many other things in life, when you focus too closely on something, it isn't easy to tell what you're looking at.

In the piggery, the physical work absorbs you and the animals are simply a pink mass you have to work around in order to do your job. How else can I explain why, after nearly six months of regular participation in the daily life of a piggery, I am forced to accept that I have failed in my goal of getting to know a pig? That I have never managed to achieve any real contact. That I have, in fact, opted to spend my time in the piggery on the pig farmer's terms.

Now, as I watch the slaughterhouse employees shove the dangling pigs farther down the cold-storage facility, and observe the seemingly endless stream of newly split carcasses, another thought starts to haunt me: at the end of 2018, more than 5.7 million pounds of unsold pork were held in cold-storage facilities across Norway.[23] That's almost a tenth of the level reported in the United States in November of the same year, incidentally—remarkable considering that the U.S. population is more than fifty times that of Norway.[24] It also adds up to more than thirty thousand pigs: thirty thousand lived lives for which no market could be found. That's equivalent in number to every single animal produced at a farm like Leiv's over a period of thirty years. So I am pained but compelled to ask: What, in the end, has been the purpose of this pig-tending work? What has been the purpose of these lives—lives that I must surely, at last, be allowed to describe as *woeful*? The fact that the minor pork-producing nation of Norway brings tens of thousands of intelligent creatures into the world to live pointless and potentially painful lives without any purpose whatsoever—surely *that* is a great animal tragedy.

AND BY THE WAY, what did John Berger mean in "Why Look at Animals?" when he wrote that our livestock was both worshipped and sacrificed in previous times? He doesn't tell us much about it, other than to say that the farmer looked the animals in the eye and valued the individual. I don't know how many of these pigs I've looked in the eye, but I do know it wasn't many. From time to time, I had a certain amount of contact with one sow, and I had some dealings with a few of the piglets when they were at their smallest. But I found that, shockingly soon, you stop relating to slaughter pigs at the individual level unless they're injured or in need of some other assistance from the person tending them. Based on my own experience, I can only conclude that almost no slaughter pigs in Norway are "worshipped" in the way Berger describes.

In this sense, I have failed to win back my dignity as a consumer of industrial meat.

At the same time, though, it's worth asking: What on earth does it mean if a person *has* looked a pig in the eye? What is the pig supposed to get out of it?

In the rare cases where pigs live outside, at a distance from the farmer and thoroughly absorbed in their natural drives, it may not be so important. The same can be said for most sheep as well as many cows, which spend part of their time outdoors and part in fully mechanized cowsheds, where the farmer no longer needs to clean, milk, or actively feed them. But that isn't true for 99.8 percent of the roughly 1.5 billion pigs that are sent to abattoirs worldwide.[25] For pigs that will never see the light of day, that have less than three square feet of a—usually concrete—floor at their disposal; for pigs that are deprived of any mental stimulation and are at the mercy of the farmers' shifting moods as they shove their way through the animals to scrape the floor clean of muck and urine-soaked wood shavings. For these animals, perhaps it may mean something to be looked in the eye. For them, eye contact may serve to protect them against the injustice that we know goes on in these places.

"What makes eye contact special?" asked Japanese psychologist and neuroscientist Takahiko Koike in a 2019 study. When we look another being in the eye, the emotional centers in our brain are activated, he concludes.[26] We build empathy. We wish them well.

Epilogue

WHILE I WAS WRITING this book in 2020, two major crises erupted in the world: one afflicting humans, the other, pigs. Both species were struck by a raging virus; both suffered fevers and coughs; and while travel restrictions and curfews kept people apart, wildlife fences set up along national borders kept contagious wild boars away from domestic herds.

At that time, no one knew how the coronavirus pandemic or African swine fever would play out, but what we did know about ASF was this: it killed around a quarter of the entire global population of domestic pigs. The disease, which spread from Africa to Georgia in 2007 and exploded in China in 2018, is considered one of the worst livestock pandemics ever seen.

Pigs' deaths are not, in themselves, liable to cause a stir. But while it's difficult to say which fate is worse for them—ASF or the butcher's knife—it's clear which is worse for the countries most affected. China, which was home to half of all the world's domestic pigs until the ASF outbreak, may have lost as many as 50 percent of them. This didn't just disrupt food provision in a country where an increasing share of the calorie intake is based on animal protein; the massive political, economic, and social repercussions of ASF have been described as "no less devastating than a war." Millions of people were left without a livelihood, and China itself calculated that the disease cost it one trillion yuan (roughly US$141 billion) between August 2018 and September 2019.[1]

If it weren't for all the innocent people affected by the crisis, it would be tempting to say that this served the Chinese authorities right, because it's hard not to see the parallels between the ASF outbreak and the early stages of the COVID-19 pandemic in 2019. In an attempt to downplay the scale of the ASF outbreak, the government engaged in systematic misreporting, did too little to alert people as contagion spread, and—once the crisis was inescapable—ordered people to keep quiet about it.[2] Yet there is one crucial difference between the two: while China managed to stem the tide of the coronavirus epidemic swiftly and effectively once it put its mind to it, displaying *apparent* openness to the outside world, ASF remains shrouded in bureaucratic secrecy, which makes it hard to grasp both the scope of the crisis and the will to halt it.[3]

In the meantime, wild boars—the source of contagion—are breeding at record rates in Europe. They're establishing themselves in Norway for the first time in a millennium and are invading towns and settlements across the entire continent, where they eat crops, destroy infrastructure, and—most importantly for now—risk killing our domestic pigs. Never before has the wild boar been so clearly defined as a pest in Europe, and many preventive measures have been introduced: the hunting season has been extended, snipers pick the boars off from helicopters, and fodder laced with poison or contraceptives has been set out at feeding stations. But nothing seems to work.

There are many good reasons for keeping wild boar populations down. All that it would take to trigger an outbreak in Norway, for example, would be for one truck driver from an affected country to discard a contaminated ham sandwich at a rest stop. Yet this conflict between wild boars and domestic pigs—in which our livestock outranks wild populations—illustrates precisely what a lot of people think is wrong with the world: whenever culture trumps nature, there are always unforeseen consequences that we sorely regret. Nowadays, for example, many in the Western world wish that the wet markets of Southeast Asia had never existed, that bats had never been traded, or that the scales of the pangolin (the animal suspected to have served as the intermediate host between bats and humans at the outbreak of the pandemic) had never been a sought-after ingredient in traditional Chinese medicine. Yet as we gawp and shudder over pictures of gutted snakes, flambéed monkeys, and peculiar pangolins in tiny cages, we rarely consider that the meat on our own plates is another facet of the same problem. The fact is that if we compared how many human deaths have been caused by viral outbreaks linked to wild and domesticated animals, respectively, our livestock would probably win. And one of the animals that has cost us the most lives is the pig.

Since the early twentieth century alone, *Sus scrofa domesticus* may have contributed to the deaths of millions of people, and it could be that the worst is yet to come.

THE NATURAL STARTING POINT for illustrating the dangers posed by pigs is another group of animals entirely: birds. At around the same time as COVID-19 broke out in Hubei, there was an outbreak of avian flu among the chicken populations in the same province. Suddenly, the Chinese were simultaneously struck by three viruses caused by the animals around them. Avian flu is the most dangerous influenza virus we know of, with a potential fatality rate of 60 percent. Luckily, however, it doesn't normally infect humans, nor can it be transmitted from one person to another and cause an epidemic. Consequently, there have been only a few, isolated human fatalities from avian flu. It's something of a paradox, really, since avian flu is the virus that caused the deadliest pandemic the world has ever seen—the so-called Spanish influenza of 1918.

No one has so far been able to say for sure how this could happen, but there are two likely scenarios. One is that an avian flu virus then in circulation mutated or altered into a form that was better adapted to humans. Another—equally likely—theory involves the pig.

First, let's deal with the technical side of things: when a virus invades a body, it attaches itself to a cell. For that to happen, the cell must have a receptor (a kind of anchor) that is adapted to the virus. If the virus and the cell don't match, the virus will never be able to exploit the new individual it has come into contact with as a host. As a species, the pig is unique in having two different types of receptors that are targeted by viruses. One enables it to carry viruses from humans or other mammals, and the other, to carry viruses from birds.

This brings us back to the theory that the pig caused the 1918 flu. When a pig is infected with different types of virus, it can act as a kind of "mixing vessel," producing new and highly potent viral strains. For example, it could produce an avian flu strain with traits that allowed it to bind to a human cell. That means the pig can become the necessary intermediary between birds and humans. Put another way: it's reasonably likely that the pig was the pangolin of the 1918 influenza epidemic.[4]

If that proves to have been the actual scenario, the pig may—in that case alone—have played a key role in wiping out more than fifty million people, or 2 percent of the global population, in 1918. Based on the current global population, the same percentage would amount to around 150 million human lives today. As if that weren't enough, this same mechanism of transmission from birds to pigs to humans is thought to have been responsible for the outbreak of two minor pandemics in 1957 and 1968. For anyone finding it hard to grasp the gloomy scenario that this implies, a 2008 research paper in the *Journal of Molecular and Genetic Medicine* makes it crystal clear: "[A]n avian influenza virus transmitted via pigs to humans poses a significant risk to cause a new influenza pandemic, possibly on the disturbing scale of the human influenza pandemic experienced during 1918–1920."[5]

OF COURSE THE PIG is quite capable of posing a viral threat to us without birds, as we found in 2009. In the early part of that year, several people in the Mexican state of Veracruz were hospitalized with severe influenza symptoms. It rapidly became clear to the Mexican authorities that the country was facing an epidemic. Mexico City locked down, but the epidemic was unstoppable. Soon several people in California and Texas fell ill with the same disease. Microbiologists in U.S. laboratories quickly concluded that the disease was caused by the HINI virus, also known as swine flu. Although it had been circulating among humans for a long time, this was a hitherto unseen variant; the source of contagion was traced back to a herd of pigs in the small Mexican town of La Gloria in 2008.[6]

In June 2009, the World Health Organization stopped counting cases, and swine flu was officially declared the first pandemic of the twenty-first century. One year on, between 11 and 21 percent of the global population had been infected— that's between 700 million and 1.4 billion people. We don't know for sure how many people died of swine flu, but some of the estimates place the number at around 575,000.[7]

Although the mortality rate wasn't especially high compared with Spanish influenza, swine flu was more than dramatic enough, because, like the 1918 pandemic, it mostly affected young people. In an ordinary flu epidemic, 90 percent of fatalities are among people aged sixty-five and older. In the case of both swine flu and Spanish influenza, 80 percent of those who died were between eighteen and sixty-five years old. Everything was topsy-turvy—and all the more tragic for it.

Since that pandemic ended in 2010, there hasn't been much talk on the topic of pigs and viral threats. However, there is every reason to discuss it: in the same year as swine flu hit, some pigs in the Philippines were also found to be carrying the Reston ebolavirus.[8] What's more, it had been transmitted to six farmers who had come into contact with the pigs. Fortunately, the Reston virus is harmless to humans—unlike the more infamous Zaire virus, which has a mortality rate of up to 90 percent. Not that this fact reassured the scientists much. As long as the Reston virus could occur in pigs, two terrifying scenarios were possible: that the harmless ebolavirus could mutate into a deadlier variant; or that pigs could become infected with the Zaire ebolavirus and transmit it to people—as monkeys, for example, have been known to do.

The credibility of these scenarios was bolstered in 2011, when researchers conducting an experiment in a Canadian laboratory found that the Zaire ebolavirus *could* be transmitted to pigs, which could then transmit it among themselves.[9] However, the biggest question of all remained unanswered. Could pigs transmit the virus to humans and cause an epidemic?

Confirmation that the scientists were onto something major—and dangerous—came the following year, when some monkeys in Africa became infected with the Zaire ebolavirus, transmitted by pigs.[10] The implication was clear to all. If the disease could be transmitted from pigs to monkeys, pigs could probably become a new source of a deadly Ebola epidemic in humans. Tension was therefore high in 2017 when a fresh Ebola outbreak occurred in the Democratic Republic of the Congo: had the scientists' predictions materialized?

The answer was quick to come. Around the time of the outbreak, several dead pigs were found in the same region, apparently killed by an aggressive viral infection. Then reports came in that the first person to have been infected was a wild boar hunter, who had become sick shortly after a hunting trip.

Tracing the source of contagion proved challenging, because the man hadn't just brought back a dead boar from the bush; he also had a monkey, which he'd sold at a local market. In other words, there were two possible sources of infection for the same person. After much effort, the scientists had to accept that neither the monkey nor the boar carcass were traceable. Even so, they concluded that the wild boar rather than the monkey had been the source.[11]

So far, there is no indication that domestic pigs have ever transmitted the deadly ebolavirus to humans. Yet it's clear that the growing swine industry established in several African countries with Chinese assistance over recent years may be a new health risk in sub-Saharan Africa.

IT'S DIFFICULT NOT TO SEE an epic aspect in current events: animals are striking back against human exploitation—their microbes the messengers that warn us of what lies ahead. Of course this can easily be written off as anthropomorphic hyperbole. We could also object that we live in an age intoxicated by a new sensitivity to nature, and that we humans tend to find the connections we are looking for. After all, diseases have been transmitted between humans and animals throughout history.

Yet if we simply brush aside the disturbing aspects of animal husbandry, we can easily start to sound like those who refuse to believe we can do anything about climate change. Just as it is possible to reduce greenhouse gas emissions, we *can* also reduce the risk of being killed by microbes borne by our livestock. One thing at least is certain: if we humans exploited the omnivorous trait we share with the pig to focus our appetite on plants rather than meat, we wouldn't suffer so many epidemics. And perhaps that would also be the most fitting way to really do honor to the pig. The animal that truly is a little like us.

Acknowledgments

FIRST OF ALL, a huge thanks to Leiv and Eirik Rugland. You opened the door to your piggery even though you didn't know what it would lead to. You are brave, honorable, hardworking people. Thank you also to the editor-in-chief at Spartacus, Nina Selvik, for her patience and belief in my project.

During my work on the book, numerous people have helped out, with rewarding conversations and useful input, manuscript reading, and other practical and psychological support. In more or less random order, they are: Kristian Ellingsen-Dalskau, Carl Andreas Grøntvedt, and Irene Ørpetveit at the Norwegian Veterinary Institute; Inger Lise Andersen and Odd Vangen at the Norwegian University of Life Sciences; Jostein Starrfelt at the Norwegian Scientific Committee for Food and Environment, University of Oslo; Erling Sehested at Norsvin; Aurora Brønstad at the Laboratory Animal Facility, University of Bergen; Ståle Julius Olsen, Terje Aukland, Jørgen Smeby, Andreas Kostøl, and Ådne Trodahl. I would also like to thank the management of Jæren Museum and Science Factory in Sandnes for the loan of office space. Thanks to my parents for being super grandparents during the final phase of writing. Finally, thanks to Ingrid, Hedvig, Solveig, and Askild. For existing—and for hanging in there while I was writing this book.

Notes

Prologue

1 The episode is cited, among others, in Fabre-Vassas, *Singular Beast*, 126, and Evans, *Criminal Prosecution*, 140.

1. An Impossible Meeting

1 Aubert, "Earliest Hunting Scene"; Ferreira, "Pig Painting."

2 Cited in Humes, *Wit & Wisdom of Winston Churchill*, 6.

3 *Nationen*, "Flere griser enn mennesker i Rogaland."

4 Pliny the Elder, *Natural History*, vol. 8, chap. 77.

5 Kirkland and Cohen, "Lisa the Vegetarian," cited in Essig, *Lesser Beasts*, 9.

6 Our World in Data, "Per Capita Meat Consumption."

7 Sanders, "Global Pig Slaughter Statistics."

8 Our World in Data, "Per Capita Meat Consumption."

9 Berger, *Why Look at Animals?*, 12–37.

10 Pollan, "An Animal's Place."

11 Shanker, "Organic Pork."

12 Statistics Norway, "Rogaland."

13 Tangvald-Pedersen, "Ingen tegn til grisekrise."

14 Shimmings, "Kan vi redde storspoven?"

2. Eating Like a Pig

1 Gould, "An Essay on a Pig Roast."

2 Gould, "An Essay on a Pig Roast."

3 Osborn, "Hesperopithecus." The anthropoid ape was named after the geologist who found the tooth, Harold Cook.

4 *New York Times*, 1922, cited in Essig, *Lesser Beasts*, 16.

5 Cited in Gould, "An Essay on a Pig Roast."

6 Gregory, "*Hesperopithecus*."
7 Quoted in Wolf and Mellett, "The Role of 'Nebraska Man.'"
8 Gould, "An Essay on a Pig Roast," 443.
9 Zielinski, "Are Humans an Invasive Species?"
10 USDA, "Feral Swine Damage."
11 Aiello and Wheeler, "Expensive-Tissue Hypothesis."
12 Navarrete, van Schaik, and Isler, "Energetics and the Evolution of the Human Brain."
13 Rozin, "Selection of Foods."
14 Hellekant and Danilova, "Taste in Domestic Pig."
15 Zaraska, *Meathooked*, 35–36.
16 Rozin, "Selection of Foods."
17 Watson, *The Whole Hog*, 33.
18 Pollan, *Omnivore's Dilemma*.
19 Wrangham, *Catching Fire*.
20 Zaraska, *Meathooked*, 37.
21 Wrangham, *Catching Fire*.

3. Quarantine
1 Moellering, "MRSA."
2 Fleming, "Penicillin."
3 Levy, *Antibiotic Paradox*, 132–33.
4 Interagency Coordination Group on Antimicrobial Resistance, "No Time to Wait."
5 Ogle, *In Meat We Trust*.
6 Hughes and Heritage, "Antibiotic Growth Promoters."
7 Olsvik, "Fremtiden vil fordømme oss."
8 Kavanagh, "Control of MSSA and MRSA."
9 Schultz et al., "Spread of LA-MRSA."

10 Van Boekel et al., "Antimicrobial Resistance."

4. The First Encounter
1 Hancox, "The Unstoppable Rise of Veganism."
2 Animalia, "Kjøttets tilstand 2019," 119.
3 Animalia, "Kjøttets tilstand 2019," 119.
4 Reuters, "Seven Stories of Sows."
5 Carroll, *Alice's Adventures in Wonderland*, 48.
6 Jenkins, "I Accidentally Bought a Giant Pig."

5. The Animal That Domesticated Itself
1 Bang-Andersen, *Svarthålå på Viste*.
2 Diamond, *Guns, Germs and Steel*, 39.
3 Aubert, "Earliest Hunting Scene."
4 Ferreira, "Pig Painting."
5 Diamond, *Guns, Germs and Steel*, 160.
6 Clutton-Brock, *Animals as Domesticates*, 22–23.
7 Galton, "Domestication of Animals."
8 Clutton-Brock, *Animals as Domesticates*, 177–83.
9 Diamond, *Guns, Germs and Steel*.
10 Villarias, "Dutch Farm."
11 Gregory, "Hallan Cemi Journal."
12 Rosenberg et al., "Hallan Çemi Tepesi"; Rosenberg

et al., "Hallan Çemi, Pig Husbandry."

13 Rosenberg et al., "Hallan Çemi, Pig Husbandry."

14 Clutton-Brock, *Animals as Domesticates*, 90.

15 Albarella, Dobney, and Rowley-Conwy, "Domestication of the Pig," 209–27.

16 Genesis 1:26 (New King James Bible).

6. Not on the Same Wavelength

1 IPCC, "Climate Change and Land."

2 Gerber et al., *Tackling Climate Change Through Livestock*; IPCC, "Climate Change 2014."

3 Garnett et al., "Grazed and Confused?"

4 Miljødirektoratet, "Klimastatus."

5 Gu and Thukral, "Soy Source"; Nepstad, "Sustainable Soy in China."

6 Moskin et al., "Your Questions About Food and Climate Change."

7 *Stavanger Aftenblad*, "Ingen dyr skaper."

8 Cited in Agamben, *The Open*, 40.

9 *Newsweek*, "Pot-Sniffing Pig."

7. The Forbidden Animal

1 Leviticus 11:8.

2 Quran 2:173 (Saheeh International translation).

3 Harris, *Sacred Cow*, 69.

4 Harris, *Sacred Cow*, 70.

5 CDC, "Trichinellosis FAQs"; Sharma et al., "High Prevalence."

6 Douglas, *Purity and Danger*.

7 Leviticus 11:2-3.

8 Douglas, *Purity and Danger*, Routledge Classics edition, xvi.

9 Redding, "The Pig and the Chicken."

10 Redding, "The Pig and the Chicken."

11 Harris, *Cows, Pigs, Wars, and Witches*.

12 Redding, "Status and Diet at the Workers' Town."

13 Zeder, "Of Kings and Shepherds," 175–91.

14 Essig, *Lesser Beasts*, 48–49.

15 Harris, *Sacred Cow*, 75–77.

16 Scurlock, "Animal Sacrifice," 393.

17 Herodotus, *The History*, 151.

18 Heilman, "57% of US Jews Eat Pork."

19 Shelach, *Praise the Lard*.

20 Essig, *Lesser Beasts*, 61.

21 Luther, *Works*, vol. 47, 212.

22 Quoted in Shelach, *Praise the Lard*.

23 Quoted in Shelach, *Praise the Lard*.

24 Rosen-Zvi, "'Pigs in Space.'"

25 Quoted in Shelach, *Praise the Lard*.

8. "Indeed, Allah Is Forgiving and Merciful"

1 Reilly, "Trump Praises Fake Story."

2 Quoted in Berenson, "Donald Trump's Pig's Blood Slander."

3 Tronstad, "Grisefett mot selvmordsbombere."

4 Associated Press, "UN Panel."

5 Shih and Kang, "Muslims Forced."

6 *Guardian*, "Inmates Tell of Abu Ghraib Abuse."

7 Ighoubah, "FBI jakter"; Møllen, "Slipper straff i grisehode-saken."

8 *Telegraph*, "Far-Right Austrian Leader Criticised."

9 Sørgjerd, "Høreradikal-provokatør og koranbrenner."

10 Tomter, "Listhaug vil ha mer gris."

11 TV2, "Første gang."

12 Quoted in Withnall, "Denmark Bans Halal."

13 Quran 2:173 (Saheeh International translation); Leviticus 11:45.

14 *Times of Israel*, "US-Born Soldier Tried for Eating Pork."

15 Quoted in Spry-Marqués, *Pig/Pork*, 166.

16 Luke 8:26–32; see also Matthew 8:28–32 and Mark 5:11.

17 Russell, *Why I Am Not a Christian*.

18 Quoted in Singer, *Animal Liberation*, 191.

19 Singer, *Animal Liberation*, 191.

20 John 1:29.

21 Mark 7:6.

22 Fabre-Vassas, *Singular Beast*.

9. Appetite and Aversion

1 Essig, *Lesser Beasts*, 86.

2 Apicius, *De Re Coquinaria*.

3 Myhrvold, "Marcus Garvius Apicius."

4 Plutarch, *Moralia*, 565.

5 Essig, *Lesser Beasts*, 73–74.

6 Beard, SPQR, 16.

7 Essig, *Lesser Beasts*, 80.

8 Henisch, *Fast and Feast*, 131.

9 Freedman, *Out of the East*, 38.

10 Freedman, *Out of the East*, 19.

11 Essig, *Lesser Beasts*, 95.

12 Essig, *Lesser Beasts*, 94.

13 Genesis 9:3–4.

14 Deuteronomy 12:23–24.

15 Houston, *Purity and Monotheism*, 145–46.

16 Ross, "The Riddle of the Scottish Pig."

17 Essig, *Lesser Beasts*, 95.

18 Essig, *Lesser Beasts*, 101.

19 Evans, *Criminal Prosecution*, 140.

20 Evans, *Criminal Prosecution*, 157.

21 Evans, *Criminal Prosecution*, 144–45.

22 Evans, *Criminal Prosecution*, 153.

23 Evans, *Criminal Prosecution*, 56.

24 Essig, *Lesser Beasts*, 109.

25 Essig, *Lesser Beasts*, 100.

10. Naked and Imprisoned

1 Smith, *Wealth of Nations*, 95.

2 Essig, *Lesser Beasts*, 113–14.

3 Dybesland, "Grisen."

4 Berge, *Svineavl*.

5 Dimery, "Chinese New Year."

6 Berge, *Svineavl*.

7 Berge, *Svineavl*.

8 Dybesland, "Grisen."

9 Løkeland-Stai and Lie, *Mellom bakkar*, 41.

10 USDA, "Hogs and Pigs," 21; National Pork Producers Council, "Pork Facts"; National Pork Board, "Quick

Facts," 94; USDA, "Meat Statistics Tables."

11 Miller, "Century of Progress."

12 Walsh, "Ending the War on Fat."

13 FAO, "Digestion, Absorption and Energy Value of Carbohydrates."

14 Ascherio et al., "Dietary Fat"; Spilde, "Da forskningen viste."

15 World Health Organization, "Reducing Free Sugars Intake."

16 Walsh, "Ending the War on Fat."

11. Against Nature

1 McClintock, "Menstrual Synchrony."

2 Sapolsky, "Human Behavioral Biology."

3 Poppick, "Invention of the Microscope."

4 Encyclopedia.com, "Leeuwenhoek, Antoni van."

5 Pain, "Ape-Man."

6 Pain, "Ape-Man."

7 Ombelet and van Robays, "Artificial Insemination."

8 Millett, Sexual Politics, 28.

9 Sharp, "The Null Case," 227.

10 Millett, Sexual Politics, 28.

11 Millett, Sexual Politics, 51–54.

12 Svineportalen, "Grundig stimulering."

13 Thomas, Man and the Natural World, 39.

14 DeMello, Animals and Society, 40.

15 Hopp, Sagaen om Gunnar, 89.

16 Hopp, Sagaen om Gunnar, 89.

17 Essig, Lesser Beasts, 67.

18 Oppian, Cynegetica, 145, cited in Salisbury, The Beast Within, 63.

19 Salisbury, The Beast Within, 63–64.

20 Salisbury, The Beast Within, 76–77.

21 Larson, Earliest Norwegian Laws.

22 Christian V's Norwegian Code, cited in Teige, "The Trial."

23 DeMello, Animals and Society, 40.

24 Liliequist, "Peasants Against Nature," 393-423.

25 Viskum, "Fortielse og straff."

26 Viskum, "Fortielse og straff."

27 Mortensen and Eilertsen, "Dyr misbrukes."

28 Norges Lover (The Laws of Norway), "Lov om dyrevelferd," para. 14c.

29 Jackman, "Is It Illegal."

30 Ege, "Nordmenn på sexferie."

31 Helljesen, "Glad for at seksuelt."

32 Sahl, "Dyre-Dan."

33 Helljesen, "Glad for at seksuelt."

12. The Human Model

1 Conner, "Galen's Analogy."

2 Gross, "Galen."

3 Gross, "Galen."

4 Guerrini, Experimenting, 16.

5 Guerrini, Experimenting, 18.

6 Corner, Anatomical Texts, 51.

7 Guerrini, Experimenting, 31.

8 Guerrini, Experimenting, 36.

9 Guerrini, Experimenting, 36.

10 Guerrini, Experimenting, 37.

11 McCarthy, "Hybrid Hypothesis."

12 Hewitt, "Chimp-Pig."
13 Watson et al., "Engineered Swine Models."
14 Lutwyche, The Pig, 31.
15 Hald and Aagaard, "Glemsomme."
16 Cooper et al., "Clinical Xenotransplantation."
17 Tena, "Xenotransplantation."
18 BBC, "Man Gets Genetically-Modified Pig Heart."
19 Bajaj, "Why Did the First Human."
20 Hayasaki, "Better Living."
21 Davis, "First Human-Monkey Chimeras."
22 Ansede, "Spanish Scientists."
23 Regalado, "Researchers."
24 Quoted in Regalado, "Researchers."
25 Farahany et al., "Ethics of Experimenting."
26 Chivers, "Tending a Fallen Marine."

13. Ugly Mug

1 Eco, On Ugliness, 427.
2 Gould, "A Biological Homage to Mickey Mouse."
3 Herzog, Some We Love, 39.
4 Lorenz, "Ganzheit und Teil."
5 Watson, The Whole Hog, 38.
6 BBC, "Russian Woman Eaten by Pigs."

14. Is Anybody Home?

1 Wittgenstein, Philosophical Investigations, 223.
2 Nagel, "What Is It Like to Be a Bat?"
3 Gould, "Sloth and Rapacity," 376.
4 Foster, Being a Beast, 205.
5 Homer, Odyssey, 139–49.
6 Plutarch, Moralia, vol. 12, 487–533.
7 Orwell, Animal Farm, 9.
8 Orwell, Animal Farm, 82.
9 Darwin, Expression of the Emotions.
10 de Waal, Are We Smart Enough, 41–43.
11 de Waal, Are We Smart Enough, 41–43.

15. Among Neurons and Neural Pathways

1 Morgen, Jane.
2 Griffin, Animal Awareness.
3 Estabrook, Pig Tales, 26–27.
4 Estabrook, Pig Tales, 26–27.
5 Associated Press, "Pigs Use Computers."
6 Estabrook, Pig Tales, 36.
7 Pig Progress, "Video Games."
8 Gallup, "Chimpanzees."
9 Darwin, Descent of Man, 5.
10 Cammaerts and Cammaerts, "Ants."
11 Koerth-Baker, "Mirror Test."
12 Broom et al., "Pigs Learn."
13 Callaghan et al., "Synchrony."
14 Woolfe, Want, and Siegal, "Signposts to Development."
15 Baron-Cohen, Leslie, and Frith, "Does the Autistic Child."
16 Premack and Woodruff, "Does the Chimpanzee."
17 Mendl, Held, and Byrne, "Pig Cognition."
18 Børresen, "Mennesket."
19 MacLean, Triune Brain.

20 Ohl, Arndt, and van der Staay, "Pathological Anxiety."

21 McMillan, *Mental Health*.

22 See de Waal, *Are We Smart Enough*, and Bekoff, *Emotional Lives of Animals*.

23 Coren, "Are Dogs More Intelligent."

24 Minervini et al., "Brain Mass."

25 Minervini et al., "Brain Mass."

26 Minervini et al., "Brain Mass."

27 Dyrevernalliansen, "Kyllingen Ross 308."

28 Dunbar, "Social Brain Hypothesis."

29 Minervini et al., "Brain Mass."

30 Schmidt, *Comparative Anatomy*, 115.

31 Mjellem, "Forståelsen."

32 Herculano-Houzel, "The Human Brain in Numbers."

33 Gibbens, "Are Dogs Smarter Than Cats?"

34 Ridgway et al., "Higher Neuron Densities" (dolphin); Herculano-Houzel and Kaas, "Gorilla and Orangutan Brains" (gorilla); Kaas, "Cortical Cell" (chimpanzee); Olkowicz et al., "Birds" (macaw); Haug, "Brain Sizes" (horse); Jardim-Messeder et al., "Dogs Have the Most Neurons" (dog).

35 Phillips, "Learning From Pig Brains."

36 Mortensen et al., "Quantitative Relationships."

37 Hippocrates, *Hippocrates*.

38 Bentham, *Works*, 143.

16. What We Talk About When We Talk About Suffering

1 Hørselshemmedes landsforbund, "Tinnitus," hlf.no/horsel/tinnitus.

2 Dagens medisin, "Ta kontroll over øresusen," January 14, 1999.

3 Singer, *Animal Liberation*.

4 Løkeland-Stai and Lie, *Mellom bakkar*, 41.

5 Løkeland-Stai and Lie, *Mellom bakkar*, 41.

6 Statista, "Dollar Sales Share of Pork in the United States in 2021, by Product Claim."

7 Animal Protection Index, api.worldanimalprotection.org.

17. Slaughter

1 Thomas, *Man and the Natural World*, 94.

2 Hardy, *Jude the Obscure*, 71.

3 Thomas, *Man and the Natural World*, 94.

4 Fitzgerald, "A Social History of the Slaughterhouse," 59.

5 Treimo, "Biffmedaljongens."

6 Vialles, *Animal to Edible*, 15–16.

7 Haugen, *Hjørnesteinen*, 9.

8 Fitzgerald, "A Social History of the Slaughterhouse," 59.

9 Vialles, *Animal to Edible*, 19.

10 Fitzgerald, "A Social History of the Slaughterhouse," 60.

11 Barrett, *Work and Community*.

12 Ford and Crowther, *My Life and Work*, 81.

13 Patterson, *Eternal Treblinka*.

14 Coetzee, *The Lives of Animals*, 53.

15 Patterson, "Animals, Slavery, and the Holocaust."

16 MacNair, *Perpetration-Induced Traumatic Stress*.

17 MacNair, *Perpetration-Induced Traumatic Stress*; see also Whiting and Marion, "Perpetration-Induced Traumatic Stress."

18 Wasley, Cook, and Jones, "Two Amputations a Week; Human Rights Watch, "'When We're Dead and Buried'"; Middleton, Reintjes, and Lopes, "Meat Plants."

19 Morris, "A Crackling Good Yarn."

20 Ponsford, "British Journalism's Greatest Ever Scoops."

21 Kevin Bonsor, "How Lethal Injection Works," Howstuffworks, people.howstuffworks.com/lethal-injection5.htm.

22 EFTA Surveillance Authority, "Final Report."

23 Løkeland-Stai and Lie, *Mellom bakkar*, 109.

24 USDA, "Cold Storage," 7.

25 World Economic Forum, "This Is How Many Animals We Eat Each Year."

26 Koike, "What Makes Eye Contact Special?"; see also Denworth, "Eye Contact."

Epilogue

1 Huang, "One Quarter of the World's Pigs."

2 Patton, "Before Corona."

3 Huang, "One Quarter of the World's Pigs."

4 Ma, Kahn, and Richt, "The Pig as a Mixing Vessel."

5 Ma, Kahn, and Richt, "The Pig as a Mixing Vessel."

6 Smith et al., "2009 Swine-Origin HINI Influenza A Epidemic."

7 CDC, "2009 HINI Pandemic Mortality."

8 Borrell, "Swine Ebola."

9 Borrell, "Swine Ebola."

10 Kupferschmidt and Cohen, "Congo's New Ebola Outbreak."

11 Nsio et al., "2017 Outbreak of Ebola."

Bibliography

Agamben, Giorgio. *The Open: Man and Animal*. Redwood City, CA: Stanford University Press, 2003.

Aiello, Leslie C., and Peter Wheeler. "The Expensive-Tissue Hypothesis: The Brain and the Digestive System in Human and Primate Evolution." *Current Anthropology* 36, no. 2 (April 1995): 199–221.

Albarella, Umberto, Keith Dobney, and Peter Rowley-Conwy. "The Domestication of the Pig." In *Documenting Domestication: New Genetic and Archaeological Paradigms*, edited by Melinda A. Zeder. Berkeley: University of California Press, 2006.

Animalia. "Kjøttets tilstand 2019: Status i norsk kjøtt- og eggproduksjon." October 31, 2019.

Ansede, Manuel. "Spanish Scientists Create Human-Monkey Chimeras in China." *El País*, July 31, 2019.

Apicius. *De Re Coquinaria*. Chicago: Walter M. Hill, 1936.

Ascherio, A., et al. "Dietary Fat and Risk for Coronary Heart Disease in Men: Cohort Follow Up Study in the United States." *British Medical Journal* 313, no. 7049 (1996): 84–90.

Associated Press. "Pigs Use Computers to Share Feelings." April 15, 1998.

Associated Press. "UN Panel Concerned at Reported Chinese Detention of Uighurs." August 10, 2018.

Aubert, Maxime. "Earliest Hunting Scene in Prehistoric Art." *Nature* 576 (2019): 442–45.

Bajaj, Simar. "Why Did the First Human Patient to Receive a Pig Heart Transplant Die?" *Smithsonian Magazine*, July 14, 2022.

Bang-Andersen, Sveinung. *Svarthålå på Viste—boplass i 6000 år*. Stavanger, Norway: Museum of Archeology in Stavanger, 1983.

Baron-Cohen, Simon, Alan M. Leslie, and Uta Frith. "Does the Autistic Child Have a 'Theory of Mind'?" *Cognition* 21, no. 1 (1985): 37–46.

Barrett, James R. *Work and Community in the Jungle: Chicago's Packinghouse Workers 1894–1922*. Champaign, IL: University of Illinois Press, 2002.

BBC. "Man Gets Genetically-Modified Pig Heart in World-First Transplant." January 11, 2022.

BBC. "Russian Woman Eaten by Pigs." February 7, 2019.

Beard, Mary. SPQR: *A History of Ancient Rome*. London: Profile Books, 2015.

Bekoff, Marc. *The Emotional Lives of Animals: A Leading Scientist Explores Animal Joy, Sorrow, and Empathy—and Why They Matter*. Novato, CA: New World Library, 2008.

Bentham, Jeremy. *The Works of Jeremy Bentham, Now First Collected*. Edinburgh: W. Tait, 1838.

Berenson, Tessa. "The Real Story Behind Donald Trump's Pig's Blood Slander." *Time*, February 24, 2016.

Berge, Sverre. *Svineavl*. Oslo: Grøndahl & Søn, 1948.

Berger, John. *Why Look at Animals?* London: Penguin, 2009.

Borrell, Brendan. "Swine Ebola." *Scientific American*, September 1, 2009.

Børresen, Bergljot. "Menneskets medfødte forutsetninger som vertskap for produksjonsdyr." In *Dyreetikk*, edited by Andreas Føllesdal. Oslo: Fagbokforlaget, 2000.

Brillat-Savarin, Jean Anthelme. *The Physiology of Taste: Or Meditations on Transcendental Gastronomy*. Translated by M. F. K. Fisher. New York: Everyman's Library, 2009.

Broom, Donald M., Hilana dos Santos Sena Brunel, and Kiera L. Moynihan. "Pigs Learn What a Mirror Image Represents and Use It to Obtain Information." *Animal Behaviour* 78, no. 5 (2009): 1037–41.

Callaghan, Tara, et al. "Synchrony in the Onset of Mental-State Reasoning: Evidence From Five Cultures." *Psychological Science* 16, no. 5 (2005): 378–84.

Cammaerts, Marie-Claire, and Roger Cammaerts. "Are Ants (Hymenoptera, Formicidae) Capable of Self Recognition?" *Journal of Science* 5, no. 7 (2015): 521–32.

Carroll, Lewis. *Alice's Adventures in Wonderland and Through the Looking Glass*. London: Penguin, 2010.

CDC (Centers for Disease Control and Prevention). "First Global Estimates of 2009 H1N1 Pandemic Mortality Released by CDC-Led Collaboration." June 25, 2012.

CDC. "Trichinellosis FAQs." Last updated September 2020.

Chivers, C. J. "Tending a Fallen Marine, With Skill, Prayer and Fury." *New York Times*, November 2, 2006.

Clutton-Brock, Juliet. *Animals as Domesticates: A World View Through History.* East Lansing, MI: Michigan State University Press, 2012.

Clutton-Brock, Juliet. *A Natural History of Domesticated Mammals.* Cambridge: Cambridge University Press, 1999.

Coetzee, J. M. *The Lives of Animals.* Princeton, NJ: Princeton University Press, 1999.

Conner, Annastasia. "Galen's Analogy: Animal Experimentation and Anatomy in the Second Century C.E." *Anthós* 8, no. 1 (2017): 118–45.

Cooper, David K. C., et al. "A Brief History of Clinical Xenotransplantation." *International Journal of Surgery* 23 (2015): 205–10.

Coren, Stanley. "Are Dogs More Intelligent Than Cats?" *Psychology Today*, December 3, 2010.

Corner, George W. *Anatomical Texts of the Earlier Middle Ages.* Washington: Carnegie Institution of Washington, 1927.

Darwin, Charles. *The Descent of Man: The Concise Edition.* London: Plume, 2007.

Darwin, Charles. *The Expression of the Emotions in Man and Animals.* London: John Murray, 1872.

Darwin, Charles. *On the Origin of Species.* Ware, UK: Wordsworth Editions, 1998.

Davis, Nicola. "The First Human-Monkey Chimeras Raises Concern Among Scientists." *Guardian*, August 3, 2019.

DeMello, Marge. *Animals and Society: An Introduction to Human-Animal Studies.* New York: Columbia University Press, 2012.

Denworth, Lydia. "How Eye Contact Prepares the Brain to Connect." *Psychology Today*, February 25, 2019.

de Waal, Frans. *Are We Smart Enough to Know How Smart Animals Are?* New York: W. W. Norton, 2017.

Diamond, Jared. *Guns, Germs and Steel: The Fates of Human Societies.* New York: W. W. Norton, 1997.

Dimery, Rob. "Chinese New Year: 8 Fantastic Pig Records to Celebrate the Year of the Pig." Guinness World Records, February 4, 2019.

Douglas, Mary. *Purity and Danger: An Analysis of Concepts of Pollution and Taboo.* Routledge and Kegan Paul, London, 1966; Routledge Classics, London, 2002.

Dunbar, Robin. "The Social Brain Hypothesis." *Evolutionary Anthropology* 6, no. 5 (1998): 178–90.

Dybesland, Svein Bertil. "Grisen og det jærske jordbruket." Jær Museum, 2015.

Dyrevernalliansen. "Kyllingen Ross 308 må fases ut." June 10, 2020.

Eco, Umberto. *On Ugliness*. Translated by Alastair McEwen. New York: Rizzoli, 2018.

EFTA (European Free Trade Association) Surveillance Authority. "Final Report From a Mission Carried Out by the EFTA Surveillance Authority to Norway From 24 to 28 November 2003." March 16, 2004.

Ege, Rune Thomas. "Nordmenn på sexferie til danske dyrebordeller." VG, September 13, 2006.

Encyclopedia.com. "Leeuwenhoek, Antoni van." *Complete Dictionary of Scientific Biography*.

Essig, Mark. *Lesser Beasts: A Snout-to-Tail History of the Humble Pig*. New York: Basic Books, 2014.

Estabrook, Barry. *Pig Tales: An Omnivore's Quest for Sustainable Meat*. New York: W. W. Norton, 2015.

Evans, E. P. *The Criminal Prosecution and Capital Punishment of Animals*. New York: E. P. Dutton, 1906.

Fabre-Vassas, Claudine. *The Singular Beast*. Translated by Carol Volk. New York: Columbia University Press, 1997.

FAO (Food and Agriculture Organization of the United Nations). "Digestion, Absorption and Energy Value of Carbohydrates." In *Carbohydrates in Human Nutrition* (FAO Food and Nutrition Paper 66). Rome: FAO, 1998.

Farahany, Nita A., et al. "The Ethics of Experimenting With Human Brain Tissue." *Nature*, 556 (2018): 429–32.

Fellini, Federico, dir. *Satyricon*. Produzioni Europee Associati, 1969.

Ferreira, Becky. "Pig Painting May Be World's Oldest Cave Art Yet, Archaeologists Say." *New York Times*, January 13, 2021.

Fitzgerald, Amy. "A Social History of the Slaughterhouse: From Inception to Contemporary Implications." *Human Ecology Review* 17, no. 1 (2010): 58–69.

Fitzgerald, Amy, Linda Kalof, and Thomas Dietz. "Slaughterhouses and Increased Crime Rates: An Empirical Analysis of the Spillover From 'The Jungle' Into the Surrounding Community." *Sage Journals: Organization and Environment* 22, no. 2 (2009): 158–84.

Fleming, Alexander. "Penicillin." Nobel Lecture, December 11, 1945.

Ford, Henry, and Samuel Crowther. *My Life and Work*. New York: Garden City Publishing, 1922.

Foster, Charles. *Being a Beast: Adventures Across the Species Divide*. London: Profile, 2016.

Freedman, Paul. *Out of the East: Spices and the Medieval Imagination*. New Haven, CT: Yale University Press, 2008.

Gallup, Gordon, Jr. "Chimpanzees: Self Recognition." *Science* 167, no. 3914 (1970): 86–87.

Galton, Francis. "The First Steps Towards the Domestication of Animals," *Transactions of the Ethnological Society of London* 3 (1865): 122–38.

Garnett, Tara, et al. "Grazed and Confused? Ruminating on Cattle, Grazing Systems, Methane, Nitrous Oxide, the Soil Carbon Sequestration Question—and What It All Means for Greenhouse Gas Emissions." Food Climate Research Network, University of Oxford, October 1, 2017.

Gerber, P. J., et al. *Tackling Climate Change Through Livestock: A Global Assessment of Emissions and Mitigating Opportunities.* Rome: Food and Agriculture Organization of the United Nations, 2013.

Gibbens, Sarah. "Are Dogs Smarter Than Cats? Science Has an Answer." *National Geographic*, November 30, 2017.

Golding, William. *Lord of the Flies.* London: Faber Educational Edition, 1962.

Gould, Stephen Jay. "A Biological Homage to Mickey Mouse." Chap. 9 in *The Panda's Thumb: More Reflections in Natural History.* New York: W. W. Norton, 1980.

Gould, Stephen Jay. "Can We Truly Know Sloth and Rapacity?" Chap. 20 in *Leonardo's Mountain of Clams and the Diet of Worms: Essays on Natural History.* New York: Harvard University Press, 1998.

Gould, Stephen Jay. "An Essay on a Pig Roast." Chap. 29 in *Bully for Brontosaurus: Reflections in Natural History.* New York: W. W. Norton, 1991.

Gregory, Joseph R. "Hallan Cemi Journal; At Dig, a Race Against Water and War." *New York Times*, August 6, 1994.

Gregory, W. K. "*Hesperopithecus* Apparently Not an Ape nor a Man." *Science* 66, no. 1720 (1927): 579–81.

Griffin, Donald. *The Question of Animal Awareness: Evolutionary Continuity of Mental Experience.* Revised and enlarged edition. New York: Rockefeller University Press, 1982.

Gross, Charles G. "Galen and the Squealing Pig." *Neuroscientist* 4, no. 3 (1998): 216–21.

Gu, Hallie, and Naveen Thukral. "Soy Source: Brazil's Share of Soybean Exports to China Hits Record." Reuters, January 25, 2018.

Guardian. "Inmates Tell of Abu Ghraib Abuse." January 12, 2005.

Guerrini, Anita. *Experimenting With Humans and Animals: From Galen to Animal Rights.* Baltimore: John Hopkins University Press, 2003.

Hald, Maja, and Emilie Aagaard. "Glemsomme grise hjælper oss tettere på Alzheimer-kur." DR, October 1, 2017.

Hancox, Dan. "The Unstoppable Rise of Veganism: How a Fringe Movement Went Mainstream." *Guardian*, April 1, 2018.

Hardy, Thomas. *Jude the Obscure.* New York: Harper & Brothers, 1896.

Harris, Marvin. *Cows, Pigs, Wars, and Witches: The Riddles of Culture.* Reissue edition. New York: Vintage, 1989.

Harris, Marvin. *The Sacred Cow and the Abominable Pig: Riddles of Food and Culture.* New York: Simon & Schuster, 1987.

Haug, Herbert. "Brain Sizes, Surfaces, and Neuronal Sizes of the Cortex Cerebri: A Stereological Investigation of Man and His Variability and a Comparison With Some Mammals (Primates, Whales, Marsupials, Insectivores, and One Elephant)." *American Journal of Anatomy* 180, no. 2 (1987): 126–42.

Haugen, Helge. *Hjørnesteinen: Kjøttsamvirket på Sør-Vestlandet 1917–2008.* Stavanger, 2008.

Hayasaki, Erika. "Better Living Through Crispr: Growing Human Organs in Pigs." *Wired*, March 19, 2019.

Heilman, Uriel. "57% of US Jews Eat Pork, and 9 Other Findings From New Pew Study." *Times of Israel*, November 4, 2015.

Hellekant, G., and V. Danilova. "Taste in Domestic Pig, *Sus scrofa*." *Journal of Animal Physiology and Animal Nutrition* 82, no. 1 (1999): 8–24.

Helljesen, Vilde. "Glad for at seksuelt misbruk av dyr nå er forbudt." NRK, January 2, 2010.

Henisch, Bridget Ann. *Fast and Feast: Food in Medieval Society.* University Park, PA: Pennsylvania State University Press, 1976.

Herculano-Houzel, Suzana. "The Human Brain in Numbers: A Linearly Scaled-Up Primate Brain." *Frontiers in Neuroscience* 3, no. 31 (2009).

Herculano-Houzel, Suzana, and Jon H. Kaas. "Gorilla and Orangutan Brains Conform to the Primate Cellular Scaling Rules: Implications for Human Evolution." *Brain Behavior Evolution* 77, no. 1 (2011): 33–44.

Herodotus. *The History.* Translated by David Greene. Chicago: University of Chicago Press, 1987.

Herzog, Hal. *Some We Love, Some We Hate, Some We Eat: Why It's So Hard to Think Straight About Animals.* New York: HarperCollins, 2010.

Hewitt, John. "A Chimp-Pig Hybrid Origin for Humans?" Phys.org, July 3, 2013.

Hippocrates. *Hippocrates: Volume II.* Translated by W. H. S. Jones. Cambridge, MA: Loeb Classical Library, Harvard University Press, 1923.

Homer. *The Odyssey.* Translated by Robert Fagles. London: Penguin Classics, 1996.

Hopp, Zinken. *Sagaen om Gunnar og Njål: Njåls saga.* Oslo: Aschehoug, 1983.

Houston, Walter. *Purity and Monotheism: Clean and Unclean Animals in Biblical Law.* Sheffield, UK: JSOT Press, 1993.

Huang, Yanzhong. "Why Did One Quarter of the World's Pigs Die in a Year?" *New York Times*, January 1, 2020.

Hughes, Peter, and John Heritage. "Antibiotic Growth Promoters in Food Animals." In *Assessing Quality and Safety of Animal Feeds*, edited by Samuel Jutzi. Rome: Food and Agriculture Organization of the United Nations, 2004.

Human Rights Watch. "'When We're Dead and Buried, Our Bones Will Keep Hurting': Workers' Rights Under Threat in US Meat and Poultry Plants." September 4, 2019.

Humes, James C. *The Wit & Wisdom of Winston Churchill*. New York: HarperCollins, 1994.

Ighoubah, Farid. "FBI jakter denne mannen etter at han festet bacon på moské-dører." *Nettavisen*, December 31, 2015.

Interagency Coordination Group on Antimicrobial Resistance. "No Time to Wait: Securing the Future From Antibiotic-Resistant Infections." Report to the Secretary-General of the United Nations, April 2019.

IPCC (Intergovernmental Panel on Climate Change). "Climate Change and Land: An IPCC Special Report on Climate Change, Desertification, Land Degradation, Sustainable Land Management, Food Security, and Greenhouse Gas Fluxes in Terrestrial Ecosystems." August 7, 2019.

IPCC. "Climate Change 2014: Mitigation of Climate Change."

Jackman, Myles. "Is It Illegal to Have Sex With a Dead Pig? Here's What the Law Says About the Allegations Surrounding David Cameron's Biography." *Independent*, September 21, 2015.

Jardim-Messeder, Débora, et al. "Dogs Have the Most Neurons, Though Not the Largest Brain: Trade-Off Between Body Mass and Number of Neurons in the Cerebral Cortex of Large Carnivoran Species." *Frontiers in Neuroanatomy* 11, no. 118 (2017).

Jenkins, Steve. "Experience: I Accidentally Bought a Giant Pig." *Guardian*, February 10, 2017.

Kaas, Jon. "Cortical Cell and Neuron Density Estimates in One Chimpanzee Hemisphere." *Proceedings of the National Academy of Sciences* 113, no. 3 (2015): 740–5.

Kalof, Linda. *Looking at Animals in Human History*. Chicago: Reaktion Books, 2007.

Kavanagh, Kevin T. "Control of MSSA and MRSA in the United States: Protocols, Policies, Risk Adjustment and Excuses." *Antimicrobial Resistance and Infection Control* 8, article no. 103 (2019).

Kirkland, Mark, and David S. Cohen. "Lisa the Vegetarian." *The Simpsons*, season 7, episode 5, aired October 15, 1995, on Fox.

Koerth-Baker, Maggie. "Kids (and Animals) Who Fail Classic Mirror Test Still Have a Sense of Self." *Scientific American*, November 29, 2010.

Koike, Takahiko. "What Makes Eye Contact Special? Neural Substrates of Online Mutual Eye-Gaze: A Hyperscanning fMRI Study." *eNeuro* 6, no. 1 (2019).

Kupferschmidt, Kai, and Jon Cohen. "Could Pigs Be Involved in Congo's New Ebola Outbreak?" *Science*, May 26, 2017.

Landbruksdirektoratet. *Produksjon og omsetning av økologiske landbruksvarer*, 1. halvår 2018. Addition to report no. 9/2018, September 17, 2018.

Larson, Laurence M., trans. *The Earliest Norwegian Laws: Being the Gulathing Law and the Frostathing Law*. Clark, NJ: Lawbook Exchange, 2008.

Levy, Stuart B. *The Antibiotic Paradox: How Miracle Drugs Are Destroying the Miracle*. Berlin: Springer Science & Business, 1992.

Liliequist, Jonas. "Peasants Against Nature: Crossing the Boundaries Between Man and Animal in Seventeenth- and Eighteenth-Century Sweden." *Journal of History of Sexuality* 1, no. 3 (1991): 393–423.

Linnaeus, Carl. *Systema Naturae*. Translated by M. S. J. Engel-Ledeboer and H. Engel. Leiden: Brill, 1964.

Løkeland-Stai, Espen, and Svenn Arne Lie. *En nasjon av kjøtthuer*. Oslo: Manifest, 2013.

Løkeland-Stai, Espen, and Svenn Arne Lie. *Mellom bakkar og kjøttberg*. Oslo: Manifest, 2019.

Lorenz, Konrad. "Ganzheit und Teil in der tierischen und menschlichen Gemeinschaft (eine methodologische Erörterung)." *Studium Generale* 3, no. 9 (1950): 455–99.

Luther, Martin. *Works*, vol. 47. St. Louis, MO: Concordia Publishing House, 1955.

Lutwyche, Richard. *The Pig: A Natural History*. Princeton, NJ: Princeton University Press, 2019.

Ma, Wenjun, Robert E. Kahn, and Juergen A. Richt. "The Pig as a Mixing Vessel for Influenza Viruses: Human and Veterinary Implications." *Journal of Molecular and Genetic Medicine* 3, no. 1 (2008): 158–66.

MacLean, Paul. *The Triune Brain in Evolution: Role in Paleocerebral Functions*. New York: Springer, 1990.

MacNair, Rachel. *Perpetration-Induced Traumatic Stress: The Psychological Consequences of Killing*. New York: iUniverse, 2005.

Marchant-Forde, Jeremy N., ed. *The Welfare of Pigs*. Dordrecht, Netherlands: Springer Science and Business, 2009.

McCarthy, Eugene. "The Hybrid Hypothesis." Macroevolution.net, 2013.

McClintock, Martha. "Menstrual Synchrony and Suppression." *Nature* 229, no. 5282 (1971): 244–45.

McMillan, Franklin D., ed. *Mental Health and Well-Being in Animals*. New Jersey: Wiley-Blackwell, 2005.

Mendl, Michael, Suzanne Held, and Richard W. Byrne. "Pig Cognition."
    Current Biology 20, no. 18 (2010): 796–98.
Middleton, John, Ralf Reintjes, and Henrique Lopes. "Meat Plants—A
    New Front Line in the Covid-19 Pandemic." BMJ 370 (July 9, 2020).
Miljødirektoratet. "Klimastatus: Klimagassutslipp fra jordbruk." 2019.
Miller, Dale. "Century of Progress." *National Hog Farmer*, Jan 1, 2000.
Millett, Kate. *Sexual Politics*. Garden City, NY: Doubleday, 1970.
Minervini, Serena, et al. "Brain Mass and Encephalization Quotients in
    the Domestic Industrial Pig (*Sus scrofa*)." PLOS ONE 11, no. 6 (2016):
    e0157378.
Mjellem, Norma. "Forståelsen av hjernefunksjon—et historisk perspek-
    tiv." *Tidsskrift for den norske legeforeningen* 11, no. 121 (2001): 1396–401.
Moellering, Robert C., Jr. "MRSA: The First Half Century." *Journal of Anti-
    microbial Chemotherapy* 67, no. 1 (2012): 4–11.
Møllen, Jon Anders. "Slipper straff i grisehode-saken." NRK, June 19,
    2014.
Morgen, Brett, dir. *Jane*. National Geographic Documentary Films, 2017.
Morris, Steven. "A Crackling Good Yarn." *Guardian*, March 1, 2004.
Mortensen, Heidi, et al. "Quantitative Relationships in Delphinid
    Neocortex." *Frontiers in Neuroanatomy* 8 (2014): 132.
Mortensen, Knut Are, and Marit Eilertsen. "Dyr misbrukes ofte sek-
    suelt." NRK, November 6, 2007.
Moskin, Julia, et al. "Your Questions About Food and Climate Change
    Answered." *New York Times*, April 30, 2019.
Myhrvold, Nathan. "Marcus Gavius Apicius." *Encyclopedia Britannica*,
    updated August 1, 2018.
Nagel, Thomas. "What Is It Like to Be a Bat?" *Philosophical Review* 83,
    no. 4 (1974): 435–50.
National Pork Board. "Quick Facts: The Pork Industry at a Glance."
    2009.
National Pork Producers Council. "Pork Facts."
Nationen. "Flere griser enn mennesker i Rogaland." June 6, 2011, updated
    May 3, 2018.
Navarrete, Ana, Carel P. van Schaik, and Karin Isler. "Energetics and the
    Evolution of the Human Brain." *Nature* 480, no. 7375 (2011): 91–93.
Nepstad, Isabel. "The History and Future of Sustainable Soy in China."
    China Dialogue, October 19, 2021.
Newsweek. "Pot-Sniffing Pig." May 3, 1992.
Nsio, Justus, et al. "2017 Outbreak of Ebola Virus Disease in Northern
    Democratic Republic of Congo." *Journal of Infectious Diseases* 221,
    no. 5 (2019): 701–6.

Ogle, Maureen. *In Meat We Trust: An Unexpected History of Carnivore America*. New York: Houghton Mifflin Harcourt, 2013.

Ogle, Maureen. "Riots, Rage, and Resistance: A Brief History of How Antibiotics Arrived on the Farm." *Scientific American* (guest blog), September 3, 2013.

Ohl, Frauke, Saskia S. Arndt, and F. Josef van der Staay. "Pathological Anxiety in Animals." *Journal of Veterinary Science* 170, no. 1 (2008): 18–26.

Olkowicz, Seweryn, et al. "Birds Have Primate-Like Numbers of Neurons in the Forebrain." *Proceedings of the National Academy of Sciences* 113, no. 26 (2016): 7255–60.

Olsvik, Ørjan. "Fremtiden vil fordømme oss for antibiotika i matproduksjonen." *Forskning.no*, December 6, 2016.

Ombelet, Willem, and Johan van Robays. "Artificial Insemination: Hurdles and Milestones." *Facts, Views and Vision in ObGyn* 7, no. 2 (2015): 137–43.

Orwell, George. *Animal Farm*. London: Penguin, 2008.

Osborn, Henry Fairfield. "Hesperopithecus, the Anthropoid Primate of Western Nebraska." *Nature* 110 (1922): 281–83.

Our World in Data. "Per Capita Meat Consumption by Type, World, 1961 to 2013."

Pain, Stephanie. "The Soviet Ape-Man Scandal." *New Scientist*, August 20, 2008.

Patterson, Charles. "Animals, Slavery, and the Holocaust." *Logos Journal* 4, no. 2 (2005).

Patterson, Charles. *Eternal Treblinka: Our Treatment of Animals and the Holocaust*. New York: Lantern Books, 2002.

Patton, Dominique. "Before Corona, China Bungled Swine Epidemic With Secrecy." *Reuters*, March 5, 2020.

Phillips, Kathryn. "Learning From Pig Brains." *Journal of Experimental Biology* 209, no. 8 (2006): ii.

Pig Progress. "Humans Can Now Play Video Games With Pigs." December 22, 2011.

Pliny the Elder. *The Natural History*, vol. 8. Translated by John Bostock. London: H. G. Bohn, 1855.

Plutarch. *Moralia*, vol. 12. Translated by Harold Cherniss and William C. Helmbold. Cambridge, MA: Harvard University Press, 1957.

Pollan, Michael. "An Animal's Place." *New York Times Magazine*, November 10, 2002.

Pollan, Michael. *The Omnivore's Dilemma: The Natural History of Four Meals*. New York: Penguin, 2004.

Ponsford, Dominic. "British Journalism's Greatest Ever Scoops." *Press Gazette*, October 12, 2012.

Poppick, Laura. "Let Us Now Praise the Invention of the Microscope." *Smithsonian Magazine*, March 30, 2017.

Premack, David, and Guy Woodruff. "Does the Chimpanzee Have a Theory of Mind?" *Behavioral Brain Science* 4 (1978): 515–26.

Redding, Richard. "The Pig and the Chicken in the Middle East: Modeling Human Subsistence Behavior in the Archaeological Record Using Historical and Animal Husbandry Data." *Journal of Archaeological Research* 23, no. 4 (2015): 325–68.

Redding, Richard. "Status and Diet at the Workers' Town, Giza, Egypt." In *Anthropological Approaches to Zooarchaeology: Colonialism, Complexity and Animal Transformations*, edited by Douglas Campana et al. Oxford: Oxbow Books, 2010.

Regalado, Antonio. "Researchers Are Keeping Pig Brains Alive Outside the Body." MIT *Technology Review*, April 25, 2018.

Reilly, Katie. "Trump Praises Fake Story About Shooting Muslims With Pig's-Blood-Soaked Bullets." *Time*, August 17, 2017.

Reuters. "Seven Stories of Sows: Inside China's High-Rise Hog Farms." *The World*, May 11, 2018.

Ridgway, Sam H., et al. "Higher Neuron Densities in the Cerebral Cortex and Larger Cerebellums May Limit Dive Times of Delphinids Compared to Deep-Diving Toothed Whales." *PLOS ONE* 14, no. 12 (2019): e0226206.

Rosenberg, Michael, et al. "Hallan Çemi, Pig Husbandry, and Post-Pleistocene Adaptations Along the Taurus-Sagros Arc (Turkey)." *Paléorient* 24, no. 1 (1998): 25–41.

Rosenberg, Michael, et al. "Hallan Çemi Tepesi: Preliminary Observations Concerning Early Neolithic Subsistence Behaviors in Eastern Anatolia." *Anatolica* 21 (1995): 1–12.

Rosen-Zvi, Issachar. "'Pigs in Space': Geographic Separatism in Multicultural Societies." In *Law and Sociology: Current Legal Issues Volume 8*, edited by Michael Freeman. London: Oxford University Press, 2006.

Ross, Eric B. "The Riddle of the Scottish Pig." *BioScience* 33, no. 2 (1983): 99–106.

Rozin, Paul. "The Selection of Foods by Rats, Humans and Other Animals." *Advances in the Study of Behavior* 6 (1976): 21–76.

Russell, Bertrand. *Why I Am Not a Christian*. London: Watts & Co., Rationalist Press Association Limited, 1927.

Sahl, Jonas. "Dyre-Dan får sin vilje: Dyresex officielt forbudt." *Ekstra Bladet*, April 21, 2015.

Salisbury, Joyce E. *The Beast Within: Animals in the Middle Ages*. London: Routledge, 2010.

Sanders, Bas. "Global Pig Slaughter Statistics and Charts." Faunalytics, October 10, 2018.

Sapolsky, Robert. "Introduction to Human Behavioral Biology." Lecture series, Stanford University, 2010.

Schmidt, Verena. *Comparative Anatomy of the Pig Brain: An Integrative Magnetic Resonance Imaging (MRI) Study of the Porcine Brain With Special Emphasis on the External Morphology of the Cerebral Cortex*. Giessen, Germany: Laufersweiler, 2015.

Schultz, Jana, et al. "Effects of Control Measures on the Spread of LA-MRSA Among Danish Pig Herds Between 2006 and 2015—A Simulation Study." *Scientific Reports* 9, article no. 691 (2019).

Scurlock, JoAnn. "Animal Sacrifice in Ancient Mesopotamian Religion." In *A History of the Animal World in the Ancient Near East*, edited by Billie Jean Collins. Boston: Brill, 2002.

Shanker, Deena. "Why It's Difficult to Find Organic Pork." *Bloomberg*, November 1, 2018.

Sharma, Rajnish, et al. "High Prevalence, Intensity, and Genetic Diversity of *Trichinella* spp. in Wolverine (*Gulo gulo*) From Yukon, Canada." *Parasites and Vectors* 14, article no. 146 (2021).

Sharp, Henry S. "The Null Case: The Chipewyan." In *Woman the Gatherer*, edited by Frances Dahlberg. New Haven, CT: Yale University Press, 1981.

Shelach, Chen, dir. *Praise the Lard*. Zygote Films, 2016.

Shepard, Paul. *Thinking Animals: Animals and the Development of Human Intelligence*. New York: Viking, 1978.

Shih, Gerry, and Dake Kang. "Muslims Forced to Drink Alcohol and Eat Pork in China's 'Re-Education' Camps, Former Inmate Claims." *Independent*, May 19, 2018.

Shimmings, Paul. "Kan vi redde storspoven?" *Vår fuglefauna* 41, no. 4 (2018): 188–92.

Singer, Peter. *Animal Liberation*. Foreword by Yuval Noah Harari. London: Bodley Head, 2015.

Smith, Adam. *An Inquiry Into the Nature and Causes of the Wealth of Nations*. London: W. Strahan and T. Cadell, 1776.

Smith, Gavin J., et al. "Origins and Evolutionary Genomics of the 2009 Swine-Origin H1N1 Influenza A Epidemic." *Nature* 459, no. 7250 (2009): 1122–25.

Solstad, Dag. *Armand V.* Translated by Steven T. Murray. New York: New Directions, 2018.

Sørgjerd, Christian. "Høyreradikal-provokatør og koranbrenner kan bli valgt inn i folketinge." *Aftenposten*, May 4, 2019.

Spilde, Ingrid. "Da forskningen viste at sukker var sunt." *Forskning*, June 30, 2015.

Spry-Marqués, Pia. *Pig/Pork: Archaeology, Zoology and Edibility*. London: Bloomsbury Sigma, 2015.

Statistics Norway. "Rogaland: fylket der det gryntes, kakles og brekes mest." August 24, 2018.

Stavanger Aftenblad. "Ingen dyr skaper sterkere følelser hos mennesker enn grisen." August 21, 2017.

Svendsen, Lars Fr. H. *Å forstå dyr*. Oslo: Kagge, 2018.

Svineportalen. "Grundig stimulering av purka gir økt grisnings-prosent." Updated May 30, 2018.

Tangvald-Pedersen, Aslaug. "Ingen tegn til grisekrise etter Brennpunkt-dokumentar." VG, July 3, 2019.

Teige, Ola. "The Trial Against Aron Åsulsen in 1693." *Skeivtarkiv*, March 1, 2017.

Telegraph. "Far-Right Austrian Leader Criticised for Anti-Semitic Facebook Picture." August 20, 2012.

Tena, Aseda. "Xenotransplantation: Can Pigs Save Human Lives?" Blog post, Harvard University Graduate School of Arts and Sciences, November 2, 2015.

Thomas, Keith. *Man and the Natural World: Changing Attitudes in England 1500–1800*. Oxford: Oxford University Press, 1983.

Times of Israel. "US-Born Soldier Tried for Eating Pork." June 1, 2015.

Tomter, Line. "Listhaug vil ha mer gris i norske fengsler." NRK, January 31, 2014.

Treimo, Henrik. "Biffmedaljongens hemmlighet." *Arr: Idéhistorisk tidsskift* 4 (2005).

Tronstad, Ole-Christian. "Grisefett mot selvmordsbombere." *Dagbladet*, February 12, 2004.

TV2. "Første gang jeg har fått gjennomslag i norsk politikk." December 4, 2019.

Uddeberg, Nils. *Medisinens historie. Lidelse og helbredelse*. Translated by Lars Nygaard. Oslo: Dreyers, 2018.

USDA (United States Department of Agriculture). "Cold Storage: November 2018 Highlights." December 21, 2018.

USDA. "Feral Swine Damage." Last updated November 10, 2020.

USDA. "Hogs and Pigs: Revised Estimates, 1965–69. Statistical Bulletin 496 (November 1972).

USDA Economic Research Service. "Meat Statistics Tables, Historical." Last updated July 27, 2022.

Van Boekel, Thomas P., et al. "Global Trends in Antimicrobial Resistance in Animals in Low- and Middle-Income Countries." *Science* 365, no. 6459 (2019): eaaw1944.

Vesaas, Tarjei. *The Seed*. Translated by Kenneth G. Chapman. London: Peter Owen, 2015.

Vialles, Noëlie. *Animal to Edible*. London: Cambridge University Press, 1994.

Villarias, Alexis. "Dutch Farm: World's First to Ever Sell Cheese From Pig's Milk." *Food World News*, September 14, 2015.

Viskum, Øystein. "Fortielse og straff. Rettsforfølgelsen av *crimen bestialitatis* i Norge 1687–1842." Master's thesis, University of Oslo, 2002.

Waagen, Ola, dir. *The Secret Lives of Pigs*. NRK, 2019.

Walsh, Bryan. "Ending the War on Fat." *Time*, June 12, 2014.

Wasley, Andrew, Christopher D. Cook, and Natalie Jones. "Two Amputations a Week: The Cost of Working in a US Meat Plant." *Guardian*, July 5, 2018.

Watson, Adrienne L., et al. "Engineered Swine Models for Cancer." *Frontiers in Genetics* 7, no. 78 (2016).

Watson, Lyall. *The Whole Hog: Exploring the Extraordinary Potential of Pigs*. London: Profile, 2004.

Whiting, Terry L., and Colleen R. Marion. "Perpetration-Induced Traumatic Stress—A Risk for Veterinarians Involved in the Destruction of Healthy Animals." *Canadian Veterinary Journal*, 52, no. 7 (2011): 794–96.

Withnall, Adam. "Denmark Bans Halal and Kosher Slaughter as Minister Says Animal Rights Come Before Religion." *Independent*, February 18, 2014.

Wittgenstein, Ludwig. *Philosophical Investigations*. Translated by G. E. M. Anscombe. New York: Macmillan, 1955.

Wolf, John, and James S. Mellett. "The Role of 'Nebraska Man' in the Creation-Evolution Debate." *Creation/Evolution Journal* 5, no. 2 (1985): 32–41.

Woolfe, Tyron, Stephen C. Want, and Michael Siegal. "Signposts to Development: Theory of Mind in Deaf Children." *Child Development* 73, no. 3 (2002): 768–78.

World Economic Forum. "This Is How Many Animals We Eat Each Year." February 8, 2019.

World Health Organization. "Reducing Free Sugars Intake in Children and Adults." Guidance summary, 2003.

Wrangham, Richard. *Catching Fire: How Cooking Made Us Human*. London: Profile, 2009.

Zaraska, Marta. *Meathooked: The History and Science of Our 2.5-Million-Year Obsession With Meat.* New York: Basic Books, 2016.

Zeder, Melinda A. "Of Kings and Shepherds." In *Chiefdoms and Early States in the Near East: The Organizational Dynamics of Complexity,* edited by Gil Stein and Mitchell S. Rothman. Madison, WI: Prehistory Press, 1994.

Zielinski, Sarah. "Are Humans an Invasive Species?" *Smithsonian Magazine,* January 3, 2011.

Index